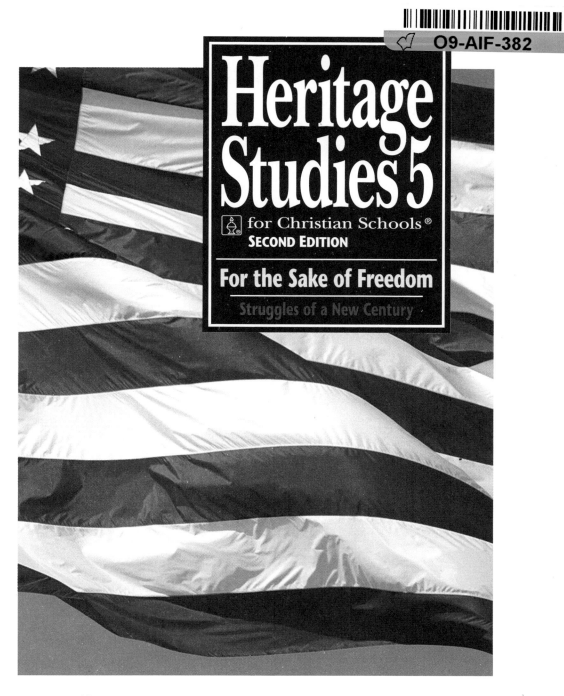

Heritage Studies 5

for Christian Schools®

SECOND EDITION

For the Sake of Freedom

Struggles of a New Century

Eileen M. Berry and Dawn L. Watkins

Bob Jones University Press, Greenville, South Carolina 29614

NOTE:
The fact that materials produced by other publishers are referred to in this volume does not constitute an endorsement by Bob Jones University Press of the content or theological position of materials produced by such publishers. The position of Bob Jones University Press, and the University itself, is well known. Any references and ancillary materials are listed as an aid to the student or teacher and in an attempt to maintain the accepted academic standards of the publishing industry.

HERITAGE STUDIES 5 for Christian Schools® Second Edition
For the Sake of Freedom

Eileen M. Berry
Dawn L. Watkins

Produced in cooperation with the Bob Jones University Department of Social Studies Education, the College of Arts and Science, and Bob Jones Elementary School.

© 1998 Bob Jones University Press
Greenville, South Carolina 29614
First Edition © 1985 Bob Jones University Press

"Exposure" by Wilfred Owen from *The Collected Poems of Wilfred Owen,* published by Chatto & Windus, was used (page 54) with special thanks to the estate of Wilfred Owen.

ISBN 0-89084-990-0

15 14 13 12 11 10 9 8 7 6 5 4 3 2 1

Contents

1

Fences Seen and Unseen

Any accurate study of the earth begins with one premise: God created all that exists. Even our best studies cannot begin to uncover the mysteries of the earth. We can measure the power of earthquakes, but we cannot say exactly what causes them nor can we prevent them. We can track a hurricane, but we cannot say for sure which way it will go. Only the One who created everything knows exactly how everything works.

The geographer who is not a Christian can discover the wonders of the world, but he will miss the wonderful testimony of God in nature. He will probably also draw some incorrect conclusions. If he accepts evolution as a fact, his estimation of time will be off by millions of years. Because he believes that this world is all man has, he will try to improve it as much as possible. How much better it is to say with the psalmist, "I will speak of the glorious honour of thy majesty, and of thy wondrous works" (Psalm 145:5).

"And, Thou, Lord, in the beginning hast laid the foundation of the earth; and the heavens are the works of thine hands."

Hebrews 1:10

The Shape of the Earth

One five-year-old says to another, "What's the difference between a globe and the earth?" The other says, "I don't know—what?" "Well," says the first, "the real earth isn't labeled." Although that is one of the less obvious differences, it is indeed a difference. What "labels" are on globes? Names of countries, rivers, mountains, and deserts? Grid lines running north to south and east to west?

The earth does not have such grid lines over it or dots and stars showing capital cities or black lines dividing countries. Such marks help us read maps and globes more efficiently. The marks also help people everywhere read maps in the same ways—whether they speak Chinese, English, or Spanish. Why is that important? Knowing how to read a map or a globe can sometimes be as important as knowing how to read words. Can you think of times when reading a map or a globe would be absolutely necessary?

Globes and Flat Maps

Look at this old map made by one of the foremost mapmakers of the world in the 1600s. What do you know about the world that he did not? What things have changed besides our knowledge of continent shapes and ocean sizes?

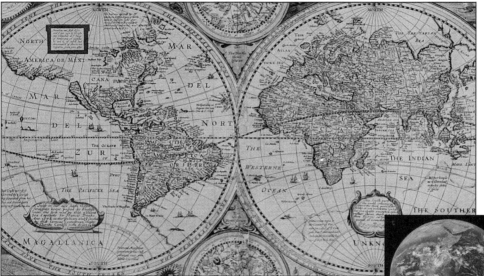

Before spacecraft could take pictures of the earth from above, people could discover land shapes only by sailing around them. Many explorers added to the knowledge of the times—Prince Henry the Navigator, who sent sailors down the coast of Africa; Bartolomeu Dias, the first to sail around the tip of Africa; Christopher Columbus, who sailed to the New World, thinking it was India; and Ferdinand Magellan, who sailed around South America and whose ships completed the first sailing trip around the world.

Ever since people have been making maps and globes, they have struggled to keep up with changes: boundary changes, new choices of capital cities, discovery of new information. In order for the maps to be accurate, these changes must be reflected on the paper or on the man-made sphere.

The word *geography* comes from Latin words that mean "earth writing" or "writing about the earth." Maps and globes represent ways that men "write" what they know about the earth. Why do you think people study the earth's surface and try to record it accurately? What activities depend on good maps? The science of making maps is called *cartography.* Look up that word and see what roots it comes from. What is a mapmaker called?

Only a globe can give the most nearly correct view of the whole earth. Why is that? The earth is a sphere. One of the first globes ever made was the handiwork of Martin Behaim of Germany in 1492. What else happened that year that may have interested Behaim? Perhaps the biggest globe in the world is in France. Made in 1824, this globe has a diameter of 128 feet (39 meters). Would that fit in your classroom?

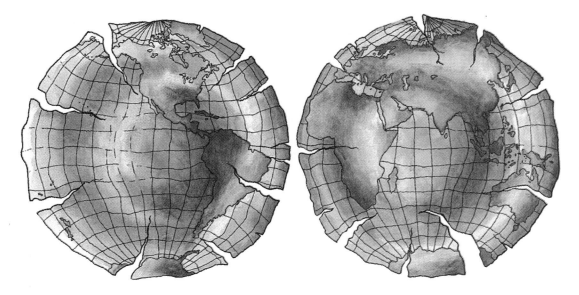

What happens to the representation of a sphere on a flat map? Many places look distorted; they appear to be a different shape or size than they really are. It is impossible to take information from a sphere and make a flat map from it without cutting or stretching the original; map-makers have been struggling with this problem for centuries.

A flat map may not represent the earth's surface as accurately as a globe does, but it can give more details. Imagine how large a globe would have to be to show all the streets in your town. Even the giant globe in France does not have room for the street names of all the cities in the world. And flat maps are far easier to carry and store.

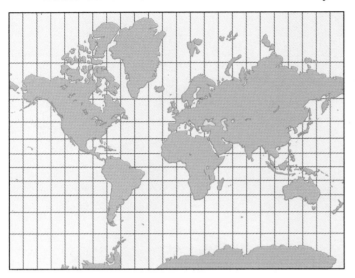

Cartographers have devised ways to make flat world maps. Some of these maps are called *projections*. Perhaps the most famous projection is the *Mercator* (or cylindrical); it shows land correctly along the equator, but the areas at the top and bottom of the map get stretched. On this map Greenland appears to be larger than South America. But actually, South America is eight times bigger than Greenland.

Interrupted projections look like cut, flattened orange peels. The shapes and sizes of landmasses are fairly accurate. But what problems does this kind of map present to travelers? It is hard to measure distances between places because of the breaks in the map.

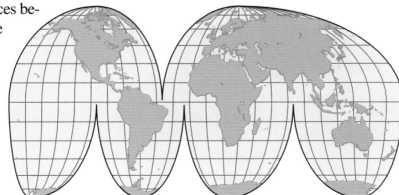

Northern Hemisphere

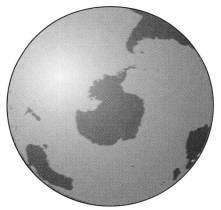

Southern Hemisphere

Latitude and Longitude

Imagine that a great belt goes around the earth, dividing it into top and bottom halves. The belt is an imaginary line called the *equator,* and the halves it forms are called the *Northern* and *Southern Hemispheres.* What do you think *hemi-* means? Find your country on a globe. Is it in the Northern or Southern Hemisphere?

At the very top of the Northern Hemisphere is the *North Pole.* And at the bottom of the Southern Hemisphere is the *South Pole.* The equator is the same distance from both poles.

Globe makers also draw a line from the North Pole through the Atlantic Ocean to the South Pole and back again through the Pacific Ocean to the North Pole. This line divides the *Eastern* and *Western Hemispheres.* Is your country in the Eastern or Western Hemisphere?

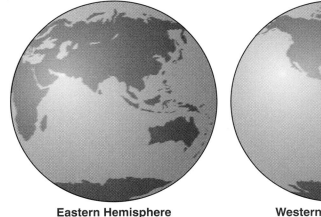

Eastern Hemisphere   **Western Hemisphere**

7

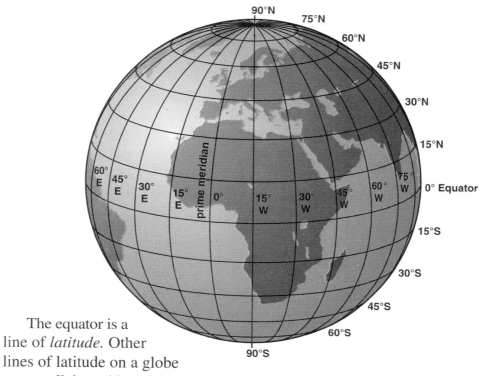

The equator is a line of *latitude*. Other lines of latitude on a globe run parallel on either side of the equator. These lines are actually called "parallels" and are labeled according to their distances from the equator, which is 0° latitude. The North Pole is 90° north latitude. What would be the parallel halfway between the equator and the North Pole?

The lines that circle a globe north to south are called *meridians* or *lines of longitude*. The meridian labeled 0° longitude is the *prime meridian*. Can you find it on the globe? New York City is 74° west of the prime meridian. Tokyo, Japan, is 140° east longitude. The meridian on the opposite side of the globe from the prime meridian is 180° longitude.

Sailors use latitude and longitude to steer their ships at sea. Surveyors use the lines to help find and set boundaries for properties. Can you find the latitude and longitude of your city or town on a map or globe?

A sextant measures the altitudes of celestial bodies.

◆ LEARNING HOW ◆

To Measure
with Latitude and Longitude

1. Get Notebook page 3, a pencil, and a map or globe and prepare to work with your Heritage Studies partner.

2. Using the map or globe and your knowledge of latitude and longitude, complete Notebook page 3.

3. After you and your partner have completed the page, exchange papers with another pair and verify their answers.

Dividing the Earth

The Continents

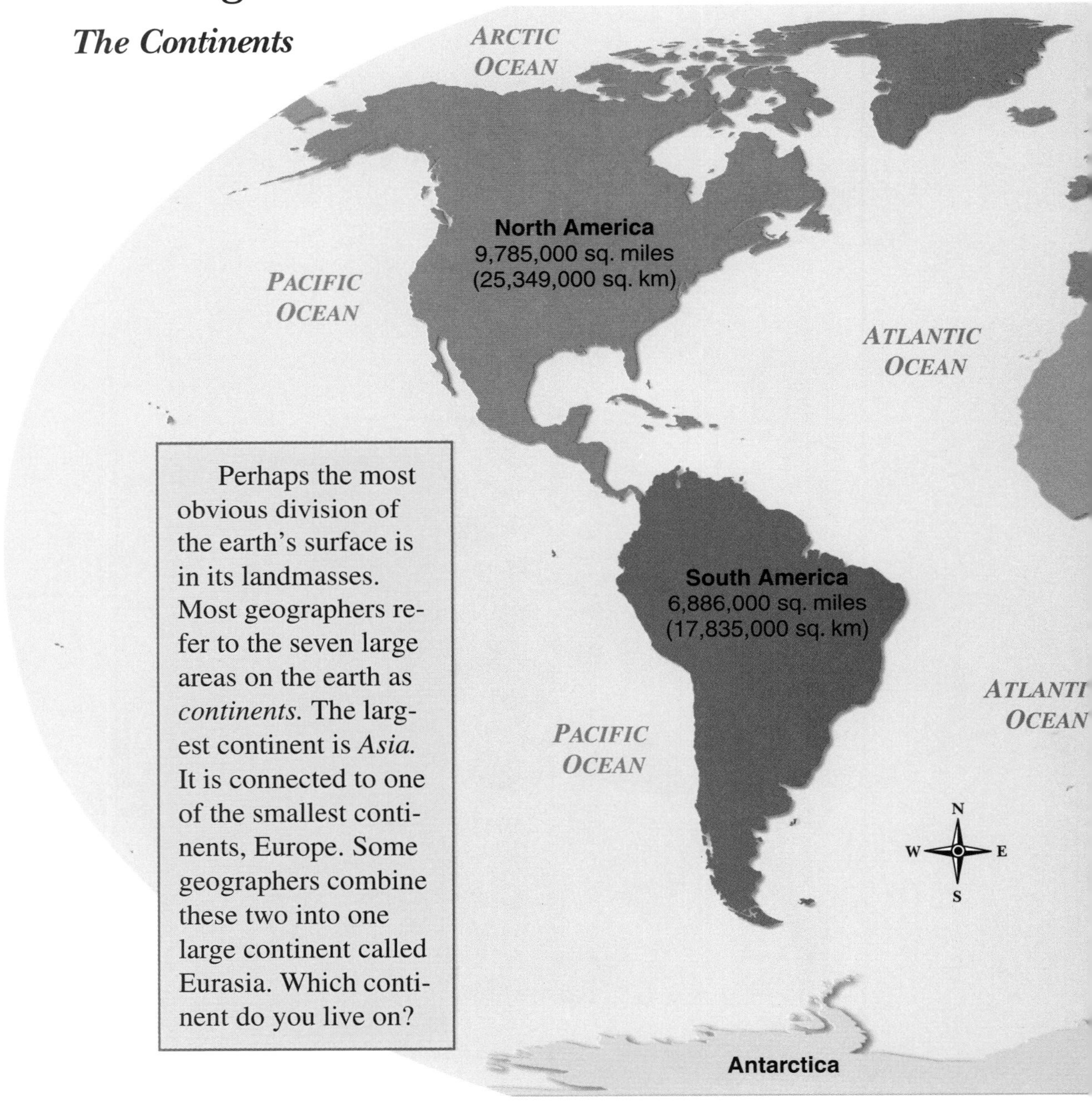

ARCTIC
OCEAN

North America
9,785,000 sq. miles
(25,349,000 sq. km)

*PACIFIC
OCEAN*

*ATLANTIC
OCEAN*

Perhaps the most obvious division of the earth's surface is in its landmasses. Most geographers refer to the seven large areas on the earth as *continents*. The largest continent is *Asia*. It is connected to one of the smallest continents, Europe. Some geographers combine these two into one large continent called Eurasia. Which continent do you live on?

South America
6,886,000 sq. miles
(17,835,000 sq. km)

*PACIFIC
OCEAN*

*ATLANTI
OCEAN*

N
W E
S

Antarctica

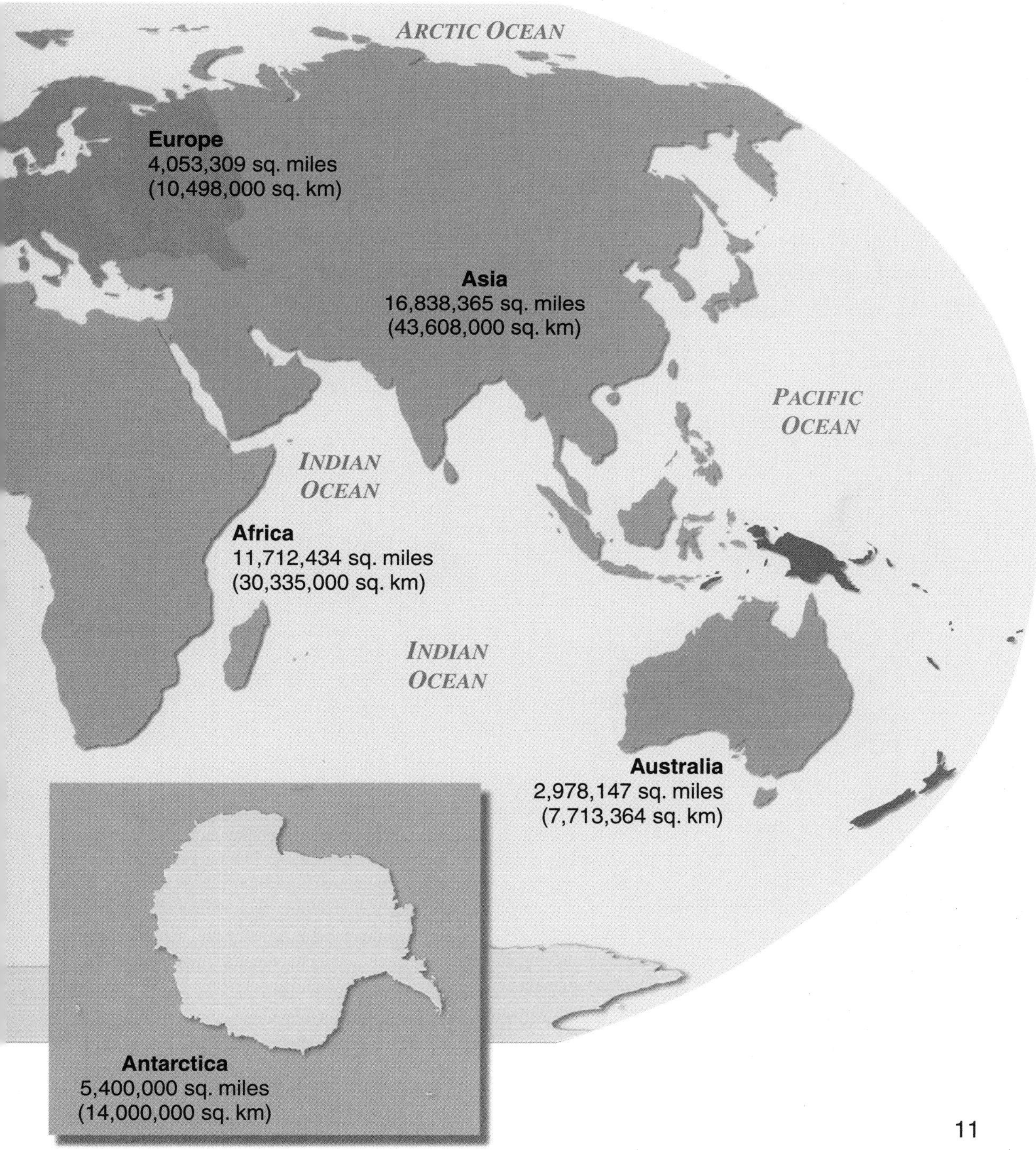

ARCTIC OCEAN

Europe
4,053,309 sq. miles
(10,498,000 sq. km)

Asia
16,838,365 sq. miles
(43,608,000 sq. km)

PACIFIC
OCEAN

INDIAN
OCEAN

Africa
11,712,434 sq. miles
(30,335,000 sq. km)

INDIAN
OCEAN

Australia
2,978,147 sq. miles
(7,713,364 sq. km)

Antarctica
5,400,000 sq. miles
(14,000,000 sq. km)

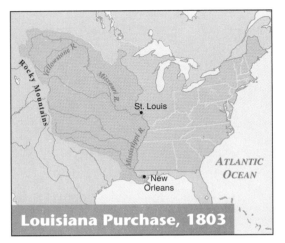

Louisiana Purchase, 1803

Political Boundaries

Maps that label features such as country borders and names of cities are political maps. Borders between countries are called *political boundaries.* These borders can change rapidly—or stay the same for hundreds of years. What do you think affects such borders? Wars and treaties do. Sale of land does. Sometimes even marriages have.

New Countries in 1991

U.S.S.R. in 1990

Cultural Boundaries

Geographers some-times divide countries or group people differently from how the people cate-gorize themselves. A map showing cultural bounda-ries would look much dif-ferent from a political map primarily because when people move, they carry their cultures with them. Boundaries often become cultural boundaries. How are the boundaries on this map different from those dividing continents?

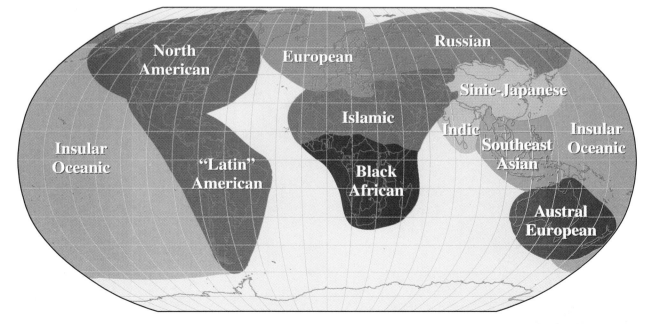

North American

European

Russian

Sinic-Japanese

Islamic

Indic

Insular Oceanic

Insular Oceanic

"Latin" American

Southeast Asian

Black African

Austral European

Time Zones

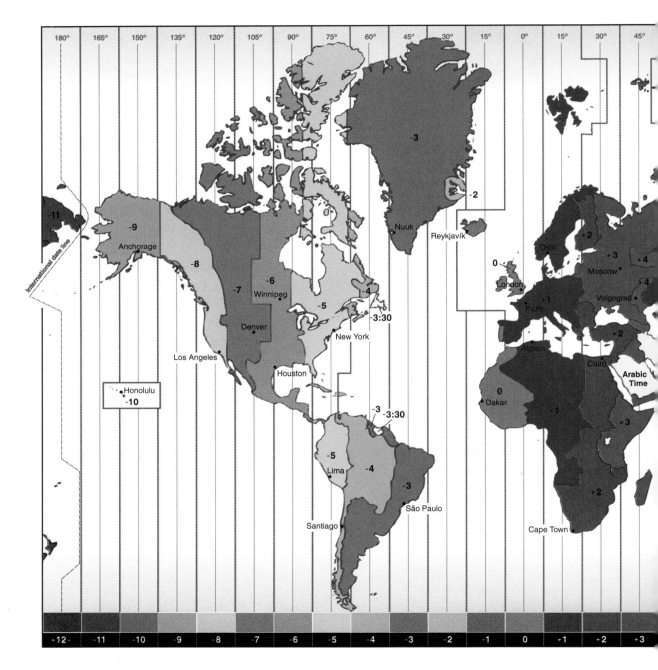

Still another way of dividing the earth is by *time zones.* Because the earth rotates on its axis, not all places can have the sun at the same time.

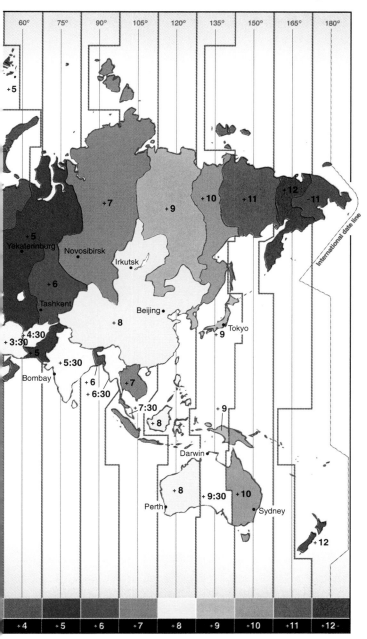

When the sun comes up in New York, it is still dark in California. Therefore, people have agreed to speak of different bands of time as time zones.

Finding the time in zones other than your own involves addition and subtraction based on the directions of east and west. For every zone you move to the east, you must add one hour to the time in your own time zone. For every zone you move to the west, you must subtract one hour from your own time. Find your own time zone on the chart. Then name a place that would show a time two hours earlier than your own.

The international date line is another division of time. It is an imaginary line running through the Pacific Ocean at about 180° longitude. A person who travels west across the date line loses a day while a person traveling east over the date line gains a day. Can you think of ways the time difference of a day might be difficult on travelers?

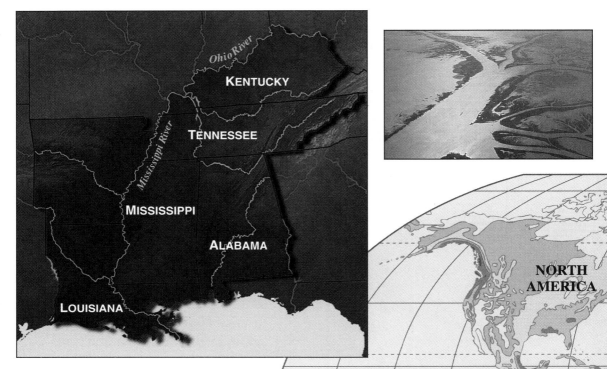

Natural Boundaries

Geographers frequently define regions according to the land: along rivers, beside mountain ranges, around lakes and seas. Such borders are called natural boundaries. Why do you think the continents of Asia and Europe are divided where they are? Why do you think North and South America are divided as they are?

Explain the borders of the states shown on this map. How many are guided by natural features? What are those features? Can you think of natural features that influenced the borders of the country or state you live in?

Environmental Regions

This map shows regions according to the amount of rainfall they receive in a year. Find your area. How much rainfall does it usually get? Follow the latitude of your area to another place on that latitude. How much rain falls there? Find another area on your latitude that gets the same amount of rain that your area does. Do the same with your longitude.

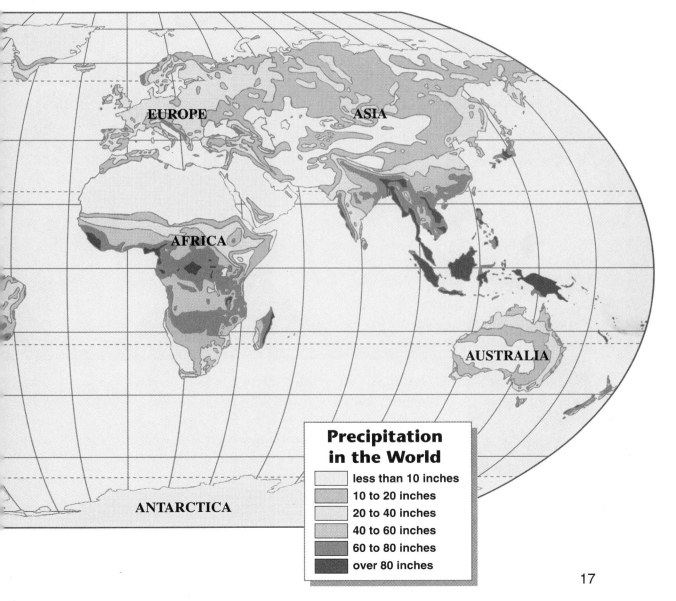

EUROPE

ASIA

AFRICA

AUSTRALIA

ANTARCTICA

Precipitation in the World

- less than 10 inches
- 10 to 20 inches
- 20 to 40 inches
- 40 to 60 inches
- 60 to 80 inches
- over 80 inches

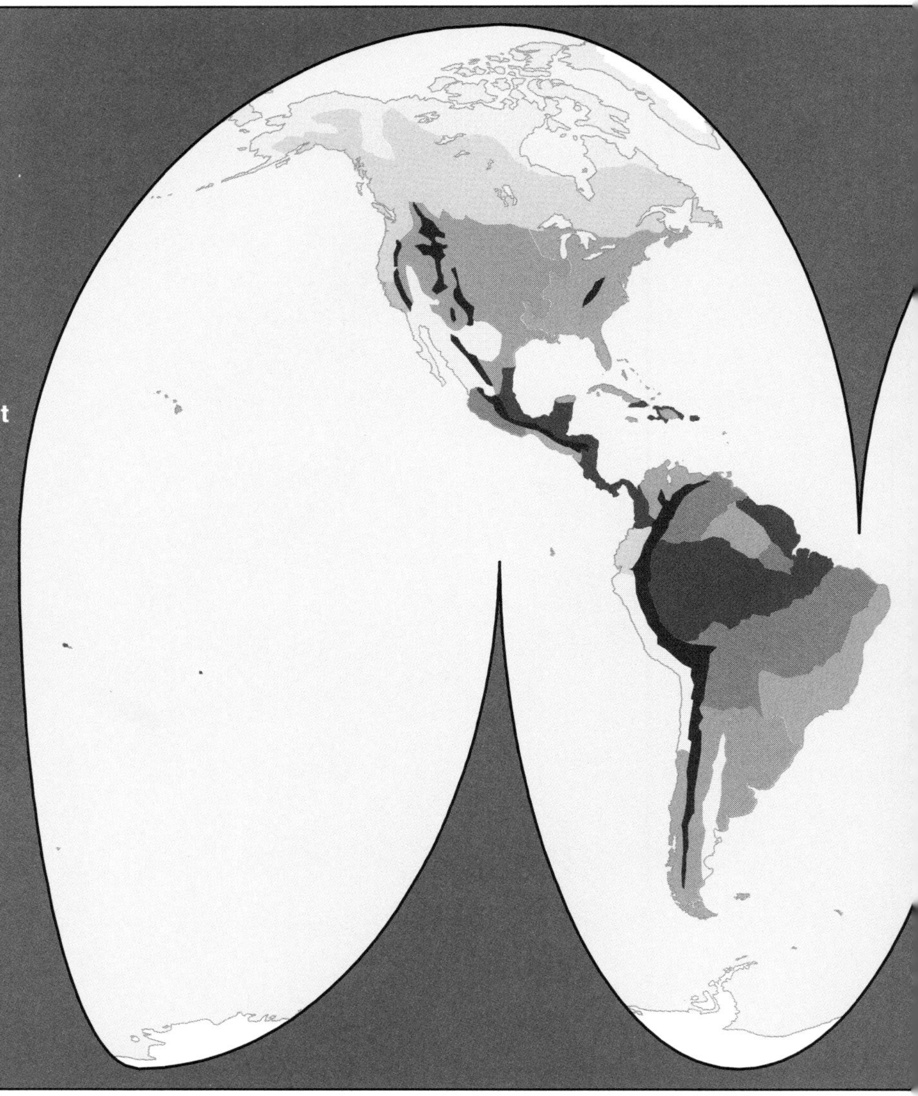
MAJOR BIOMES
OF THE WORLD
Coniferous Forest
Deciduous Forest
Tundra
Grassland
Desert
Tropical Rain Forest
Chaparral
Savanna
Mountains

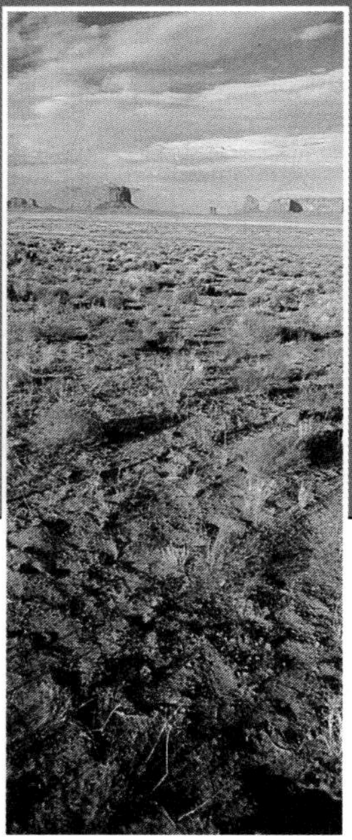

Rainfall affects much about a region—what vegetation can grow there, why people settle there, what kinds of work they do. Other factors that influence how a region is settled and used are temperature, abundance of natural resources such as minerals and fuels, and the lay of the land. Some people like to live in the mountains; others prefer the plains and valleys. What is the region like where you live?

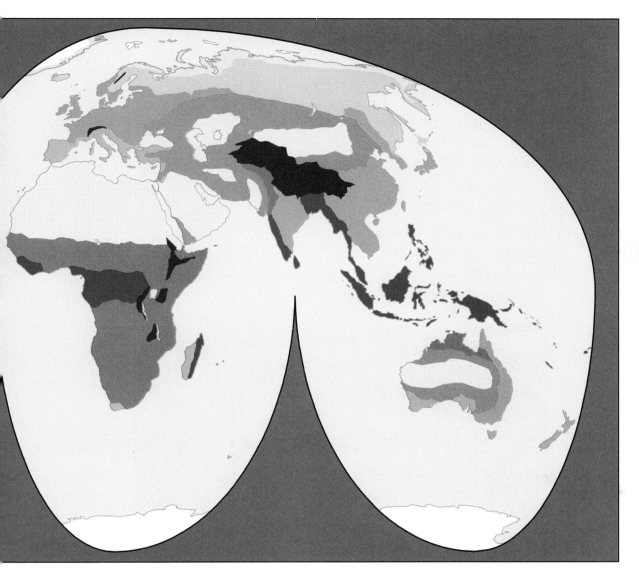

Combinations of temperature, rainfall, soil, and landforms create distinct environments. When we put the temperatures, precipitation, soil, and plants together, we have a *biome*. The name comes from two words that mean "life" and "group." These environments influence the way people live and work in them. Can you think of how the place you live in affects the work that people do?

What is the environment where you live? What other places have the same conditions?

To Interpret and Graph Data

1. Get felt-tip pens of many colors, this textbook, and any books your teacher may recommend. Your teacher will give you a graph page.

2. Select a region of the world or write down the name of the region your teacher chooses.

3. Use your textbook as well as other sources to find the information asked for on the graph page.

4. Put the information on the graph page in the form required by the particular graph you have.

2

Getting There Faster

Henry was thirteen years old in the spring of 1877. He wanted to sleep late and tinker with watches and get out of all the farm work he could. His father got up early every day and let Henry sleep in. And he gave Henry more tools than most boys in those days could ever hope to have.

Henry was the oldest child; he had three brothers and two sisters. His parents worked hard and long, but they made a good home for their children. Everything seemed rather slow and changeless to Henry. And then something happened that changed his life forever—and in turn changed America.

In March of 1879, Henry's mother died. Fifteen-year-old Henry was stunned. She had been the light of the whole house, his own guiding star. Although she died during childbirth, Henry blamed the hard work of the farm for her death. And somehow the horses that pulled the plow represented in his mind all the work that he believed had killed his mother. He promised himself that he would invent a machine that would replace horses.

Henry Ford at age seventeen;
also shown with Model T on page 21

That boy was Henry Ford. He did indeed put the horse out of the carriage business almost entirely: he made an automobile that the average person could afford. Later, his tractors put the plowhorses out to pasture as well. And eventually there were more cars and tractors in America than there had ever been horses. The little farm boy from Michigan became the man who revolutionized modern transportation.

The Automobile

Try to imagine for a moment the streets and roads around your school without any cars or trucks on them—only wagons and horses and people walking. What would be different? Noise levels? Speed? The number of people going by in an hour? Indeed these would be significant differences. But other things would have to change as well. Think of the people who attend your school. Do they live close by or far away? If there were no cars, those students who live more than five miles away would probably go to school somewhere else.

But the people who worked on inventing the automobile merely wanted to find a quicker way to get from one place to another. They did not envision the many other changes that the automobile would bring.

Early Autos

As early as 1801, some Englishmen had put steam-powered carriages on the road. In 1860, Thomas Rickett drove all around Scotland in his

Cugnot, a French engineer, designed this steam tractor to carry artillery in the 1770s. It was the first self-propelled vehicle.

steam carriage. He caused a stir with his "noisy" machine, and soon there was a big debate over such "horseless conveyances."

People who wanted to stop steam cars were happy when the "Red Flag Law" was passed in 1865. This English law said that such vehicles could go only two miles an hour in town and four miles an hour on the open road. Furthermore, someone had to walk in front of the car carrying a red flag. Carriages pulled by horses could go ten miles an hour. Do you think this law made people want horseless carriages? Railroad owners were especially happy with the law. Why do you think that was?

Besides such laws, the cars themselves had many drawbacks. For one thing, they were large and heavy. They had to carry fuel such as coal to keep the boiler going and water to make steam. The body of the car had to be heavy to hold up all the machinery that made it run. Some early cars looked more like train engines.

A steam carriage of the mid-1800s

24

Would you like to ride a bicycle like this one?

The bicycle was extremely popular in the 1880s and 1890s. A few people tried to make steam-powered bicycles. A Frenchman, Leon Serpollet, produced a much lighter steam engine for his tricycle than had ever been made before. In the 1860s, Jean Joseph Lenoir patented the first internal combustion engine—one that runs on gasoline. Later, the German inventor Gottlieb Daimler further developed the gasoline engine, providing the basis for most car engines that are used today.

The American Interpretation

Although some wealthy people in England and elsewhere had motor cars, the cars were not trustworthy. In fact, most drivers took a team of horses with them in case of breakdowns. But in America, Henry Ford was determined to make a reliable car that average people could own. He built his first car at his home in 1896. It took him several years to get a patent. But in 1908, he introduced the *Model T,* a sturdy, simple car.

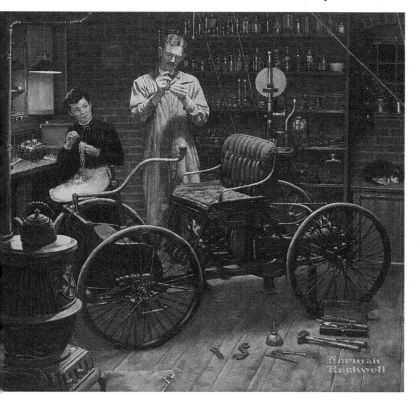

Henry Ford built this Quadricycle in his small workshop behind his home in Detroit, Michigan.

Painting by Norman Rockwell; From the Collections of Henry Ford Museum and Greenfield Village

The Model T was large enough for a family to ride in comfortably.

A flat tire on a Model T could often be easily pumped up again.

The Model T became one of the most famous cars in history. In England and other countries, as well as in the United States, it sold faster than any other car. It was easy to drive (only two gears) and easy to fix, even if it broke down on the road.

At first, drivers did not need licenses to operate a car. They could pay for two hours of instruction from the Ford Motor Company and then drive off on their own. Or, if they preferred, they could simply drive off. What do you think spurred the making of laws about owning and driving cars?

Owning cars changed people's lives. Driving gave them more freedom than they had previously enjoyed, something always appealing to Americans. They could now live in one town and work in another. Why would people want to do that? And they could take trips on their own schedules, not the railroad's schedules. What other things do you think changed?

Names from the Past

When you go past a car sales lot and see cars called Dodge and Chevrolet, you are seeing a little piece of the past. Early in the twentieth century, some individuals and several sets of brothers started car-making companies that are still around today.

David Dunbar Buick, born in Scotland and reared in Detroit, opened the Buick Motor Company in 1903. His cars had a better engine than earlier cars: they got more power from a gallon of gasoline. One

A 1904 Buick

of his workers, Walter Percy Chrysler, became president of the Buick company. Chrysler later founded the Chrysler Corporation and made the famous Chrysler automobile.

Louis Chevrolet came to the United States from Switzerland to sell an invention. Instead he became a driver in the newest sport in America: car racing. Later, in 1911, he helped form the Chevrolet Motor Company, having ideas of his own about how cars should be made. The company became part of the General Motors Corporation. Louis and his brother Arthur tried to start an airplane company too.

Louis Chevrolet behind the wheel of an early racing Buick

John and Horace Dodge were a wild and brawling pair who owned a machine shop in Detroit, Michigan. They had invested in the Ford Motor Company. They also sold parts to Ford's factory. With the money they made (and it was a good amount), they produced their own line of cars in 1914. Their car had twenty-four horsepower; Ford's Model T had only twenty. The Dodge Company became part of the Chrysler Corporation in 1928.

Stanley Steamers, powered by steam engines, continued in production until 1924.

Other brothers in the car business were Francis and Freelan Stanley, who made the respected "Stanley Steamers"; Fred and August Deusenberg, who produced an automobile that many people think was the finest car of its time; and John and Warren Packard, who had been making a very popular car since 1900.

The names of these earliest car makers "echoed" in show-rooms and car lots for decades; and some, like Ford, are still "echoing" today.

A Deusenberg from the late 1920s

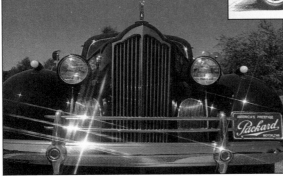

A 1940 Packard

On today's robotic assembly lines, machines do the work that people used to do.

Another Change Ford Made

Not only did Henry Ford change America by making a car many people could afford, he also changed the way America manufactured goods. When Ford first started making cars, each one had to be put together in his shop, at the rate of one car every twelve or fourteen hours. The Model T sold for $850. That rate and that price did not suit Ford. "We can do better," he said.

Why would he want to do better? He had sold six thousand Model T cars in one year. How much money did he bring in? Ford was sure that a lower-priced car would benefit everyone: more people could have cars and he would make more money. Do you think he was right?

Ford had heard of a meatpacking business in Ohio that used an *assembly line*. In an assembly line, each worker does one part of a total job instead of each doing one complete job. In the meatpacking company, each person did his work on a side of pork and then moved to the next piece. Some companies making rifles and typewriters had also been using the same system. Ford began to think cars could be made on assembly lines.

Can you tell which parts are being manufactured on these early Ford assembly lines?

Other car makers had tried the assembly line and given it up. Ford made a major change, however. He made the assembly line itself move, not the workers. He built a factory with conveyor belts and overhead cranes to move the car being assembled from worker to worker. The new system was a success: now a Model T rolled out of the factory in one and one-half hours. How much faster was that than the old method? Do you think the price of cars went down?

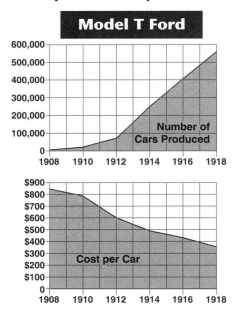

Model T Ford

Number of Cars Produced

Cost per Car

Ford's idea spread to other companies. Before long, clothes and household goods were being made quickly on assembly lines. And the prices went down. More people could afford to buy more things. Why is that good for the economy of a nation? Much of America's modern comfortable living is due to the assembly line.

Ford's company made more than fifteen million Model T cars before the last one was made in 1927. Not until the Volkswagen hit the American market in the late 1940s was another car as popular.

An Assembly Line Works

1. Get the materials your teacher tells you.

2. Go to the "station" you have been assigned.

3. When the whistle blows, begin your work. Keep doing your job until the whistle blows again.

4. Assess your production rate. How can it be improved? How can you do your part more efficiently?

Collecting Antique Automobiles

People have many different reasons for buying and driving antique cars. For a few, it is a matter of thriftiness—why buy a new car when the old one still runs? For most others, it is a good investment, like buying a gem or a work of art. Because the car is rare, it is valuable.

Still others like to own vintage cars, collectible autos named for their style. Collectors think these cars are beautiful or historical or remarkable for some reason. They want to preserve a part of the past—and enjoy it.

Collectors take their cars to shows all over the world. They like to look at others' automobiles and display their own. For some it is a hobby; for others it is a business. Restoring and maintaining vintage cars takes much skill and money. Do you know anyone who collects vintage cars?

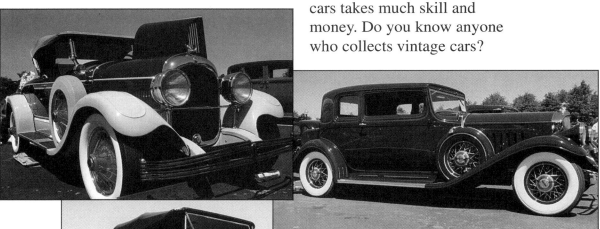

Clockwise from upper left: a 1928 Chrysler, a 1932 Pierce Arrow, and a restored 1911 Model T

The Airplane

A Greek myth tells of a boy named Icarus, who had a pair of feathered wings and learned to fly. His father warned him not to fly too high, but Icarus did anyway. He got too close to the sun, and the wax holding the feathers on his wings melted. The boy fell from the sky into the sea.

The First Flying Machines

In more modern times, there have been other Icaruses with different wings—but with much the same results. In England about A.D. 1050, a man named Eilmer made some wings from linen stretched over wooden frames. He went to a high tower and pushed off into a fair wind. He flew almost an eighth of a mile before he crashed. He broke his legs and was lame for the rest of his life.

Otto Lilienthal kept his gliders balanced by constantly shifting his weight back and forth.

Later, people tried to glide on the air currents rather than fly like birds. Around 1890 a German, Otto Lilienthal, made gliders that looked much like birds' wings and tails. In fact, he made sixteen kinds of gliders and tried over two thousand flights with them. He never could stay in the air for a great distance (fifteen seconds was his longest flight), but he helped prove that flying might not be an impossible dream after all.

At the same time, other people were experimenting with making flying machines. Octave Chanute, an American, had seen Lilienthal and his gliders. He returned home full of ideas for a better glider—one with rubber joints so that the wings could move with the wind.

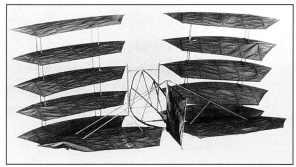
Chanute's glider

Samuel Langley, head of the Smithsonian Institution, was building his *aerodrome,* which carried a gasoline engine. Although small models of the aerodrome had flown quite well, the *Great Aerodrome,* with Charles Manly as its pilot, lurched off the top of a houseboat on the Potomac and slid right into the river. The newspapers jeered at Langley's soggy flying machine. The next day the *New York Times* claimed that man would not fly until scientists had worked for another ten million years.

Langley's aerodrome

But on a windy beach in North Carolina, just nine days later, two brothers were going to prove the newspaper wrong—and change the world beyond anyone's wildest expectations.

The Wright Idea

When Orville and Wilbur were boys, their father bought them a toy helicopter made of paper, cork, and bamboo. They played with the "bat," as they called it, until it completely wore out. Then they used it as a pattern to make others that were bigger and better. Wilbur later said it was that toy that caused him and Orville to become interested in flying.

When Orville was seventeen, he made his own printing press and set up a shop. Business was good and he had to hire a helper. Wilbur and Orville also had a bicycle repair shop. When that business became so large that they had four shops running, they put the hired man in charge of the print shop and started designing bicycles as well as repairing them. During the winter, when business was slow, the brothers used their tools and know-how in their lifelong hobby: making a flying machine.

The Wrights wanted to know all that they could about flying, so they wrote to the Smithsonian Institution for information. They received a list of books, some written by Langley and Chanute. They wrote to both men and had replies from both. Before long, Chanute and the Wright brothers were good friends.

This building in Dayton, Ohio, housed the Wright Cycle Company.

Wilbur and Orville read everything they could about new inventions and discoveries of every kind. When they read about gliders, machines that fly by riding the air currents without engine power, they decided to build a glider for themselves. They took their glider by train all the way to Kitty Hawk, North Carolina, where good winds always came in from the ocean and where the hills were layered with soft sand for landing.

The glider flew—but only for a few seconds at a time. The brothers went home to experiment some more. They built a wind tunnel, a six-foot-long narrow box with a fan at one end and a glass top. Why do you think it had a glass top? When they flew a model glider in the tunnel, they could watch what happened to it in different wind levels. Their calculations of air pressure and the effects of different wing surfaces were so accurate that modern computers only confirmed, not corrected, them.

After they finished the tests in the wind tunnel, the brothers built a better glider and went back to Kitty Hawk. The next year they took a third glider to the banks of North Carolina and were greatly pleased with how this one flew. Now they were ready to add an engine to the flying machine.

Modified gliders

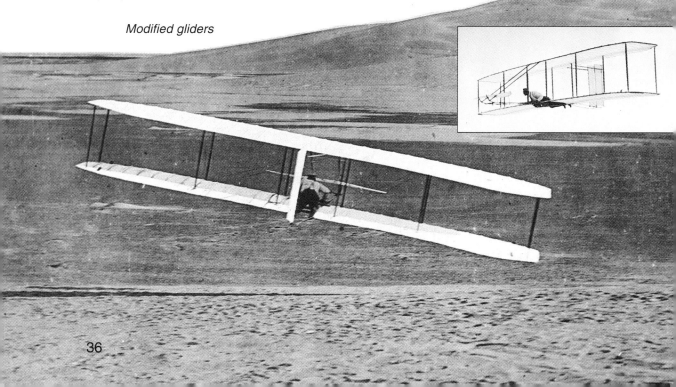

The Wrights knew that the key was to build an engine that had much power but was not heavy. They asked several engine makers to design an eight-horsepower engine that would not weigh more than two hundred pounds. Everyone they asked said that it could not be done. So the brothers set to work and built their own engine: it weighed just 179 pounds and had more than twelve horsepower. And they had accomplished this job that "could not be done" in only six weeks.

The Wrights' propeller went through many changes from the 1903 version (left) to the 1909 version (right).

But they had to make another invention before they could complete their flying machine—a propeller. For several months, they tested many different shapes and filled up five notebooks with their formulas and sketches. Orville wrote in his diary that the problem took up so much of their time that they "could do little other work." Then they made a major discovery: a blade that turned worked on the same principles as wings that sliced forward through the air.

The Wrights made a propeller with blades shaped like the wings of their machine. Then they were ready for their most important trip to Kitty Hawk.

Kitty Hawk, North Carolina
December 17, 1903

Late morning

Orville Wright aboard the Flyer *as it lifts from the ground*

The wind was brisk and the air was raw—so cold that the Wrights had to keep going into the camp building to warm their hands. They put up the red flag to signal their helpers to come; the Wrights were going to try to fly the machine.

Four men and a boy showed up. With their help, the Wrights laid out the track and set the *Flyer* on it. Orville and Wilbur shook hands; one of the helpers said they shook hands a long time, "like two folks parting who weren't sure they'd ever see one another again." Then Orville got onto the *Flyer*.

Orville let the engine run a little while; then he slipped the wire that held the flying machine, and the machine started forward. It moved slowly against the wind for about forty feet. Then, on its own power, the *Flyer* lifted from the ground. It went up about ten feet and then dipped and rose again, swaying and lurching in the wind. Wilbur and the others cheered, and one man operated the camera that Orville had set up, catching forever the first moment a man really flew.

38

The *Flyer* stayed up for twelve seconds and traveled only 120 feet. But it had stayed up by its own power and had landed on high ground. The Wrights had truly done what many said was impossible. They flew the *Flyer* three more times. That afternoon Orville and Wilbur walked four miles to send their father a telegram. In part it said, "Success four flights Thursday morning . . . inform Press home Christmas." What do you think their father thought when he read that message?

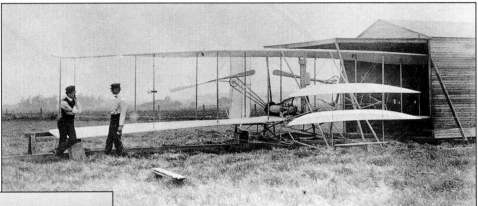

The Flyer II *could fly for five minutes at a time.*

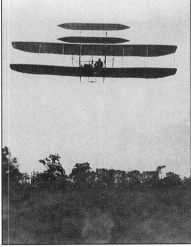

The Flyer III *stayed aloft for 39 minutes—a new record.*

That winter, the brothers worked on improving the flying machine. In the spring they went to a neighbor's field and began testing the *Flyer II*. In order for the airplane to be useful, it had to do more than fly in a short, straight line. So Wilbur began to experiment with turning in the air. Soon both brothers were flying in complete circles over the field.

The next winter, they built *Flyer III,* a plane that gave the pilot more control over turns and landings. With this airplane, they could stay in the air for more than thirty minutes at a time. And they could land many times without making repairs. They were ready now to show the world. However, there were few people in the world ready to believe that man could fly.

When the Wrights offered the invention to the United States War Department, they were turned down immediately. No one even came to see the airplane. The army had given much money to Langley, only to see the aerodrome fall into the river. The army leaders were not about to spend more money

Orville Wright demonstrated the Flyer's *capabilities for the army in 1908.*

so badly. For two years, the Wrights did not fly or show their invention to anyone. Why do you think that was? They were waiting for a patent because they did not want anyone to steal their idea. And they still hoped the United States government would give them a contract to make airplanes for the army.

Finally in 1908, the army decided to give the Wrights a chance. But the army wanted proof that the Wrights' machine could fly 125 miles at forty miles per hour with two men aboard. So Orville and Wilbur took to the air again, this time with a passenger—Charlie Furnas, a mechanic friend of theirs. There could be no doubt anymore. The age of air travel had arrived.

The Wright brothers on the back steps of their home

Air Traffic Controller

Who would have guessed on that day in 1903 that in a few decades there would be so many airplanes over airports that they would need a

traffic director? Without the tower and the quick, sharp-eyed people in it, large airports would be in chaos. Air traffic controllers tell all pilots when and where to take off and to land. Their job is to get the most aircraft in and out of the airport in the safest and most efficient way.

Although controllers have good eyesight, there are days when heavy fog or other weather conditions cut visibility. Then the controllers must rely fully on their equipment. The Instrument Landing System uses radio signals to locate planes. Large airports also use the Microwave Landing System, which gives even more precise information to the controllers and pilots.

The most important characteristic of an air traffic controller is an ability to remain calm in hectic hours and in an emergency. Some busy airports like Chicago O'Hare International and Dallas-Fort Worth International each have nearly one million take-offs and landings in a year.

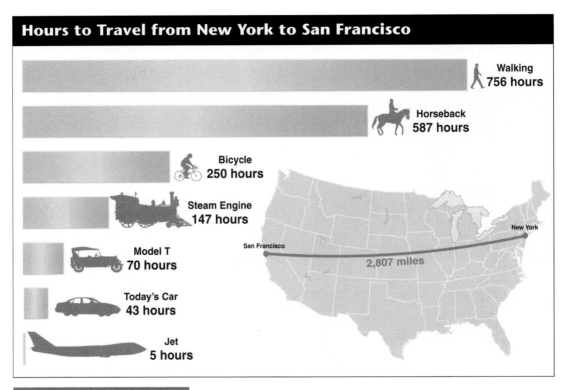

Hours to Travel from New York to San Francisco

Walking — 756 hours

Horseback — 587 hours

Bicycle — 250 hours

Steam Engine — 147 hours

Model T — 70 hours

Today's Car — 43 hours

Jet — 5 hours

San Francisco — New York — 2,807 miles

Since Then

Modern travel is immensely different from travel just one hundred years ago. Imagine what Wilbur and Orville Wright might think of the space shuttle. Think how the sleek cars of today would look to Henry Ford. And consider how it would be to have to ride to church in a buggy or travel to another state in a wagon. It would certainly slow down life in this decade.

In 1903, when the Wright brothers made the first short flights in an engine-powered machine, they little dreamed that sixty-six years later, Neil Armstrong would step down from a far different craft onto the surface of the moon. Or that Armstrong would carry with him a small piece of cloth from the *Flyer,* which had skimmed the air at Kitty Hawk one cold December day not so long before.

3

The War
to End All Wars

The European Powder Keg

The year was 1914. In the United States, life was good for most people. Nearly everyone had a job and plenty of food to eat. People everywhere—bankers, factory workers, farmers, and college students—talked about President Woodrow Wilson's recent election.

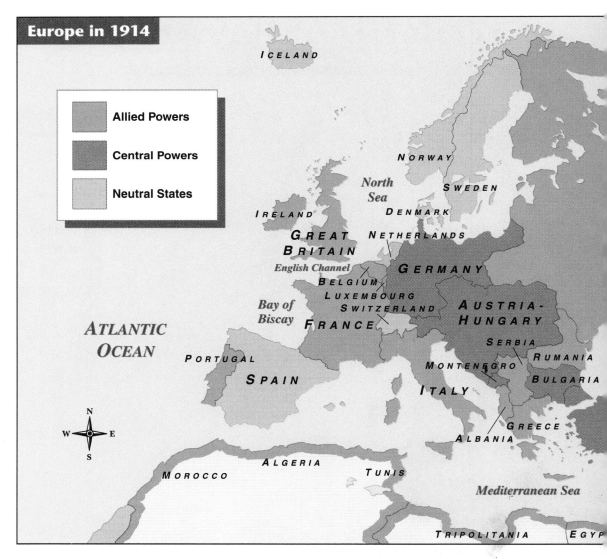

Europe in 1914

Allied Powers

Central Powers

Neutral States

ICELAND

NORWAY

North Sea

SWEDEN

DENMARK

IRELAND

GREAT BRITAIN

NETHERLANDS

English Channel

GERMANY

BELGIUM

LUXEMBOURG

SWITZERLAND

Bay of Biscay

FRANCE

AUSTRIA-HUNGARY

SERBIA

RUMANIA

ATLANTIC OCEAN

PORTUGAL

MONTENEGRO

BULGARIA

SPAIN

ITALY

GREECE

ALBANIA

MOROCCO

ALGERIA

TUNIS

Mediterranean Sea

TRIPOLITANIA

EGYPT

But across the ocean in Europe, life was not so peaceful. Several nations wanted to enlarge their boundaries, even if that meant taking land that other countries already owned. They wanted to have the strongest armies and navies. They were all competing with one another to make the best products and to sell the most products. The people of each nation thought that their nation was the best one in Europe. Some of these people would stop at nothing to advance their nation's goals.

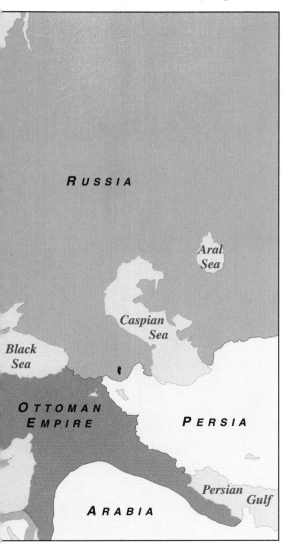

Germany, Russia, Austria-Hungary, and France were four of these powerful nations. Their extreme patriotic feelings were called *nationalism*. Great Britain was also powerful, but it was separated from the rest of Europe by the English Channel. Great Britain did not desire to expand its territory in Europe, and for many years its navy had been the strongest on the seas. More than anything, Great Britain wanted to stay out of the tension on the continent.

But Great Britain would not be able to avoid tension for long. Several years earlier, it had formed an agreement to side with France and Russia if they went to war. This is called an *alliance*. France, Russia, and Great Britain named their alliance the Triple Entente *(ŏn tŏnt′)*. In 1882 Germany, Austria-Hungary, and Italy had also made an alliance. They called their group the Triple Alliance.

Can you find each of these nations on the map?

Some people referred to Europe in 1914 as a "powder keg." Do you know what they meant by that? Gunpowder will explode the moment a spark touches it. People meant that relations between countries were so tense that it would take only a "spark" to cause them to explode into war. The spark came on June 28, 1914.

Archduke Ferdinand (left) with Emperor Franz Josef

The Powder Keg Ignites

Find Serbia on the map of Europe. In 1914 Serbia was a small, independent kingdom. Bosnia had been independent too, before it became part of Austria-Hungary. The Serbs felt that Bosnia should belong to them, and they hated Austria-Hungary.

A group of Serbs thought of a way to get back at the Austrian government. They planned to kill Austria's archduke, Francis Ferdinand, when he visited Bosnia.

On the twenty-eighth of June, a young Bosnian Serb named Gavrilo Princip fired shots into the archduke's car as it passed. Both Ferdinand and his wife died from their gunshot wounds.

The government of Austria-Hungary was outraged. Kaiser Wilhelm II of Germany urged his Austrian allies to attack Serbia immediately. Instead, Count Leopold von Berchtold, its foreign minister, sent Serbia a note with some harsh demands. He wanted Serbia to give up most of the rights it had as an independent country. Do you think Serbia was willing to agree to these demands?

Serbia agreed to some, but not all, of Austria's demands. That was not good enough for Austria. Austria-Hungary took the advice of Germany and declared war on Serbia on July 28.

Spreading Flames

But Serbia could not fight Austria-Hungary alone. It had to have help. Russia prepared its army to help Serbia. When Russia's army began preparing for war, Germany declared war on Russia.

During the German invasion of Belgium, Belgian troops used straw for camouflage in the straw-covered field.

Do you remember the Triple Alliance and the Triple Entente? Italy had promised to side with Germany and Austria-Hungary in a war. But now it decided to withdraw from the Triple Alliance. Great Britain had promised to help France and Russia.

Great Britain did not want a war. But something happened that made Great Britain angry. The Germans invaded Belgium, a tiny neutral country between France and Germany. Belgium was under Great Britain's protection, so the British declared war on Germany and Austria-Hungary the next day. It seemed as though an entire continent had gone to war.

Early in the war, the German soldiers wore helmets like this one.

*"Help us win!" pleads the German poster.
The French poster declares, "We'll have them!"*

In each of the countries at war, a holiday spirit filled the air. Crowds of people swarmed the streets. Bands played and people sang. Long lines of volunteers waited to enlist as soldiers. Posters went up in every city, urging men to join the armed forces. Newspapers and magazines published political cartoons that poked fun at the enemy.

"War is a glorious thing," most people thought. "How noble it would be to fight for one's country!" No one expected the war to last very long.

Sir Edward Grey, the British secretary for foreign affairs, was one of the few people with a solemn face. "The lights are going out all over Europe," he told a friend. "We shall not see them lit again in our lifetime." What do you think he meant by this remark?

Germany and Austria-Hungary called themselves the *Central Powers*. Since the German army was much larger and better trained than that of Austria-Hungary, the Germans did most of the actual fighting for the Central Powers. Russia, France, and Great Britain called themselves the *Allies*.

The Central Powers had a plan to conquer the Allies. They named it the Schlieffen *(shlē′ fen)* Plan, after the German official who had thought of it. The Schlieffen Plan called for the Germans to attack France first, to capture Paris quickly, and then to march east and defeat Russia.

"In six weeks it will all be over," read a telegram that the German general sent home to Kaiser Wilhelm II of Germany.

French troops marching through a village on their way to the Battle of the Marne

But things did not happen that easily for the Germans. Before they got to Paris, they ran into French troops at the Marne River. The French soldiers fought so fiercely that the German troops had to retreat. After the Battle of the Marne, the Germans realized that they would have to abandon their Schlieffen Plan. The French were not going to be defeated quickly.

War on the Western Front

The Germans and the Allies began a "Race to the Sea." Both sides wanted to be the first to take control of the ports along the English Channel. If Germany could control the ports, it would be able to prevent the British from sending help to France.

At the Belgian city of Ypres *(ē′ prə),* the Allied army finally stopped the German advance toward the English Channel. The battle lasted an entire month, and thousands of soldiers died. Today Flanders, Belgium, has fields dotted with white crosses where many of these men are buried.

By the end of November, both armies had dug trenches to shelter themselves. These trenches snaked for nearly six hundred miles from Belgium to Switzerland. The war had reached a *deadlock,* which means that neither side was gaining ground. Most people had thought the war would be over by Christmas. Do you think many still believed this?

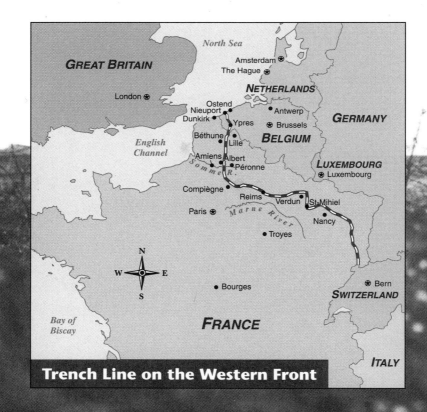

Trench Line on the Western Front

What was life like for soldiers in a trench? Trenches were about six and a half feet deep and only wide enough for two men to stand abreast. Sometimes soldiers tried to cover the muddy ground with boards. But often mud was knee-deep on the floor of a trench. Lice and bad smells were problems because soldiers had to go without bathing for days— sometimes weeks—at a time. And rats constantly scurried underfoot.

Some of the officers lived in furnished underground rooms. But most soldiers had only crude dugouts cut into the trench walls.

At the top of the trenches were *parapets,* little fences made of sand-bags and tangles of barbed wire, to discourage enemy attacks. Soldiers fired their machine guns over the parapets. Each side had a system of four trenches—a frontline trench with two support trenches behind it and a reserve trench farther back. Soldiers could move between trenches through underground tunnels.

Between enemy trench systems was a stretch of land called "no man's land." Littered with dead bodies, barbed wire, and muddy shell holes, the area was hard for soldiers to cross during an attack.

Western Front
Christmas of 1914

A dusting of snow covered the muddy battlefields of the western front on Christmas Eve, 1914. Soldiers had hung paper lanterns along the lines and decorated Christmas trees.

A familiar sound rose from the battle lines in the hushed darkness. The men were singing. Germans and British alike blended their voices in Christmas carols.

Soldiers in their dugouts heard the music and climbed up over the parapets of their trenches to join the singing. Germans in pointed caps shook hands with British in khaki-colored berets. Christmas greetings were exchanged in German and English.

The guns were silent all the next day. Some exchanged gifts, and a few held soccer matches. For just that day, the men forgot about the war and celebrated a holiday.

Many officers were angry with their troops. They did not believe it was right to make friends with the enemy, even on a holiday. After 1914 Christmas truces were forbidden.

In 1915 it became clear that the war would last a long time. The soldiers were able to defend themselves easily from their trenches, and direct attacks were too risky to be tried often.

Weapons of World War I

Machine guns had not been in use long. These guns were the most important weapons of the war. In one minute a soldier's rifle could fire fifteen shots, but his machine gun could fire 450 shots. Aircraft were also

Machine gunners protect themselves with gas masks at the Battle of the Somme.

equipped with machine guns. A Dutchman named Anthony Fokker had invented a mechanism that allowed the machine gun to shoot between an airplane's spinning propeller blades without hitting them. This mechanism allowed machine guns to be mounted on an airplane.

Another new weapon was gas. Most gases were contained in shells and spread when the shell exploded. At first only tear gas was used. Then the Germans introduced more deadly gases like chlorine gas and mustard gas. These gases were poisons that suffocated the victims and burned their skin. Mustard gas was especially hard to defend against because it was invisible and had no odor. To protect themselves, soldiers wore large, clumsy masks that covered their entire heads.

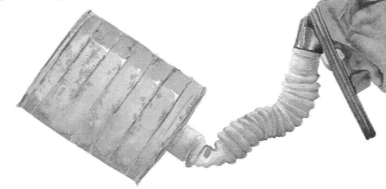

Writing Poems

A soldier huddled on the dirt floor of his dugout in an Allied trench, pen in hand. Distant machine gun fire rattled like popcorn on a hot stove. Somewhere a shell exploded, and a man's cry of pain echoed over the battlefield. The soldier closed his eyes for a moment, ran his hand over his damp brow, and began to write:

> Our brains ache, in the merciless iced east winds that knive us . . .
> Wearied we keep awake because the night is silent . . .
> Low, drooping flares confuse our memory of the salient . . .
> Worried by silence, sentries whisper, curious, nervous,
>   But nothing happens.
>
> Watching, we hear the mad gusts tugging on the wire,
> Like twitching agonies of men among its brambles.
> Northward, incessantly, the flickering gunnery rumbles,
> Far off, like a dull rumour of some other war.
>   What are we doing here?
>
> —from "Exposure" by Wilfred Owen

Poets write poetry to make people think about something in a new way. Poems written during World War I can help us to better understand how people felt about the war.

Wilfred Owen wrote many of the best poems about World War I. He died from an illness at the age of twenty-five in 1918, shortly before the war ended.

In a famous poem called "In Flanders Fields," John McCrae expressed his feelings about the soldiers who died.

> In Flanders fields the poppies blow
> Between the crosses, row on row,
> That mark our place. . . .
> . . . Short days ago
> We lived, felt dawn, saw sunset glow,
> Loved and were loved, and now we lie
> In Flanders fields.

Wilfred Owen wrote, "We only know war lasts, rain soaks, and clouds sag stormy." During 1915 the Germans and the Allies tried several offensive moves, but none were successful. The western front remained deadlocked, and the war continued.

The western front was only part of the war. The Allies made an unsuccessful attempt to take control of a peninsula in Turkey called Gallipoli. France and England wanted to open a supply route to Russia. On the eastern front, the Germans, under the command of two brilliant generals, Paul von Hindenburg and Erich Ludendorff, were winning. The fierce Russian Cossacks, an army on horseback, had retreated before the smaller German army.

On the high seas, the British navy swept the sea clear of German surface ships. So the Germans used submarines, called U-boats, to sink enemy ships. On May 7, 1915, a German U-boat torpedoed the *Lusitania,* a passenger ship traveling from New York to Liverpool. Over one thousand people died when the ship sank. One hundred twenty-eight of them were Americans.

A German U-boat

The New York Times *reports the sinking of the* Lusitania.

How do you think the Americans felt about the sinking of the *Lusitania?* They were shocked and angry. They felt that the Germans had violated important laws by sinking an unarmed ship that carried defenseless civilian passengers. Many Americans believed that the United States should become involved in the war.

A few weeks after the *Lusitania* incident, Italy joined the war on the side of the Allies. Do you remember which side Italy had been on before the war started? It had been in league with Germany and Austria-Hungary in the Triple Alliance. But now the Allies promised Italy lands in Austria, Africa, and Turkey if they won the war. The offer was too good for the Italians to refuse.

The Central Powers gained new allies too. Turkey joined after defeating the British at Gallipoli, and Bulgaria joined them just in time to help them defeat Serbia. In the East, at least, the Central Powers were winning.

Battles and Bravery

Early in 1916, the Germans on the western front decided it was time to break the deadlock. They planned to capture Verdun *(ver • dŭn′)*, a French city surrounded by three rings of fortresses. They thought that Verdun would fall quickly, since many of the French soldiers who normally manned these fortresses had left their posts to fight on the front.

For two days in February, the Germans bombarded Verdun's fortresses with shells, machine gun fire, and poison gas. Then German foot soldiers began marching forward. They expected to find all the French defenders dead. Instead, French soldiers rained gunfire on them when they tried to advance. The French were not defeated yet.

A poilu, or French soldier

The Battle of Verdun

General Henri Philippe Pétain arrived two days later to take command of the French forces. Under his leadership, the French rallied. *"Ils ne passeront pas!"* they cried, meaning "They shall not pass!" The French were determined that the Germans should not have Verdun. For ten months they fought bravely, and their determined efforts saved Verdun. But more than five hundred thousand French soldiers died in the battle. German losses were almost as great. Verdun was the longest and bloodiest battle of the war.

Military cemetery at Verdun, France

The Battle of the Somme

In July of 1916, British commanders on the western front thought of a plan to help the French soldiers fighting at Verdun. They would attack the Germans at a point along the Somme River. This might lure some of the Germans away from Verdun and relieve the French.

The Battle of the Somme lasted four months. The Germans finally retreated, but over one million lives had been lost on both sides. A British soldier called this battle "the glory and the graveyard of our army."

During this battle, the Allies introduced a new offensive weapon—the tank. These giant vehicles looked more like water carriers than weapons, but they were equipped with huge guns. Soldiers driving tanks could crush anything in their paths. They could even drive tanks over the tops of trenches. When Germans first saw the tank, they called it a *Schutzengrabenvernichtungsautomobile,* meaning "an automobile built to destroy trenches dug in the ground."

Tanks advance through the Argonne Forest in France.

The Battle of Jutland

At the same time as the Battle of Verdun, another important battle took place at sea. The Battle of Jutland was fought in the North Sea off the coast of Denmark. The British Grand Fleet, the finest navy in the world, clashed with the German High Seas Fleet in May of 1916.

HMS Warspite *participated in the Battle of Jutland.*

The battle was quick and bitter; it lasted less than thirty minutes. The British lost fourteen ships, among them the *Queen Mary,* with a crew of 1,266 men. The Germans lost eleven ships. Neither side could really claim a victory, and neither wanted to admit a defeat.

It was now 1917, the third year of the war. Even after costly battles and millions of sacrificed lives, the Allies and the Central Powers were still deadlocked. Everyone was tired of fighting. Woodrow Wilson, the president of the United States, encouraged the European leaders to consider settling for "peace without victory." Do you think either side was willing to agree to his proposal?

Both the Allies and the Central Powers believed that "peace without victory" would mean giving in to the enemy, and neither was willing to do that.

America Joins In

President Woodrow Wilson had just been re-elected in 1916. His campaign slogan had been "He kept us out of war." But now people in the United States, President Wilson included, were leaning more and more toward joining the war in Europe.

Early in 1917, the Germans did two things that outraged Americans. First, Kaiser Wilhelm II declared all ships to be fair game for German submarine attacks, with no restrictions. Second, the Germans planned to convince Mexico to join the war on the side of Germany. If it agreed, Mexico would receive Texas and other land in the southwestern United States.

President Wilson before Congress

President Wilson spoke to Congress on April 2, persuading them of the need to make the world "safe for democracy." What do you think he meant by this? On April 6, 1917, the United States declared war on Germany and joined the Allies.

American soldiers marching onto French soil were a welcome sight for the Allies. The Americans were nicknamed "doughboys," probably because the buttons on their uniforms resembled an English dumpling by that name.

Uniform button of an American soldier in WWI

On the Home Fronts

At home in each of the countries at war, life had changed. Most of the men had gone to the battlefronts. Women took over men's jobs in factories and on farms. Women were delivering the mail, acting as chauffeurs and waiters, and even making weapons for the soldiers.

Woman welding in an arsenal

Children helped the war effort too. Girls sewed clothing and rolled bandages to be sent to the battlefields. Boy Scouts ran errands and wrote letters for wounded soldiers in war hospitals. Some teenage boys trained to be army officers while still in school. Most families planted gardens and grew their own vegetables, since food was in short supply. Products like meat, bread, butter, and sugar had to be carefully rationed or saved for special occasions. In the United States, Herbert Hoover created a system of "meatless days," "sweetless days," and "heatless days" to help with the rationing.

People who lived in towns near the fronts had to take special precautions, since cities were often bombed or raided during the war. Schoolchildren and mothers learned how to put on gas masks and go to the nearest bomb shelter in case of an enemy attack.

Boy Scouts help wounded soldiers in Great Britain.

To Conserve Food

1. Label three separate sheets of paper with the headings "Day One," "Day Two," and "Day Three."

2. Under "Day One," plan a lunch menu for a "meatless day." No meat may be included.

3. Under "Day Two," plan a lunch menu for a "sweetless day." No candy or dessert foods may be included.

4. Under "Day Three," plan a lunch menu for a "heatless day." None of the foods included may be hot or require cooking.

5. Choose one of your menus to take home with you. Prepare the foods listed for your lunch one day this week. You may work with a parent on this part of the project.

Trouble in Russia

While America was entering the war, Russia was changing politically. For several years there had been political unrest in Russia. In March of 1917, the Russians revolted and forced their czar, Nicholas II, to give up his throne.

A man named Vladimir Ilich Ulyanov, who called himself Lenin, came to Russia in April. Over the next several months, he organized his own political party. His followers were called Bolsheviks. The Bolsheviks staged a second revolution in November. Lenin promised the Russian people peace, land, and bread.

With all the hardships of war, do you think the Russians listened to Lenin? They did. Many men left the war and went to Moscow, Russia's capital, to help set up Lenin's new government. Germany now had to fight on only the western front.

Political conditions in Russia were so unstable that, only a few months after being publicly welcomed by his party members, Lenin had to disguise himself as a Finnish railway worker to avoid arrest.

Childe Kassam, Allies Day, May 1917, *The National Gallery of Art, Washington, D.C.*

Can you name the Allied nations represented by these flags?

The war dragged on through 1917. Offensives from both sides ended in more casualties. After one of these battles, many French soldiers gave up and went home, deserting their general, Robert Nivelle. Nearly three hundred thousand British soldiers died after an offensive against the Germans at Passchendaele *(päss' chən • dāl • ĕ)* in Belgium.

By spring of 1918, over six hundred thousand American troops had arrived at the fronts to give fresh help to the Allies. Over two million American soldiers came. In July the Allies, under the command of Frenchman Ferdinand Foch, were ready to move forward against the Germans.

At the Second Battle of the Marne, the Allies drove the Germans behind the Marne River once again. Then they broke through the Germans' mighty Hindenburg Line in the forest.

Now the fighting became more fierce than ever before. It was becoming more and more apparent that the Germans were losing.

Sergeant Alvin York

Alvin York grew up on a farm in the hills of Tennessee. As a boy he learned how to shoot a rifle and a pistol, and he became a skilled marksman. He also learned that Jesus Christ had died for him, and he accepted Him as his Savior.

York was a young man when World War I began. He believed that it was wrong for a Christian to kill people in war. When the United States entered World War I, he asked that his name be left out of the draft pool.

But the government would not listen to York's protests. He was drafted into the United States Army. After thinking and praying for a long time, York changed his mind. He decided that it would be wrong for him to refuse to serve his country. So York went off to Europe to fight in the war.

On October 8, 1918, York performed a deed that made him a hero. He faced an entire platoon of German soldiers alone, firing his rifle at them from a kneeling position. After some of the Germans had fallen, he forced the rest of them to surrender. Single-handedly, York took 132 German prisoners.

Soon York was promoted to sergeant. After the war, he was awarded the Congressional Medal of Honor for his bravery. He had saved many American lives by his heroism. When congratulated, he gave the Lord the credit for his actions. "God will be with you if you will only trust Him," he said.

The End at Last

By early November, all of the Central Powers except Germany had surrendered. Germans at home were starving. Nearly every German family had lost one of its members in the war. Weary German leaders met with General Foch in a railroad car in Compiègne Forest to sign the armistice. On November 11, 1918, at 11:00 A.M., the war officially ended.

The Allied troops went wild with joy. Soldiers cried and laughed and slapped each other on the back. Four years of fighting were over.

But there was sadness too for many families. More than six million people would have physical disabilities for the rest of their lives because of wounds received in the war. And more than ten million people had lost their lives in World War I. Rows and rows of white crosses on French and Belgian battlefields were silent reminders of the high cost of peace.

Delegates from various countries watch as the German leaders sign the Treaty of Versailles in the Hall of Mirrors.

Woodrow Wilson met with David Lloyd George, the British prime minister, and Georges Clemenceau, the French premier, along with leaders of twenty-nine other Allied nations. Their job was to make up a peace treaty. Discussions were held in Paris to determine what they would put in the treaty.

Wilson had fourteen points that he wanted the treaty to include. But not all of the other leaders agreed with him. Many of them wanted the treaty to punish Germany.

In the end, the treaty placed all of the blame for the war on the Germans and required them to pay for the damages they had caused. It took away a great deal of territory from Germany, Austria-Hungary, and other nations who had fought on the side of the Central Powers. It limited the number of men Germany could have in its army. It made Germany give up many of the ships in its navy. The Allies wanted to weaken Germany so that it would be unable to stir up more trouble in Europe. Do you think their plan worked?

On June 28, 1919, German leaders signed a treaty at the Palace of Versailles in the Hall of Mirrors. It was an official acceptance of the Treaty of Versailles. The Germans were then obligated to meet the demands in the treaty.

(From left to right): Allied leaders David Lloyd George of Britain, Vittorio Orlando of Italy, Georges Clemenceau of France, and Woodrow Wilson of the United States

People had called World War I "the war to end all wars." Was this an appropriate title for the war? People soon realized they had been too optimistic in assuming there would be no more war after this one.

"Come, behold the works of the Lord, what desolations he hath made in the earth. He maketh wars to cease unto the end of the earth; he breaketh the bow, and cutteth the spear in sunder; he burneth the chariot in the fire."

Psalm 46:8-9

Many problems had been left unsolved. Germany remained extremely bitter about its defeat in World War I. Europe was still divided into systems of alliances between nations. And several countries were developing dangerous new political ideas.

But for a while, the world enjoyed peace.

4

Nations of the Earth

It is difficult to think of studying the whole world at once. There are so many peoples, so much land, so many events through so long a time. Therefore, histo-

rians and geographers usually use three main elements to organize the study of places: culture, history, and geography. These divisions make it easier to understand why people and places are what they are.

Cultures of the World

At seven o'clock in the morning in Minnesota, an alarm clock rings. A boy rolls over to turn it off and thinks of a race he will run at school that day. In Syria, a bell chimes, and a boy goes to prayers with his father. In China, a buzzer sounds, and a boy begins to study. All over the world, every day, people go about their routines with many different

purposes. The patterns that all those activities make are called *cultures*.

All peoples of the world have customs or characteristics that make them different from all other people. Most cultures cherish the differences and strive to preserve them. What are some things that make your country or city different from other countries and cities?

This church is a small group within the Masai culture in Kenya.

A *culture* is a way of life. It is the combination of languages, religions, government, economy, customs, and arts of a group of people. What can you say about your culture? The culture to which you belong consists of many smaller groups. For example, your community is a small group within your state, and your church is a small group within the context of your community.

What choices do you make during the day? On what do you base these choices? What you have been taught by parents, teachers, and friends affects what you believe and the choices you make. These people close to you are yet another group to which you belong. You are an important part of all the groups within your culture. You make a difference in your family, church, community, state, and country. It is a Christian's responsibility to make the right choices so that he can have a godly influence on those around him.

Hudson Taylor

A Christian also has a responsibility to learn about the cultures of other places, for this knowledge will make him a better ambassador for Christ. Hudson Taylor, missionary to China, believed in learning the culture of others. Despite disapproval from other English missionaries, Taylor had his head shaved except for a section in back. Into those remaining hairs he had a pigtail woven. (He later grew his own.) He purchased Chinese clothing, including a long silk outer gown with full sleeves that marked him as a teacher. He was eventually received by the Chinese— and so was his message.

Histories of the World

Perhaps you think the title of this section should read "History of the World."

The Parthenon in Greece

That would be a rather large subject for one or two pages. The title is meant to suggest that every nation has a unique history, a smaller story that is part of the whole large story of man on the earth.

Covered bowl from China

Nonwritten Sources

History is the record of activities and events in the lives of all the people who have ever lived. Historians use many means to put this long story together. They study nonwritten sources such as fossils and *artifacts,* objects made by people. They listen to stories and legends passed on from generation to generation. What problems might such sources present?

Marble sculpture from Rome

Digging Up the Past

Until the early 1900s, most of the digging into places of the past was in search of treasures to sell or hoard. The tomb of the Egyptian pharaoh Tutankhamen yielded incredible wealth—solid gold artifacts and a gold

mask that is an art treasure itself. Some discoverers were mainly interested in the money the artifacts would bring as well as the prestige of owning things that had once belonged to a famous king.

Today, however, the goal of such searches is to learn about the people of long ago. The great Viking ships, for example, are carefully removed from the earth and even more carefully preserved—not for their market value but for what they can tell us about how the Vikings lived.

Archaeologists, people who excavate ancient sites, work with soil specialists, chemists, and even botanists and zoologists, looking at every part of a dig and searching for any clues to help unravel the mystery of earlier days. Using small spades and soft brushes, archaeologists and their helpers sort through everything, even ancient trash dumps. To them, even broken pottery is a treasure— of information.

73

Written Sources

Historians also read accounts from people who actually lived in the times they wrote about. The Gospels are *primary* historical sources. Matthew, Mark, Luke, and John wrote of events that they had been part of. They give contemporary accounts. Why are such accounts valuable to historians?

Other primary sources are those written during the same time as the events, but the writer may not have actually seen what he writes about. When a newspaper prints a story from another newspaper without sending out its own reporter, it creates a primary source but not a first-person report. Sometimes all the best sources are destroyed in a fire or are lost at sea. It is then that the other sources increase in importance.

Secondary sources are those that are made by people who study the original sources later on, after the events have passed. For example, the eruption of Mt. Vesuvius in A.D. 79, recorded forever in the artifacts preserved in the ash, was depicted in a painting in 1785. Although the painter, Angelica Kauffman, may have studied primary sources, she was not living when the volcano erupted. Her painting is a secondary source. Why are secondary sources useful?

Giovanni Battista Carlone, Jacob Shown the Coat of Joseph, The Bob Jones University Collection

What can we learn from this secondary source about life in Joseph's day?

World Geography

Geography is the study of a place—the land, the climate, the natural resources, and the way all those things influence the inhabitants. The first chapter of this book discussed latitude and longitude, climate, natural boundaries, and biomes. But there are other parts of a good geography study as well.

"The earth is full of the goodness of the Lord."

Psalm 33:5

Natural Resources

God has placed many treasures in and on the earth for our good. The very ground we walk on is rich with treasures—the soil itself is a treasure. The rich vegetation that springs from the soil is a gift, as are the minerals in the earth. The sun, fresh water, wildlife, and the seas are all great gifts. How we use these gifts shows our respect for the Giver, the Lord God. Some people choose to worship the gift, the earth, instead. What are some ways people worship the earth?

Some regions of the world have more natural resources than others. People must use the resources that they have to produce food, shelter, and clothing. Look at the chart. What resources are most plentiful where you live?

Natural Resources

Forests	provide wood for fuel, paper, lumber, and other products
Fuel and mineral deposits	provide fuels and materials for industries
Soil	for growing plants for animal and human food
Sun	provides light and warmth for plants, animals, and man
Water	for growing plants, for animal and human needs, and for producing energy
Wildlife	for food, study, and enjoyment

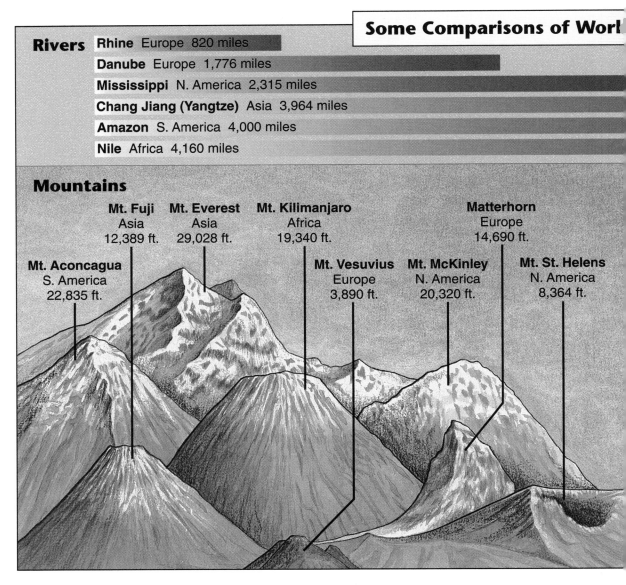

Rivers

Rhine Europe 820 miles

Danube Europe 1,776 miles

Mississippi N. America 2,315 miles

Chang Jiang (Yangtze) Asia 3,964 miles

Amazon S. America 4,000 miles

Nile Africa 4,160 miles

Mountains

Mt. Fuji
Asia
12,389 ft.

Mt. Everest
Asia
29,028 ft.

Mt. Kilimanjaro
Africa
19,340 ft.

Matterhorn
Europe
14,690 ft.

Mt. Aconcagua
S. America
22,835 ft.

Mt. Vesuvius
Europe
3,890 ft.

Mt. McKinley
N. America
20,320 ft.

Mt. St. Helens
N. America
8,364 ft.

Lay of the Land

Topography refers to the land features of a region. You have already discussed a few of these features as natural boundaries—rivers, lakes, and mountains. What other features might an area have? Some areas have waterfalls and canyons; others have streams and swamps; still others have caves and valleys.

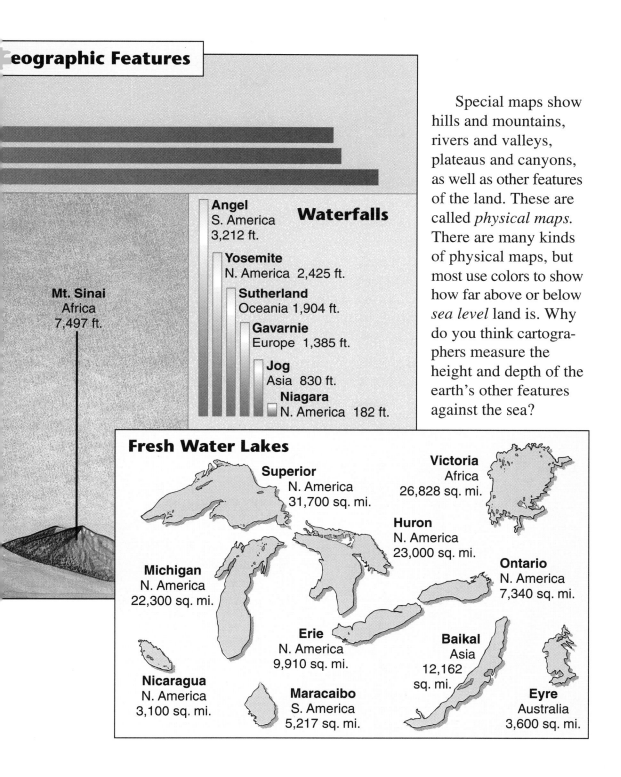

Special maps show hills and mountains, rivers and valleys, plateaus and canyons, as well as other features of the land. These are called *physical maps.* There are many kinds of physical maps, but most use colors to show how far above or below *sea level* land is. Why do you think cartographers measure the height and depth of the earth's other features against the sea?

Mt. Sinai
Africa
7,497 ft.

Waterfalls

Angel
S. America
3,212 ft.

Yosemite
N. America 2,425 ft.

Sutherland
Oceania 1,904 ft.

Gavarnie
Europe 1,385 ft.

Jog
Asia 830 ft.

Niagara
N. America 182 ft.

Fresh Water Lakes

Superior
N. America
31,700 sq. mi.

Victoria
Africa
26,828 sq. mi.

Huron
N. America
23,000 sq. mi.

Michigan
N. America
22,300 sq. mi.

Ontario
N. America
7,340 sq. mi.

Erie
N. America
9,910 sq. mi.

Baikal
Asia
12,162
sq. mi.

Nicaragua
N. America
3,100 sq. mi.

Maracaibo
S. America
5,217 sq. mi.

Eyre
Australia
3,600 sq. mi.

77

Nations and Capitals

In addition to topography, cities and towns are important in the study of geography. What is the capital city of your country? Do you know how it became the capital? What does it mean for a city or town to be a capital? Usually it means that the government carries on much of its business there, that many officials work and live there, that laws are made there, and that it is the chief city in the country.

L'Enfant's plan for the city of Washington

The capital of the United States is Washington, D.C., a city that makes up the entire District of Columbia. The District of Columbia is not a state, but sixty-nine square miles set aside for the capital.

The site for Washington, D.C., was chosen by President George Washington. Part of the land he chose belonged to Maryland and part to Virginia. Both states gave the territory to the United States government. In 1791 Washington hired Major Pierre Charles L'Enfant to plan the city.

Why do you think President Washington hired a planner rather than letting the city grow as it would on its own? Why do you think a special site was necessary for the national government?

The U.S. Capitol under construction

78

In 1800 the United States government moved from Philadelphia to Washington, D.C. The streets of the new city were made of dirt. The Capitol building sat at the end of the "Grand Avenue," which today is known as "the Mall." In 1814, during the War of 1812, British soldiers captured the city and burned down the Capitol, the White House, and other buildings.

By 1819, the buildings were rebuilt. The Capitol was even bigger and grander. Although many had hoped that the city would grow quickly, it remained much smaller and less influential than the older cities of New York, Boston, and Philadelphia.

By looking at the graph on this page, you can see the rise and fall of the population of Washington, D.C. What was happening in the 1860s that caused the city's population to double? What about 1915 through 1920? Why do you think the population has decreased since 1960?

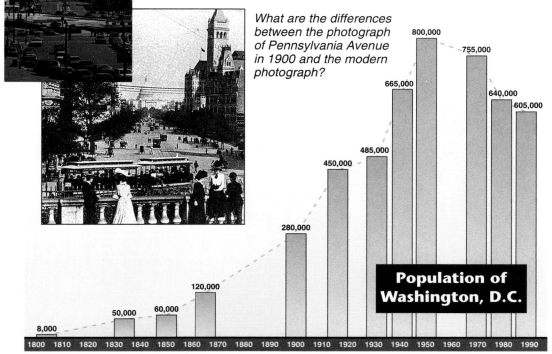

What are the differences between the photograph of Pennsylvania Avenue in 1900 and the modern photograph?

Population of Washington, D.C.

Year	Population
1800	8,000
1830	50,000
1840	60,000
1860	120,000
1900	280,000
1910	450,000
1920	485,000
1930	665,000
1950	800,000
1970	755,000
1980	640,000
1990	605,000

What nations of the world can you name without looking at this map?

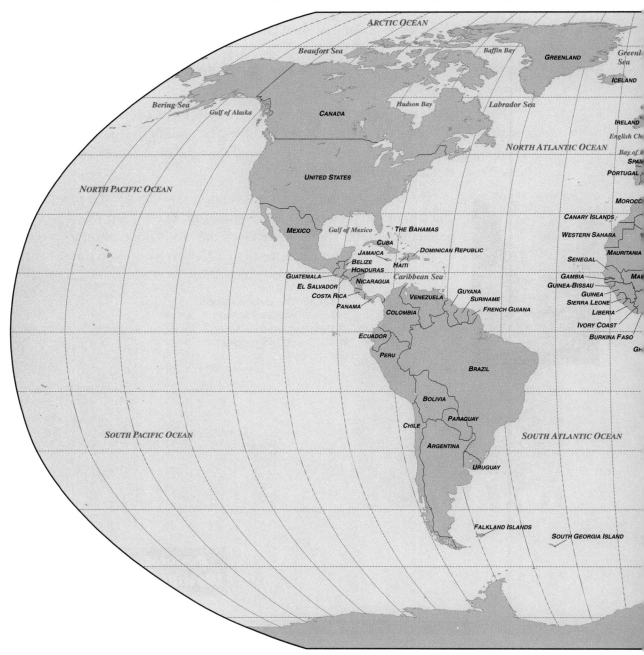

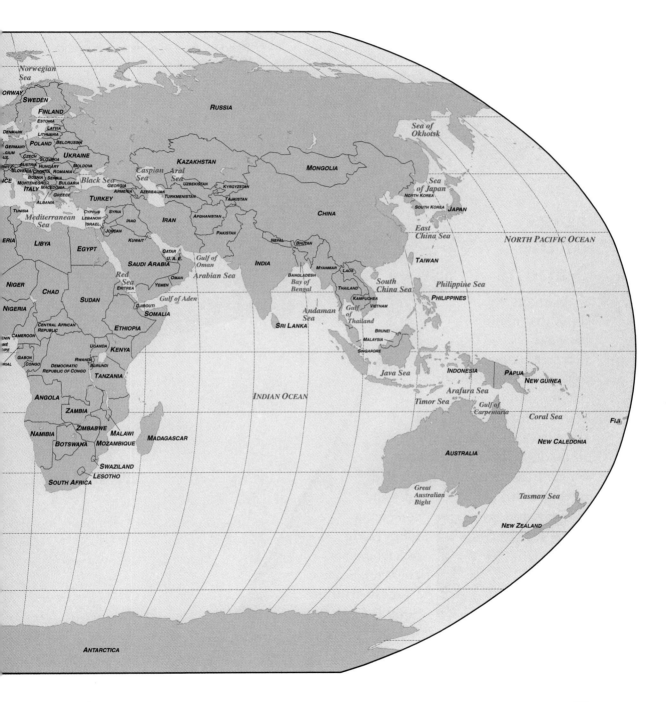

The letters on this Roman flag
stand for the Latin phrase meaning
"Senate and people of Rome."

Flags of the Nations

Perhaps you think that nations have always had flags to represent themselves to the world and to stir patriotism in their own people. However, national flags have been around only since the 1700s. Before that, banners and streamers represented rulers (such as kings or lords) and sometimes ideas (such as a religion or courage). Some Chinese art from 3000 B.C. shows cloth attached to the tops of poles. These early flags were probably made of silk.

> *"Thou hast given a banner to them that fear thee, that it may be displayed because of the truth."*
>
> **Psalm 60:4**

Early flags were used in battle. Sometimes they indicated the direction of the wind to help those who had to shoot arrows at the enemy. Sometimes they helped leaders locate their armies. Eventually flags bore symbols that stood for the people they represented. Do you know what the stars and stripes on the United States flag represent?

Each state in the United States has a flag. You can see the flags in the Resource Treasury at the end of this book. What are some symbols these flags use? Some flags represent individuals, such as the president of the United States, or organizations, such as the United Nations.

This flag was carried by Edward III's troops in a battle between the English and the French in 1346.

83

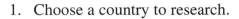
To Research Other Countries

1. Choose a country to research.

2. Get Notebook pages 32-33.

3. Find the information by looking in the books that your teacher provides or recommends.

4. Prepare a report to present to the class.

5

States in the Spotlight

Prologue

What if the entire history of the United States were presented as a play and the fifty states were the characters? Which part would you play?

Imagine what the costumes for this play might be like. We might see characters dressed in the denim overalls of a farmer, in the colored beads of a Comanche warrior, or in the dusty hat and boots of a cowboy. Each character would represent a different state. What type of clothing would your state character wear?

What would your state's role be like? Some roles would be sad; some might be a little frightening; some would even involve hardship and bloodshed. Yet each role would be a proud one, and all the characters would have one important thing in common—freedom.

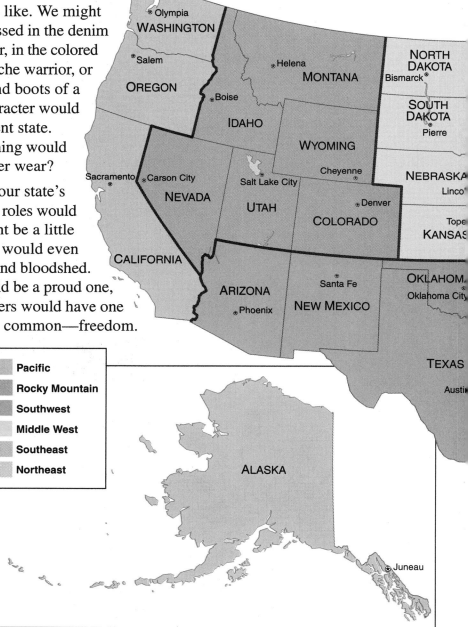

The background scenery for this play could be a map of the United States. How many of the states can you name? In which state and region do you live? What is your state's capital?

NEW HAMPSHIRE

MAINE

VERMONT

Augusta

Montpelier

MASSACHUSETTS

Concord

Boston

Albany

Providence

NEW YORK

RHODE ISLAND

Hartford

CONNECTICUT

PENNSYLVANIA

NNESOTA

Trenton

Paul

MICHIGAN

Harrisburg

NEW JERSEY

WISCONSIN

Madison

Lansing

OHIO

Dover

DELAWARE

Columbus

Annapolis

)WA

INDIANA

W.

MARYLAND

es Moines

ILLINOIS

Indianapolis

VIRGINIA

Richmond

Springfield

Charleston

VIRGINIA

Jefferson City

Frankfort

MISSOURI

KENTUCKY

Raleigh

Nashville

N. CAROLINA

ARKANSAS

TENNESSEE

Columbia

Little Rock

ALABAMA

Atlanta

S. CAROLINA

Jackson

GEORGIA

LOUISIANA

Montgomery

Baton Rouge

MISSISSIPPI

Tallahassee

FLORIDA

Honolulu

HAWAII

N

W   E

S

87

The Northeast

The Northeast region includes eleven states. Do you know which ones they are? Many of these states would have major parts in a play about America's history.

One of the leading roles would belong to Pennsylvania. Can you remember some events that took place there? In 1776 the Declaration of Independence was written and signed at the Second Continental Congress in Philadelphia. Later, in 1787, America's leaders wrote the United States Constitution in this city. Philadelphia was also one of the early capitals of the United States.

To get from Pennsylvania to Massachusetts, which direction would you travel? Massachusetts would also have a leading part in our historical play. Boston, the state capital, was a center of activity before and during the War for Independence. British soldiers killed five colonists in an event called the Boston Massacre in 1770. Later, Boston patriots dumped British tea into the harbor because they thought the tax on tea was unfair. Do you remember what this event was called?

Maryland would be likely to have a singing part in our play. America's national anthem, "The Star-Spangled Banner," was composed there in 1814 by Francis Scott Key as he watched the flag flying over Fort McHenry in Baltimore's harbor.

The American flag still flies over Fort McHenry today.

88

What about costumes for the states of the Northeast? Perhaps Vermont would enter the stage dressed as a Green Mountain Boy, one of a group of Vermont settlers that formed a military force in 1770. The Green Mountain Boys made history in 1775 when they captured Fort Ticonderoga from the British.

New York might wear a crown and a long gown and carry a raised torch to represent the Statue of Liberty. The statue, a gift to the United States from France, stands in New York Harbor. It has become famous as a symbol of America's freedom.

Rhode Island might choose the costume of the Narragansett, one of its earliest peoples. Buckskin leggings and a necklace of bone, shells, and beads would make up this wardrobe. Rhode Island's Narragansett Bay takes its name from this people.

Delaware would likely wear the colorful dress of a Dutch or Swedish settler. A group of colonists from Hoorn in the Netherlands were the first European settlers in the Delaware region. Later, Swedish people also formed a settlement there.

Maine might come on stage dressed in work clothes, carrying the tools of a shipbuilder. People have been building ships in Maine ever since 1607, when English colonists built a boat called the *Virginia*. The first sea battle fought during the War for Independence took place off the coast of Maine in 1775. Today, boats and ships built in Maine are often used for fishing, one of the state's largest industries.

Do you have any ideas for the characters of New Jersey, Connecticut, or New Hampshire? What important events have happened in these states? What kinds of costumes might these state characters wear?

In this Chattanooga cemetery are the graves of many Confederate soldiers.

The Southeast

The Southeast region is made up of twelve states. The states of this region have had a difficult role to play in America's history. Many of them might have battle scars from the terrible war fought in this region. What was this war called?

Eleven southeastern states seceded from the Union and formed their own country, called the Confederate States of America. Some of our play's most tragic scenes would show the Confederacy fighting against the Union. Often family members, even brothers, fought each other in the Civil War.

But pleasant things happened in the Southeast too. In 1791 residents of Maryland and Virginia gave part of their land to America's government.

The Capitol Building in Washington, D.C.

The government wanted to build the city of Washington, D.C., there. Washington, D.C., is now the capital of the United States of America. It is the place where the president lives and where the government makes laws for the country.

Think about which states in the Southeast might have leading roles in our play.

Virginia would definitely have a major part in the play. The first permanent English settlement was formed in Virginia at Jamestown in 1607. Two major wars ended in the state of Virginia. The War for Independence ended in Yorktown in 1781 when Lord Cornwallis surren-

The surrender ending the Civil War took place in the McClean House in the town of Appomattox Court House, Virginia.

dered to George Washington. And the Civil War ended in Appomattox Court House. Do you remember the names of the two generals who reached an agreement there in 1865? How many presidents can you name who came from Virginia? There are eight of them.

South Carolina played a key role in the Civil War. In 1860 it became the first state to secede from the United States. The Civil War began in the harbor of Charleston, South Carolina. What fort did Confederate troops fire upon to begin the fighting?

Fort Sumter was the stage for the Civil War's opening scenes.

Tennessee would have some tragic scenes in its role. During the Civil War, a major battle was fought at Shiloh. Although the Union eventually won the battle, each side lost over ten thousand men. Following the war, an epidemic of yellow fever swept through the city of Memphis. Out of 19,600 people in Memphis, over 5,000 died.

Georgia's role in our play would require a special prop. A machine invented in 1793 near Savannah, Georgia, influenced the history of the entire United States. Eli Whitney was the inventor's name. Do you remember the name of his invention? How did it change life for many Americans?

Mississippi would probably have a part right before a scene change in our play. A major turning point in the Civil War occurred in 1863 when Union soldiers won a battle at Vicksburg, a busy port city on the Mississippi River.

The Vicksburg National Military Park

Some of Louisiana's lines in our play might be in French. Louisiana was part of the region that the French explorer La Salle claimed for France in 1682. The first European settlers in Louisiana were from France; and later, French-speaking people from Canada, called "Cajuns," settled there also. Today the city of New Orleans has a French Quarter where some people still speak a French dialect and enjoy French cooking.

The French Quarter in New Orleans is famous for the lacy ironwork that adorns its buildings.

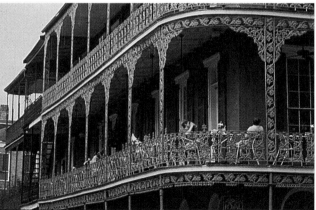

Daniel Boone

How would the states of the Southeast be dressed? Perhaps Kentucky would wear what Daniel Boone wore—a black felt hat and rugged clothing. Daniel Boone cut the first path for travelers through the Appalachian Mountains. In 1775 he led a group of pioneers from Virginia to Kentucky through the Cumberland Gap. He called his trail the Wilderness Road.

West Virginia might wear the costume of a coal miner. Mining has been an important part of the area's history since John Salling discovered coal there in 1742. After further growth of the railroad in the mid-1800s, coal mining became one of the state's largest industries.

Florida might choose the plumed hat and full-sleeved coat of a Spanish explorer in honor of Juan Ponce de León. Ponce de León discovered and named Florida in 1513 while searching for the "Fountain of Youth" he had heard of in legends. Spaniards formed the first permanent European settlement at St. Augustine in 1565.

We still have North Carolina, Alabama, and Arkansas left in the Southeast. What scenes from their histories would you choose to highlight in our play?

To Read a Historical Map

1. You will need Notebook page 40, a pencil, and the map on text pages 86-87.

2. Compare the historical map on Notebook page 40 to the map on text pages 86-87. In what year was the historical map an accurate map of the United States? What war was about to take place at the time this map shows? What things have changed since the time of the historical map?

3. Count the number of states that are shown on the map in your textbook. How many have been added since 1861? Draw in one state on the historical map that has been added to the Union since 1861 and label it on the map.

The Middle West

The middle of our play would bring the states of the Middle West region to the stage. The Middle West has twelve states. Can you remember all of them? Many of these states were part of the territory that made up the Louisiana Purchase. The United States bought this land in 1803. Do you remember which country sold the land?

Iowa was one of the states carved out of the Louisiana Territory. Its part in our play would have some battle scenes. In 1832 Chief Black Hawk, the leader of the Sauk and Fox people, fought with United States troops over the land where his people lived. He was forced to give up a section of Iowa's land to the white settlers, and people called it the Black Hawk Purchase.

Illinois would have a principal part in our drama because one of America's greatest leaders lived and worked there. Today he is buried in Springfield, the capital of Illinois. Do you know the name of this great leader? Chicago, Illinois, is another famous United States city. Did you know that Chicago was nearly destroyed by a great fire in 1871?

Lincoln's tomb in Oak Ridge Cemetery is a much-visited site.

Do you remember which Middle West state is divided into two separate land areas? Michigan is made up of the Upper Peninsula and the Lower Peninsula. What sort of part would it have in our play? Perhaps we would have an old-fashioned car on stage. Henry Ford invented the first working automobile in Detroit, Michigan, in 1896. Detroit began as a fort called Pontchartrain, built by a Frenchman in 1701.

Missouri's part in our play would involve some arguing. It became part of the United States as a result of the Missouri Compromise in 1820. Many people wanted it to be a slave

Henry Ford invented this quadricycle in 1896.

state, and many wanted it to be a free state. It was admitted as a slave state. Do you remember which other state was admitted as a free state

Dred Scott

at the same time? Another event that caused people to argue was the Supreme Court's ruling about a slave from Missouri named Dred Scott. In 1857 the Supreme Court decided that Scott could not have his freedom, even though he had lived in a free state for a time. The ruling also stated that slavery could not be against the law in United States territories.

Kansas would be involved in some violent scenes in our play. Before Kansas became a state, people fought over whether it should be slave or free. An abolitionist named John Brown led a raid on a Kansas settlement at Pottawatomie Creek, and he and his men killed five settlers. Other incidents like these gave this state the nickname "Bleeding Kansas."

South Dakota's part in the play would stir up some excitement in the audience. In 1874 General Custer's soldiers discovered gold in the Black Hills. Gold hunters rushed to South Dakota, and many were not disappointed. Gold is still the chief product of South Dakota's mines today. A tragic event in this state's history took place in 1890. Hundreds of Sioux were killed at Wounded Knee Creek after their leader, Sitting Bull, was arrested by the United States Army and died in the struggle that followed.

The city of Deadwood served as the "capital" for Black Hills gold hunters.

The Cincinnati Red Stockings were undefeated in their first season of professional play.

The Middle West region's costumes would be colorful and varied. Ohio might come dressed in the uniform of a Cincinnati Red Stocking. The Red Stockings became the first professional baseball team in 1869. Do you know what the Cincinnati team is called today?

Wisconsin might wear the blue uniform of a man from the Iron Brigade. This group of men, mostly from the state of Wisconsin, fought for the Union during the Civil War. The troops were commanded by several different Wisconsin generals.

The Mayo Clinic

Perhaps Minnesota would wear as its costume the white lab coat of a medical doctor. In 1889, William Mayo and his two sons started the Mayo Clinic in Rochester, Minnesota. Over the next century, it became one of the world's foremost centers of medical research.

Can you imagine costume ideas for the states of Nebraska, North Dakota, and Indiana?

The Southwest

Let's bring the Southwest region to center stage. This region has the fewest number of states—only four. Can you name them all?

What do you remember about the Trail of Tears? Oklahoma's part in our play would include this journey by people from five Native American groups. In 1859 Oklahoma was set aside to be Indian Territory. Groups of Creek, Choctaw, Chickasaw, Seminole, and Cherokee had to leave their homes in southeastern states and move to Oklahoma. Many grew sick and died on the journey. Later, even the land that was supposed to belong to them was opened for white settlers. Fifty thousand people, nicknamed "boomers," poured into Oklahoma to build homes on the first day that the land opened. Some even entered the land before it was open for settlement. Do you remember what nickname these people were given?

Cold weather was only one of the many hardships the Native Americans endured on the Trail of Tears.

Arizona was part of the land the United States gained from Mexico after the Mexican War. Its part in our play might include a treasure hunt. The first European to explore Arizona was a Spanish priest named Marcos de Niza in 1539. He was looking for the Seven Cities of Cíbola, thought to contain gold. Do you think he found them?

Fragments of Anasazi pottery

*Archaeological finds show
that the Anasazi wore sandals.*

What kinds of costumes would the Southwest states wear? Perhaps New Mexico would come on stage in the fur robes and feathers of the Anasazi people. The Anasazi were farmers who grew corn, beans, gourds, and cotton. They made their homes in the walls of cliffs. The Spanish explorer Coronado found their villages while he, like Marcos de Niza, searched for gold in the Southwest.

Texas might choose to carry the Lone Star flag and a rifle in memory of its struggle for freedom from Mexico in the 1830s. A small band of Texans defended the Alamo mission against the Mexican army in 1836. Finally the Mexicans wore them down and killed all of them. But the struggle was not over. Under the command of Sam Houston, Texans defeated the army of Mexico a month later at the Battle of San Jacinto. For ten years Texas was an independent republic, flying a flag with a single star.

In 1835, Texan men formed a group called the Rangers to defend settlers from bandits and outlaws.

101

Designing Costumes

Have you ever seen a play that made you wish you could be in it? What appealed to you about that play? Maybe one thing was the costumes of its characters. Costumes help audiences better understand a play. Costumes tell about the place and time of the play's action, and they can give clues about the characters' personalities. How do people design costumes?

The first thing a costume designer must do is research. He reads the script of the play and perhaps even watches a rehearsal or two. He must be familiar with the play's setting, or the location and time period in which the action happens.

Historical plays require a designer's special attention. He needs to find out exact details about how people from that time period dressed. Even fabrics and colors of materials are important. What if a designer included the

color yellow in a costume for a Puritan? Puritans never wore yellow; they considered it a haughty color. But yellow might work well in another setting. To some early colonists in America, the color yellow symbolized optimism and happiness.

Scene from Hamlet, *Bob Jones University Classic Players*

Where could a costume designer go to find out these details? Library books are always a helpful source of information. The designer could

also study letters or paintings from the era of the play. These might give him extra hints about fashions of the day, such as folding up one corner of an apron or giving a plume a stylish tilt over the brim of a hat.

Next, the designer makes a sketch of his idea to show the director of the play. The stage crew might need to give its approval to the sketches too. Full hoop skirts for a play set in Civil War times might not be practical if the actors have only a small amount of room to move about on stage.

The last step is actually making the costumes. Cast members must be measured first, and then the fabrics must be purchased, cut, and sewn. But the work is worthwhile when performance night arrives. As different characters come onto the stage in their costumes, the satisfied smiles and admiring eyes of the audience tell the designer he has done his job well.

Scene from Hamlet, *Bob Jones University Classic Players*

The Rocky Mountain Region

Our play's next act belongs to the Rocky Mountain region. Six states make up this region in the northwestern section of the United States. Part of the Rocky Mountain Range can be found in all of these states except one. Can you name them?

Montana would have some turbulent scenes in its part. In 1876 General George Custer and his men fought Sioux and Cheyenne warriors near the Little Bighorn River. The two tribes defeated Custer and his men in a battle called "Custer's Last Stand." A year later, Chief Joseph, the Nez Perce leader, tried to move his people across the Canadian border. He wanted them to settle there rather than on the reservation where the United States government wanted them. After a one-thousand-mile trek, he and his people were captured at Big Hole in the Montana Territory.

Utah's part in our play would begin when a fur trader named Jim Bridger explored the Utah region in 1824. When he tasted the water in the Great Salt Lake, he thought he had found the sea. Do you know why? Later, members of a religious group came to live in Utah. Do you remember which group settled there?

What sort of costumes would we see when the Rocky Mountain states enter the stage? Colorado might wear boots and carry a backpack as mountain climbers do. In 1806, explorer Zebulon Pike discovered one of the most famous peaks in the Rocky Mountain range. He named the steep mountain with its curved top Pikes Peak. The Colorado mountaintops are the tallest in the Rockies.

Nevada might carry mining tools as part of its costume. When Henry Comstock found a rich source, or *lode,* of silver and gold near Virginia City in 1859, he named it the Comstock Lode. Miners poured into Nevada hoping to become rich, and many did.

Buffalo Bill

Perhaps Wyoming would be dressed in a fringed jacket and a cowboy hat like one of its famous people, "Buffalo Bill" Cody. Before retiring to his Wyoming ranch, Buffalo Bill acted in a traveling show that gave people his view of the Wild West.

Idaho might come dressed as missionary Eliza Spalding. She and her husband established the Lapwai Mission Station in the Idaho Territory. Eliza was one of the first women to settle in the Northwest.

The trans-Alaska pipeline

The Pacific

The final act brings the Pacific region to the stage. This region contains five states. Can you name all five?

Alaska and Hawaii would be the two youngest members of our cast. Alaska joined the United States in January of 1959. Secretary of State William Seward first purchased the territory from Russia in 1867. Do you remember any of the names people called Alaska? "Seward's Folly" and "Icebergia" were two of them. But Americans soon learned that Alaska was rich in resources. One of these resources was oil. In 1977, workers completed the trans-Alaska pipeline. This pipeline can carry one and a half million barrels of oil a day from Alaska's north coast to its south coast, where it can be shipped out and sold.

Liliuokalani was the last queen of Hawaii.

Hawaii became a state in August of 1959. The first people to live in the islands were Polynesians. Now people from many different countries live in Hawaii. Kings and queens ruled the islands until 1894. Then the islands formed a republic. Do you remember how many islands make up Hawaii? There are over a hundred in all but only eight main islands. On December 7, 1941, a U.S. naval base at a harbor on the island of Oahu was bombed by Japan. Do you know the name of the harbor?

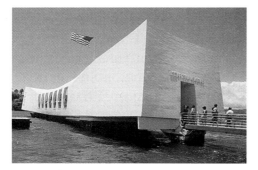
Today a memorial at Pearl Harbor honors those who died aboard the U.S.S. Arizona.

What kinds of costumes could we expect the Pacific states to wear? Washington State might wear a warm coat and carry a bundle of furs. Fur traders were frequent visitors to the Washington territory in the 1700s, and many even settled there. Robert Gray, the leader of a fur-trading expedition, discovered the mouth of the Columbia River in 1792. Now this river is part of the boundary line between Washington and what other state?

Lewis and Clark recorded their findings in a journal. They gave peace medals to the Native American chiefs they met.

Oregon might dress as Meriwether Lewis or William Clark, two explorers who first traveled the route that became the Oregon Trail. In the 1840s, over nine hundred settlers braved the difficult trail from Independence, Missouri, to the Willamette Valley in Oregon.

Perhaps California would dress as one of the Hupa or Yurok people. They lived in the northwestern part of California before any white settlers came. They were skilled woodworkers. They even made their own tools. They fashioned canoes for traveling on rivers and on the sea, and they were also expert fishermen.

107

Epilogue

How do you think the audience will react to our play? Certain scenes might make them laugh; others might bring tears to their eyes. A lot of scenes might make them think about the future.

The drama is not over yet. It will keep going on as long as there is a United States of America. What parts will your state act out in future scenes? Do you like the direction the play is taking? What can you contribute to the next act?

> "Only fear the Lord, and serve him in truth with all your heart: for consider how great things he hath done for you."
>
> **I Samuel 12:24**

6

The Roaring Twenties

By 1926 downtown Chicago traffic looked like this.

The doughboys had come home. Ticker tape parades, waving flags, brass bands, and cheers greeted the soldiers as they marched through American streets again. Americans were glad that the Allies had won the war and even gladder that the war was finally over.

But when the cheers died away, many people felt let down. It was time to turn from patriotism and high ideals to the practical business of daily living. Many people realized that life in America would never be the same as it had been before World War I.

Life was picking up speed. Business was booming. More people were driving cars. Women had begun to dress differently—now many were wearing silk stockings and skirts above the ankles. Even the music was faster. The decade of the 1920s has been given names like the Jazz Age, the Dazzling Decade, and the Roaring Twenties. The 1920s had so many different names because so many different things happened. It was indeed a decade of change.

New Feelings, New Freedoms

Two important amendments were added to the Constitution shortly after World War I. The Eighteenth Amendment, ratified in 1919, out-

Despite the ban on alcohol, police often discovered underground breweries like this one in Detroit.

lawed the manufacturing, transporting, and selling of alcoholic liquor in the United States. People called this ban on alcohol *Prohibition.*

Women of the United States had been working for many years to have another amendment passed. These women wanted *suffrage,* which is the right to vote. Elizabeth Cady Stanton, Susan B. Anthony, and other leaders who fought for this cause were known as *suffragettes.* They collected women's signatures on petitions asking the government to let them vote. By 1920, enough states ratified the proposed amendment that it became the Nineteenth Amendment. Women were allowed to vote for the first time. That same year, women voted in the election that made Warren G. Harding president.

Harding promised a "return to normalcy" for the United States. Most Americans wanted nothing more than for life to return to normal. The soldiers wanted to forget the horrible sights they had seen on the battle-fields. People were ready to stop rationing their food and reading lists of

the names of dead soldiers. They wanted to relax; they wanted a chance to become rich; and they wanted to enjoy life again.

Sometimes suffra-gettes held parades in city streets.

◆ LEARNING HOW ◆

To Make a Petition

1. Think of an idea for a new rule in your school. Make sure your idea is a positive one—something that would be helpful for everyone in the school and would make the school run more smoothly.

2. Write a paragraph at the top of Notebook page 46, explaining your idea and why the new rule is needed.

3. Present your idea to the following people: a parent, an older student, a younger student, a teacher, and someone else from your class.

4. Collect signatures from each person on your Notebook page.

5. Give the petition to your teacher.

Model T's at a Ford factory in 1925

New Products, New Pastimes

"The business of America is business," Calvin Coolidge said, shortly after he was elected to the presidency in 1923.

Business was good in the 1920s. Factories had found ways to *mass produce* their products. For example, Henry Ford's automobile corporation produced car parts on an assembly line. His company was able to make more than one thousand cars per day. His employees used interchangeable parts, which made cars cheaper to repair. Do you remember which inventor pioneered the idea of interchangeable parts in the 1700s?

Because interchangeable parts made producing cars faster and less expensive, Henry Ford was able to gradually reduce the price of an automobile. In 1908 his Model T sold for $850. By 1924 he had brought the price down to $290. Between 1920 and 1921, he sold over a million cars.

In 1907 Woodrow Wilson had called the automobile a "picture of the arrogance of wealth." But now, in the 1920s, many more than just wealthy people were driving automobiles. Between 1920 and 1925, the number of cars in America skyrocketed from eight million to seventeen million.

When people became discontented with the Model T, the Model A was developed.

As more and more people bought cars, they traveled more often and farther away. The more they traveled, the more money they spent. What kinds of things do travelers need to spend money for? Businesses like gas stations, hotels, and restaurants profited from the increase in travel.

People in the 1920s were finding other things to spend their money on as well. More and more people were putting electricity into their homes. Now they could use appliances like washing machines and refrigerators for the first time.

Radios were becoming more common. Families who had radios would often spend entire evenings listening to them. They could hear news, information, sports, and comedy programs. Even more than newspapers, radio helped Americans feel closer to each other.

How were Americans getting the money to pay for these new items? Many people bought items on *credit.* Banks loaned them money for the item, and they gradually paid the banks back in small payments called *installments.*

Others earned extra money by investing in *stock.* Do you know how a person comes to own stock?

At the stock exchange, people can purchase parts of companies. These parts are known as *shares,* and if you own shares, you are said to own stock in a company. When the company makes money, part of that money goes to its shareholders. If you own stock in a company whose business is doing well, there is a good chance you will get back more money than you spent to buy the shares.

Before the 1920s, very few people could afford to buy stock. Stock trading was done mostly by wealthy businessmen. But now that business was doing well and more people were prospering, more people were buying shares in companies. And their earnings, called *dividends,* were usually worth their investment.

The Younger Generation

What would it have been like to be a teen-ager during the 1920s? No doubt there would have been many temptations facing a young person, just as there are today. Partying and movie-going were favorite pastimes. A new style of music called *jazz* was popular, and many were learning a fast new dance called the *Charleston*.

Standards of dress and behavior that parents had upheld for years were being broken down. Up until the decade of the twenties, girls were expected to wear ankle-length skirts. Cosmetics were considered immodest, and every well-bred young lady wore her hair long.

Now young girls' skirts fell just to their knees. Rouge and lipstick were fashionable, even among girls who had been well brought up. Young women all over America sat in barbers' chairs and had their hair cut short around their faces in the new "bobbed" style. Girls who dressed this way were called *flappers*.

Have your parents taught you certain ways in which you should or should not act? These codes of behavior we learn are called *manners*. During the 1920s, many young people began ignoring these codes. It became acceptable for boys and girls to ride alone together in cars. People "crashed" parties that they hadn't been invited to. Some girls smoked cigarettes and drank alcohol along with boys. Many thought the idea of manners was old-fashioned.

Do you think there were any teenagers who refused to go along with the new ideas? Those who did not accept the new ideas often found it hard to be different from their friends.

New York City During Prohibition

Although the Eighteenth Amendment made it illegal for anyone to make or sell alcohol, many people disobeyed the law. Some people made

Izzy Einstein and Moe Smith in disguise

their own alcoholic drinks. And some restaurants, soda fountains, and even candy shops had back rooms or basements where alcohol was sold in secret. Such places were called *speakeasies*. How do you think they got this name?

Sometimes policemen accepted money from the owners of speakeasies and kept quiet about them. But two New York police agents stood up for the law. Izzy Einstein and Moe Smith wanted to stop the illegal buying and selling of liquor.

They wore disguises to get into speakeasies. Izzy was especially known for his creative costumes. Once he carried a violin, pretending to be a musician. At another place he wore a football uniform. And another time he stood out in the cold until his skin turned blue, so that Moe could rush him into the building as a frostbite victim. Once inside, Izzy and Moe would always pour some liquor into the flasks that they carried in their vest pockets. The liquor was the evidence that allowed them to arrest the owners of the speakeasies.

Izzy and Moe's fame spread. When people began to recognize them, they added false mustaches and rubber noses to their disguises and continued their work. The two agents worked just in New York City at first, but soon other cities wanted to hire them for difficult jobs. Over a five-year period, Izzy and Moe made 4,392 arrests.

The young people of the 1920s often referred to themselves as "the lost generation"—a name that at first referred to those lost during the war. Can you think of another way that the young people were "lost"?

In spite of efforts by policemen like Izzy and Moe, the drinking went on. People crowded into speakeasies all over America to drink

alcohol, dance, and have a good time. Do you think they found lasting happiness in these activities?

A young man with large, sad eyes was often seen at the tables of such places. He was a writer, and his novels were very popular. He wrote about the younger generation of his day, basing his stories on things he had actually experienced and observed. He went restlessly from one party to the next, seeking a cure for the emptiness he felt inside. He even went to Paris for a time with his wife and young daughter but returned penniless to America. He never got control of his drinking and spending, and he died of a heart attack at the age of forty-four.

F. Scott Fitzgerald's writings are still read and studied today because they reflect the attitudes and values of a whole generation. He once wrote: "In the real dark night of the soul, it is always three o'clock in the morning." What do you think he meant? What do you believe was the real problem with Fitzgerald's soul?

118

Some people during the 1920s were concerned about souls. They saw the despair of people around them—people searching for joy in places where they would never find it. And they wanted to help.

One man with such concern for souls was Billy Sunday. Before he came to Christ, Sunday was a baseball player for the Chicago White Stockings. He heard the gospel in a service at the Pacific Garden Mission, and he trusted Christ to save him from his sin and give him a new life. A few years later, he gave up generous contracts from two different baseball teams because he believed the Lord wanted him in full-time evangelistic work. He quit baseball and became a preacher.

During the 1920s, Billy Sunday preached to thousands of people in cities and towns all over the United States. He told them that Christ had died to pay for their sins. He encouraged them to put their trust in the Lord and not to look to alcohol and a sinful lifestyle for happiness.

Billy Sunday put the same energy into preaching as he had put into baseball.

Bob Jones was another evangelist who ministered during the 1920s. He held most of his meetings in the southern part of the United States. Meetings like his and Billy Sunday's were called *revivals*.

Many people gathered for this revival meeting held by Bob Jones Sr.

Many people repented of their sin and trusted Christ after attending a revival meeting. Do you think everyone who attended revivals became Christians? What things might have held people back from trusting Christ?

Perhaps some people were more interested in making money than in spiritual things. In 1924 and 1925 the most popular way to invest money was to buy real estate in Florida. Advertisements declared Florida "an emerald kingdom by the southern seas." The value of land was high because so many people wanted to live there. In Miami, land worth thirty dollars an acre in 1910 was selling for seventy-five thousand dollars an acre in 1925. Some people who bought Florida land actually moved there; others sold their land to someone else for a higher price and made large profits.

But the "Florida boom," as it was called, could not last forever. Soon sales and land values started to go down. And in 1926 a hurricane hit the Florida coast, killing 115 people in Miami. Over seventy-six million dollars of property was lost. Hundreds of people in other parts of Florida lost their lives in flooding. Do you think many people were interested in moving to Florida after the hurricane?

About fourteen thousand homes were damaged or destroyed in the Miami hurricane.

Babe Ruth

Do you have any heroes? Some people in the 1920s were more interested in worshiping heroes than in worshiping God.

Some heroes of the 1920s were sports figures. People flocked to baseball games, hoping to see Babe Ruth hit a home run. They listened to Jack Dempsey's boxing matches on their radios. They cheered Gertrude Ederle with a ticker tape parade after her swim across the English Channel.

Some heroes were actors and actresses. In the early 1920s, the films had no sound. People watched the silent screen and read the captions at the bottom to find out what the actors were saying. One of the most popular actors was Rudolf Valentino. After his death in 1926, mourners lined the street for nine blocks outside the funeral parlor, hoping to view his body.

Some heroes were famous not for their noble characters or actions but only because people were fascinated by their lives. Al Capone was held in awe by the public because of his wealth and power. He headed up a group of men in Chicago who earned millions of dollars through illegal activities. People called this network of men the *underworld* or *mobsters*. Capone and his gang were blamed by many for the murders of seven of their enemies in an event called the St. Valentine's Day Massacre of 1929.

Al Capone

Charles Lindbergh
(1902-1974)

The twenties was an age of heroes. But one man stands out above the others as the greatest hero of the decade.

Dawn had just broken over Roosevelt Field, Long Island, on May 20, 1927. A crowd of five hundred people watched as a twenty-five-year-old pilot from Minnesota stepped up into his gray-and-white monoplane, the *Spirit of St. Louis*. Charles Lindbergh was about to attempt to fly solo from New York to Paris—a feat that had never been done before.

Lindbergh started his engines. Armed with sandwiches, a bottle of water, and four hundred fifty gallons of gas, he felt he was prepared. The *Spirit of St. Louis* sped down the runway and lifted into the air.

The long flight was a fairly smooth one. Toward morning of the next day, Lindbergh became worried when sleet began to cling to his plane. For a moment, he wondered whether he should go back. Later he said, "I decided I must not think any more about going back."

In the early afternoon of May 21, Lindbergh flew over Ireland. He knew he was on the right track to France. Once over France, he followed the Seine River into Paris and landed at the city's airport, Le Bourget.

French people swarmed up to the plane, surrounding it almost before Lindbergh brought it to a stop. His first words to the crowd were, "Well, here we are. I am very happy."

Lindbergh's flight of over 3,600 miles had taken a little over thirty-three hours. He was hailed as a hero, not just in the United States and France, but all over the world. In the next few days, he was showered with praise, fan letters, job offers, and even some proposals of marriage. People nicknamed him the "Lone Eagle" and wrote songs about "Lucky Lindy." But through it all, Charles Lindbergh kept his modest smile. "My flight has not done anything to advance the cause of civilization," he said. "Yet I am not unaware that it marks a date."

On leaving Paris, Lindbergh circled the Eiffel Tower twice in his gray-and-white plane. Just before flying away, he dipped the plane low over the Arc de Triomphe. A message fluttered down onto the Place de la Concorde. "Good-bye, dear Paris," it read. "Ten thousand thanks for your kindness to me."

Arthur Schomburg

Some heroes of the 1920s were African Americans. It was during this decade that many African Americans in Harlem, New York, began to preserve their culture in the forms of literature and art. This artistic movement among the black people of Harlem was called the *Harlem Renaissance.*

A Harlem man named Arthur Schomburg had an idea. He decided to start a collection of books, pamphlets, poems, and pictures. All of the works in his collection were either by or about African Americans.

As his collection grew larger and larger, African American poets and writers began coming to look at it. They wanted to find out about their history and to get ideas for writing. Arthur Schomburg kept collecting, even during his travels to other parts of the world. By 1926 he had collected over five thousand books, three thousand manuscripts, and two thousand pictures.

The Carnegie Foundation bought the collection from Schomburg and donated it to the New York Public Library. Today this collection is located in Harlem at the Schomburg Center for Research in Black Culture.

Langston Hughes, poet

Why do you think people in the 1920s were so interested in money and heroes and having fun? Do you think people today are still interested in these things?

In 1928, prices of stock were higher than they had ever been before, and they continued to rise. More than one and a half million people were involved in buying and selling stock. Experts called this period of time "the Big Bull Market."

A bowl of soup was common fare for the poor in the 1930s.

In 1929 Herbert Hoover became president of the United States. The nation seemed to be prospering, and it looked as if America's economy was getting better and better.

But in October of 1929, America's prosperity came to a sudden end. The stock market crashed—the prices of stock fell to rock bottom before people could sell what they owned. Now everyone's shares were worth next to nothing. Thousands of people became poor overnight.

The Roaring Twenties were over. For many, the fast-paced life of travel and parties would soon slow down. Laughing faces would become much more solemn in the decade to follow.

People have called the decade of the 1920s the Golden Age of Sports, the Get-Rich-Quick Era, and the Dry Decade. What name would you give to the 1920s?

What can you learn from studying a past decade? Think about the decade in which you live. In what ways is it different from the 1920s? In what ways is it the same? Perhaps some of the lessons learned in the twenties could apply to your decade today. Can you think of a name to describe the present decade?

"In the day of prosperity be joyful, but in the day of adversity consider: God also hath set the one over against the other, to the end that man should find nothing after him."

Ecclesiastes 7:14

7

Why Prices
Go Up

Supply and Demand

How many different brands of gasoline can you name? Can you name some of the many brands of soft drinks? Why do you think there are so many? Not all people like the same brands of products, so companies and businesses offer a variety to choose from.

When you buy any type of product, you are a *consumer*. Consumers have much influence over what kinds of things are sold by the *manufacturers,* or those who make the products.

For example, imagine that you always buy a CocoCrunch-Bar—your favorite kind of candy bar—but the company that makes the Coco-Crunch-Bar changes the ingredients. The new candy bar does not taste at all like the old one, so you stop buying that brand. All of your friends agree that the old CocoCrunch-Bar was much better than the new one; they stop buying the new one too. What do you think the company will do if no one buys the new candy bar?

The company will probably change back to the old recipe because the company is losing business. The change back to the old recipe is a change that is consumer-driven. A consumer-driven product is one that is determined by the wants and tastes of the consumer—by his demands regarding the product.

The *demand* is what and how much the consumer wants to buy. In a sense, he "demands" that the manufacturers make certain things. One way that a consumer tells companies what he wants is by what he actually buys, as in the CocoCrunch-Bar example. When you and your friends stopped buying that brand, you were actually demanding that the company change back to the old ingredients.

Why are these people boycotting meat?

Can you think of other ways a consumer can tell the manufacturers he does not like a certain product? Some buyers may write letters to a company. Others may boycott the product or store. When people boycott, they refuse to buy or use a product or go to a certain store. It is their way of protesting against something they do not like. Do you think boycotting influences businesses?

The *supply* is what businesses or companies produce. Supply can come from sources such as farms, ranches, factories, or stores. The supply depends on the demand. Companies are going to produce only what will sell the best. They want to make a good *profit*. A profit is the extra money a company makes from its product. If the candy bar company did not want to lose its profit, it would have to change its supply. How would a company change its supply? By going back to the first recipe that everyone liked.

The Economy in War and Revolution

At first, the American Civil War helped the *economy*—especially in the North. The economy is the way a country handles its money and materials. The federal government bought a lot of supplies such as steel,

iron, clothing, and food from Northern companies. How do you think this exchange of supplies helped the North? The money the government gave for the supplies allowed businesses to expand and make more products.

As the war kept on, however, money grew scarce. To pay for goods, the government printed

Most of the artillery used during the Civil War was manufactured in the North.

more money so that it could buy more products. Did more money help? No. With more money, people demanded more than could be supplied. Because the demand was greater than the supply, prices rose.

People in the South had a harder time because they lacked many of the supplies that the North had. This lack of goods caused the prices for the goods the South *did* have to soar. The prices became so high that a pair of regular shoes cost about two hundred dollars!

The effects of the war were not changed overnight. Rebuilding an economy is a long process. Balancing supply and demand takes time too. The government could not help by printing more money or by taxing the people. Today the government is careful in how it interferes with the economy. Instead of adjusting the money supply, the government allows the law of supply and demand to work by itself. This policy is an "echo" from lessons America learned long ago.

Communist and Capitalist

Do you think every country runs on consumer-driven supply and demand? Some countries are *communist*. In these countries, the government determines the supply. Leaders decide what items to produce and then determine a set price for those items. Can you think of some problems with this system?

Sometimes a communist government, because of poor planning, will not produce what the people need. How does it affect the citizens when not enough food items, such as bread or canned goods, are produced? The government prices may be low, but there may not be enough goods for everyone to purchase. Some people must go without.

Do you think all of these people will be able to purchase meat from this Russian sausage shop?

When there is not enough of a certain item that people need, such as food, gasoline, or water, there is a shortage. Shortages are hard. People must stand in long lines, sometimes not even getting what they wait for. When they finally do get to buy the product, they must pay a high price.

Colonial Economics

In early America, most of the land had been chartered to companies or to people in the courts of England. The settlers were allowed to work on this land, but most of the crops they produced were used by everyone. What system is similar today? Neither the land nor the crops harvested belonged to the individuals who worked them.

In 1623 William Bradford put an end to group ownership of land and supplies in Plymouth Colony. He divided the land among the settlers, allowing the individual families to work their own land and to keep their own crops. The settlers could decide for themselves what they wanted to do with their property. How was this system similar to capitalism?

Captain John Smith of Virginia noticed a good change in the people of his colony. John Smith wrote, "When our people were fed from the common store, glad was he who could slip from his labor." But when they had their own land, he wrote, "they will do in a day" what they used to do in a week. Why do you think the settlers worked harder on their own land? What "echoes" of this philosophy do you see today?

Do you ever stand in long lines in stores? Is it because there is not enough of something? Your reasons for standing in line are usually different from the reasons that someone in a communist country would stand in line.

In the United States, the supply is not determined by the government as it is in a communist country. Instead, individual people decide what and how much to produce. They make their decisions based on what the consumer wants. What is this system called? It is a consumer-driven economy.

The kind of government that uses supply and demand in this manner is a *capitalist* government. The United States is capitalist, allowing individual people to own the businesses and goods.

How might the owner of a bakery decide which items to produce in greater quantity?

Have you ever seen several businesses of the same type on one street? How is this arrangement good for the economy?

Monopolies

Can you think of why both the manufacturer and the consumer might like a capitalist system? People want to make their own choices about the way they earn and spend money.

One benefit of a consumer-driven economy is *competition*. When you run in a race with your classmates, you *compete* with them for first place. In the same way, manufacturers compete for the consumer's business. Manufacturers try to please the buyer with good products and low prices. Competition often leads to lower prices.

What do you think happens when competition does not exist between businesses? Without competition, a *monopoly* can occur. Have you heard this word before? A monopoly exists when only one business sells a product. Because just one business sells a certain product, the business can charge as much as it wants. How does this monopoly affect the consumer?

With a monopoly, the consumer does not have a choice when he selects a product. To understand monopolies, go back to the CocoCrunch-Bar example. When you do not like the new CocoCrunch-Bar, you can stop buying it and buy another brand. Pretend, though, that the Coco-Crunch-Bar Company is the only company that makes candy bars. Whenever you buy a candy bar, it is one that the CocoCrunch-Bar Company has made.

How does a monopoly affect consumer-driven supply and demand? Because the CocoCrunch-Bar Company is a monopoly, it can charge as much as it wants. The company does not depend so much upon the tastes of the consumer. Why? The company gets all the profit from any candy bars sold. How can a monopoly become unfair to the consumer?

136

Monopolies can be worse when they control items that people need, such as gasoline, food, or electricity. These types of products are called *resources*. Resources are valuable products that people must have in order to live—natural products like land, water, and sunlight. Some resources, such as coal, oil, and natural gas, give us power, light, and heat.

Can you think why a monopoly of these products can hurt the consumer? Because a consumer needs these things to live, he must buy them regardless of the cost. Since everyone needs resources, the government makes laws to prevent businesses from having a monopoly of certain resources.

Where do we get these resources? Many are found naturally in the earth. Resources are an important part of a nation's economy. Countries such as the United States have many natural resources. Developing these resources so that they may be used is important. How do you think the supply of resources affects the way Americans live? When a country is rich in resources and develops them well, it tends to have a higher *standard of living,* or way of life. Why do you think people can live better when there are more natural resources?

Mild regions of the United States have peaches as a natural resource.

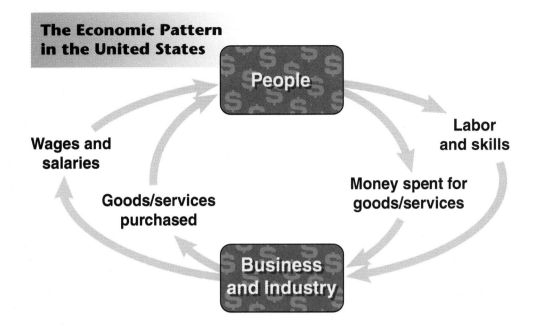

The Economic Pattern in the United States

People

Labor and skills

Wages and salaries

Money spent for goods/services

Goods/services purchased

Business and Industry

As you can see, businesses and consumers depend on one another. Without businesses, consumers would have to supply their needs themselves. This process would take a lot of time or would even be impossible in most situations. Without the consumers, the businesses would go *bankrupt,* or run out of money.

Was there ever a time when the consumer had to make a lot of the products he needed for himself? In the Colonial days of America, people usually mastered one skill and used that skill to produce goods that they could trade. Do you remember what this system of payment was called? Trading goods for other goods is called *bartering.* Do you think a barter system would be possible in the United States today?

As the nation grew, there was more money available. People could then pay for products with money instead of with skills. Yet they still had to use their skills to earn the money. Production continued to be slow, and sometimes demand was not met by supply. Then in the 1800s, the American Civil War marked the beginning of mass production and the Industrial Revolution.

Money

When you buy a CocoCrunch-Bar, you pay for it with money. Where did that money come from? Maybe your parents gave it to you as a present or as payment for jobs you did. But where did they get the money?

People must work for the money they use to buy things that they need and want. When people work, their *employers* pay them. Where do employers get money? Their money comes from the products they make and sell.

Do you think there would ever be enough money for everyone in the United States to buy what he needs or wants? Who actually makes the bills and coins that we get paid with or use to buy products?

The United States has a main banking system called the *Federal Reserve System.* It controls the amount of bills and coins in *circulation.*

If there is not enough money in circulation, business will slow down. If there is too much money, prices will become too high. Why do prices rise? When there is not enough money, people must stop buying, leaving the manufacturers and businesses with all the products they have already made. Because there are so many products and so few buyers, the prices drop. With these low prices, many of the businesses cannot make enough money, so they cannot pay their employees. What happens then? Businesses that cannot pay their employees must take away jobs from some of their workers. Why would losing a job under these circumstances be harmful?

When there is more money in circulation, people are paid more and demand more products. Manufacturers then hire more workers to meet this demand, and the economy grows.

Too much money may hurt the economy if the manufacturers cannot meet the consumer demand. What happens when the demand is greater than the supply? Prices go up. This process is called *inflation.*

Minting Money

Have you ever examined a quarter and wondered how it was made? *Minting* is the process of making coins. The place where coins are made is called the *mint*.

Mint sculptor holding a large model

The minting of coins involves many steps. The government chooses a design for its coins. What design is on a quarter? An artist will first make the design out of plaster. Some models are almost twelve times larger than a real coin. Why do you think the plaster models are so big? The artist can carve details more easily on this larger model.

This tool, called a hub, is created when the coin-sized image is cut into steel.

These quarter dies were made from the hub at the top of the photo.

The plaster model is then used to make a *die* of the coin. A die is made from steel and presses the design of the coin onto thin sheets of metal. Coins are stamped out of these sheets.

Minting coins requires careful work. In what ways would a minting artist have to be careful? What happens if he makes a mistake? Would you like to have a job working at a mint?

Needs and Wants

When prices are high because of inflation, what do you think people do? They must try to save money. How can they save? One way is by buying only those things that are *needs*. Needs are those things such as food, clothing, and shelter. How are needs different from *wants?* Do you think every person has the same wants?

Which product is a need? Which is a want?

Another way to save money is by planning a *budget*. A budget is a plan that determines how money will be spent. With a budget, a person decides ahead of time how he will spend his money. How would this plan help save money? A budget can help a person make wise decisions about spending and saving his money.

The way people spend or save money affects the law of supply and demand. Do you know why? When people do not spend as much, there is plenty of supply and prices are lower. When people spend more, the supply diminishes, and prices go up. Because people earn their own money, they are free to spend it as they choose. In what ways can this freedom be helpful or harmful?

To Plan a Budget

1. Get Notebook page 57 and a pencil.

2. Pretend that you earn ten dollars each week. Decide how much money you will spend in each category on the Notebook page.

3. Fill in the amounts of money you will spend for each category. Do not spend more than your ten dollars for that week. Compare your amounts in the different categories. Have you spent more for certain items than for others? What things are more important? Which things could you get along without?

John Maynard Keynes
(1883-1946)

Were you interested in math when you were four years old? John Maynard Keynes was. John was born in Cambridge, England, in 1883. For his elementary education, he read poetry and went to plays. He gained an interest in the economy from his father, Dr. John Neville Keynes, who studied economics.

Keynes at age six

When he was fourteen, John went to Eton College, a secondary school, on a scholarship he had won in a math contest. Keynes, as most people called him, was a good student. He enjoyed all subjects. He graduated from Cambridge University, where he later taught economics and edited a journal on the economy.

Keynes took great interest in political and economic affairs. He wrote several books on economics and developed a plan suggesting that the government be involved with regulating the market and the law of supply and demand. Many other economists disagreed because they believed that the government should not get involved with the economy.

Keynes as a nineteen-year-old Eton graduate, 1902

After the Great Depression in the United States, Keynes made several proposals for the government to take action. He believed that a government could help its country by taxing and borrowing. He also believed that in times of economic depression, the government should spend money to help the economy. Can you think of reasons that people would disagree with this theory? When times are hard, people try to save as much money as they can. How would this saving affect supply and demand?

Keynes also proposed that people save during inflation when prices are higher. What would saving do to the supply and demand? His ideas were surprising for his time. Other economists disagreed with him. After World War II, however, countries started to listen to some of John Maynard Keynes's ideas.

Keynes wrote several books about the economy. He even met with President Roosevelt to discuss the New Deal. His ideas have greatly contributed to the workings of the economy in England, the United States, and other countries around the world.

*Keynes
in later life*

How is this boy affecting the law of supply and demand?

The Economy and You

Consider supply and demand, money, capitalism, and budgets. Why is it important to learn about economics? Someday you will have a job and will earn money to provide for your needs. In the future, and even now, when you buy things in the store, you are affecting the law of supply and demand.

You, as a consumer, are very important to the economy. You can affect not only your own community but also the nation, which, in turn, affects other countries.

The economy is always changing. Some years are more stable than others. Why does it change so much? There are many factors that affect supply and demand. These factors include resources, jobs, trade with other countries, war, and the money supply. While you may not have control over these things, you can be careful about how you spend your money and which products you choose to buy.

> "He that is faithful in that which is least is faithful also in much."
>
> **Luke 16:10**

The Market System Works

1. Get Notebook page 58, a pencil, and the materials your teacher gives you.

2. Listen as your teacher tells you the rules of The Economy Game.

3. Choose your position or take the position your teacher assigns you. Get your money from the bank. Choose who will go first, following your teacher's directions.

4. Play the game for a predetermined amount of time or until one player has five times the money he had originally.

8

Hard Times

False Promises

Have you ever wanted something that cost a great amount? Because you did not have enough money, you had to save for a long time to buy it. Was it hard to wait and save your money? During the 1920s many Americans decided not to wait. They bought what they wanted whether they had enough money or not.

In the 1920s it seemed that there was plenty of money. Wages were high and borrowing from banks was easy. No one stopped to think about the future and how much he was spending. But people were not as prosperous as they thought. What could make them think they had plenty of money when they did not?

Many people spent more than they had earned. They bought new cars and stoves and washing machines on *credit*. Buying on credit means

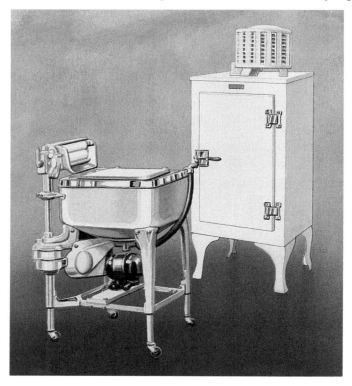

that they paid only a small part of the price at first, and then they made payments called *installments*. If buyers could pay all of their installments, they and the businesses were happy. But many people bought more than they could pay for.

A 1920s washing machine (left) and refrigerator

150

When some people bought many items on credit, they found that they were unable to make their installment payments. Businesses received less money in payment. Why was that? Also, banks lent money to people who were not able to pay it back.

Factory owners produced more and more goods, more than the American people could buy. Because the factory owners could not sell all the goods they had made, they produced less. What do you think happened? Not as many factory workers were needed. Many lost their jobs. Those workers who had purchased items on credit did not have the money to pay their installment bills.

The businessmen who had sold the items on credit were not paid on time. Because these businesses were losing money, they had to let some of their workers go. Now more people were out of work and needed money. Those who had saved money in banks went to get it out.

But the bankers had not been wise in their practices. They had lent money to people who were not able to pay it back. Sometimes they lent so much money that they had little left. When people who had deposited money in the banks went to withdraw their money, the banks did not have enough money in the vaults to give to them.

The Crash

What Is the Stock Market?

Stocks are papers showing that someone has paid to be part owner of a company. Each stock represents one *share* in the business. The place where people can buy and sell stocks is called the *stock exchange.* The business of buying and selling stocks at the stock exchange is called the *stock market.* Why do you think people want to own part of a company? When a company makes money, part of the money goes to stockholders.

Buying stocks became a popular way to *invest* money, that is, to spend money with the promise of getting more back. Money paid to stock-owners is called *dividends.* For a while, stocks paid good dividends to shareholders.

Why do you think the stock market attracted so many people? Part of the reason was that it looked like a way to make extra money without having to work long hours to get it. Another reason was that investing in America's companies was patriotic. That is, it meant the investor believed in America's future.

A day at the stock exchange in 1920

The Stock Market Works

1. Your teacher will give you one hundred dollars in play money.

2. Go to the "trading floor" and see the "stocks" your teacher has there. Check what the prices of the stocks are today.

3. Purchase some stocks and track what happens to them in the "market." Record your losses or earnings.

Shaky Market

Someone who thinks the stock market prices will go up is called a *bull.* This person wants to buy low and sell high to make a quick profit. Sometimes people "bullish on the market" will buy new shares to try to make the market go up. On the other hand, someone who tries to sell shares because he thinks the market prices will go down is called a *bear.*

In the late 1920s, many people put their money into stocks. Was the market a bull or a bear market then? But the prices went up too quickly, and the stocks were not worth the money. If, for example, someone had to pay four hundred dollars for a share, he would have to wonder whether he could ever get that money back in dividends. With prices high, many began to worry about the stocks they already owned and refused to buy more.

Black Thursday

People then tried to sell their stocks. So many people wanted to sell their stocks that there were few buyers. Prices began to go down. What kind of a market was this—bull or bear? When stockholders saw that their stocks were losing value, what do you think happened?

People began selling stocks even faster, trying to get some money for them before they became worthless. On October 24, 1929, now known as Black Thursday, this selling only sped up the rate at which stocks lost their value. It would have been better for investors to wait, to hold onto their stocks and wait for prices to level out. But they did not; they caused a *panic*. What do you think that means?

Some big banks tried to help keep prices up. They bought a lot of stocks. It helped, but not for long. When the prices dropped again, the banks could not help. They had already put too much of their money into the market. The stock market was on the brink of disaster.

An anxious crowd outside the stock exchange waits for word about the market.

Black Tuesday

On Tuesday, October 29, 1929, prices went so low that the stock market in New York City *crashed.* That means the stocks lost more than half their value. Few people wanted to buy stocks, not even for a dollar a share.

Part of the problem came from the way people had been buying stocks. Many had borrowed money to buy them, hoping to sell at a profit. That way they could pay off their debt and still make money.

In the late 1920s, operators at the stock exchange took many calls from people wanting to sell their stock.

What do you think the stock market crash did to the economy? For one thing, it showed people that they could not keep borrowing and spending money as they had been doing. It also meant that for many people life would change drastically—and suddenly.

The Depression

Since many banks had invested people's money in the stock market, they did not have money on hand to pay out to those who wanted their money. What do you think happened? There was a *rush* on the banks. The first people in line got most of their money. Others got nothing at all.

> *"He that trusteth in his riches shall fall: but the righteous shall flourish as a branch."*
>
> **Proverbs 11:28**

People rush to withdraw their money from a bank in danger of failing.

The leaders of the Treasury Department thought there would be trouble and closed the banks for a *bank holiday.* Although everyone knew that there was no "holiday," most people accepted the pause quietly. They thought that surely things were as bad as they could get and would get better soon. They did not anticipate what the next few years would bring.

Wealthy and poor alike lost their money and possessions. Nearly everyone became poor. One of every four people who wanted to work could not find a job. Families lived on small amounts of food and could not buy new clothes. Try to imagine what it would be like to have only one or two shirts or dresses to wear.

In the cities people worked for pennies a week. Men who had once been wealthy sold apples on street corners. Others who had no work stood in long lines at *soup kitchens* to get a small portion of soup or bread. Many times people got what food they could from garbage dumps.

Many of the men who sold apples and stood in bread lines had once been successful businessmen.

By the spring of 1930, more than four million people had no jobs. The next year there were eight million people without work. And ten months after that, thirteen and a half million workers were looking for jobs. Almost one-third of all the people in the United States who were able to work could not find work.

New York, New York
Wednesday, March 12, 1930

7 A.M.

This boy went every day to buy a loaf of bread for his family.

He ran with the nickel to the store, fearing someone would take his money.

When he went home with the bread, he ran even faster because someone always tried to grab the loaf from him.

When he grew up, he became a track athlete.

159

Many farmers had borrowed money to purchase more land and improve their farms. What do you think happened to the farmers who could not pay on their loans? Some of them had to give up their land and their homes. Others tried to make the best of things, producing grain and animals to sell wherever they could.

The trouble was, however, that they could no longer get the same prices for their goods. Wheat had sold for $1.05 a bushel in 1929; in 1932 a bushel sold for only $0.39. Cotton had earlier brought $0.17 a pound; after the crash it sold for $0.06 a pound. How could farmers make enough to live on and pay their debts at that rate?

What can you say about the prices in 1933 by looking at the chart of prices? What about the prices in 1923? Compare the prices in 1933 to the prices in 1903 and 1913. Then compare the prices in 1923 to the ones in 1933. How would the change in prices affect the farmers?

Fifty Years of Prices

	1903	1913	1923	1933	1943	1953
eggs 1 doz.	$0.26	$0.34	$0.50	$0.29	$0.57	$0.70
milk ½ gal.	$0.14	$0.18	$0.28	$0.21	$0.31	$0.47
potatoes 10 lb.	$0.17	$0.17	$0.30	$0.23	$0.46	$0.54
sugar 5 lb.	$0.28	$0.27	$0.50	$0.26	$0.34	$0.53
butter 1 lb.	$0.28	$0.38	$0.55	$0.28	$0.53	$0.80

Dust storms brought devastation to many midwestern farms. Many Oklahoma families like this one took refuge in California.

Just when farmers thought the worst had passed, terrible droughts hit, and the few farmers who had held onto their land could not produce anything to sell. When massive windstorms whipped through the dry land of the central United States, great clouds of dust covered the land. Several states came to be called the "dust bowl." Do you think the farmers were able to harvest good crops during this time? With no crops to sell, the farmers were unable to repay their loans.

For years before, some farmers had plowed the prairie's natural grass and planted wheat. Wheat cannot hold down the topsoil of the plains the same way the original grass can. The farmers did not know that droughts hit the central part of the United States every twenty to thirty years. When the droughts came, winds swept up the dry soil and turned it into enormous dust clouds. At times the blowing dirt was so thick that it blotted out the sun.

The man who took most of the blame for the depression—or at least the criticism—was President Herbert Hoover. Places where people lived in boxes or roughly made shanties were called "Hoovervilles." Old newspapers were called Hoover blankets. Cartoonists drew unflattering pictures of the president. And many people said the trouble was all his fault. But the seeds of trouble had been growing years earlier.

President Calvin Coolidge had said, "The business of America is business." He meant that as long as businesses were doing well, America would do well. What he and many Americans did not stop to think about was that while many businesses seemed sound, they were running on credit.

By the time the spending habits and the stock speculating caught up with America, Coolidge was out and Hoover was in. Hoover thought that if he did nothing, America would work itself out of the depression. He refused to let the government lend money to the needy for fear they would get lazy. He believed, as Coolidge had, that business would right itself.

A "Hooverville" in Seattle, Washington

163

During Roosevelt's campaign in Indianapolis, he was welcomed by a two-mile-long parade.

Starting Over

After two and one-half years of fear and unhappiness, Americans were looking for relief.

In 1933 Franklin Delano Roosevelt (often known as FDR) became the president. He promised everyone relief from the depression with

his plan, the *New Deal.* His idea was for the government to plan projects and to pay Americans to do the work.

When he was sworn into office, FDR gave a speech that he believed would give everyone a breath of hope. The new president said, "The only thing we have to fear is fear itself—nameless, unreasoning, unjustified terror which paralyzes needed efforts to convert retreat into advance." What did he mean? Do you think people believed he was right?

FDR speaks at his first inauguration in 1933.

The media poked fun at the grim face Hoover wore on FDR's inauguration day.

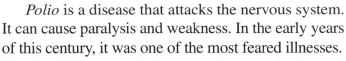

Franklin Delano Roosevelt
(1882-1945)

While sailing one afternoon when he was thirty-nine years old, Franklin Roosevelt fell overboard. Although he was a strong man and used to the water, he took a chill. The next day he was so tired he could not get dressed, and his leg dragged. Soon he could not stand at all or hold a pen. He knew what these symptoms meant even before the doctors told him: polio.

Polio is a disease that attacks the nervous system. It can cause paralysis and weakness. In the early years of this century, it was one of the most feared illnesses. Mostly children got it; but sometimes, as in Roosevelt's case, an adult

came down with it. People with polio rarely recovered fully. Roosevelt, however, refused to give up trying to walk again.

Before he got polio, Roosevelt had been running for vice president on the Democratic ticket with presidential nominee James Cox. Although the Cox-Roosevelt team lost to the Harding-Coolidge team, Roosevelt was making a name for himself in the Democratic Party. He had high hopes of winning another election. After his illness left him unable to stand alone or without leg braces, many told him to give up trying for public office.

Roosevelt with his family in 1919

165

FDR was not about to give up. While he recuperated, he wrote letters to important Democratic leaders all over the country. In 1928 some of those leaders asked him to run for governor of New York. He did, and he won. Rather than allowing his struggle with polio to ruin his career, FDR overcame his personal tragedy to serve his country.

He became president in 1933, just when the banks were failing and the country was sliding into the worst of the depression. The new president gave many radio talks, which he called "fireside chats." Why do you think he called them that? In them he explained what he was doing and what he hoped would happen with his plans. Some people liked him a great deal; others thought he was taking too much power.

Roosevelt was re-elected as governor in 1930.

He pleased enough people, however, to get re-elected—and re-elected. Ever since George Washington had refused to run for a third term, no president had served more than twice. But FDR served a third term and

was elected to a fourth. But just eighty-three days after his fourth inauguration, he died. A speech he had written for the next day said, "The only limits to . . . tomorrow will be our doubts of today."

In his fireside chats FDR explained his ideas for the nation's future.

The New Deal

Under the New Deal, millions of Americans went back to work. They built roads, bridges, and dams throughout the country. Besides giving people jobs, these projects improved transportation and helped prevent floods. One program, the *Civilian Conservation Corps,* also known as the CCC, planned and built many of America's national parks.

FDR had so many new programs and organizations in action, each one called by the first letters of its name, that they were known as the "alphabet agencies."

FDR's National Recovery Administration insured fair competition for businesses.

This political cartoon presented FDR as a doctor trying to treat Uncle Sam's ailments.

This early group of workers from the Industrial Workers of the World and Arizona Metal Miners are ordered out of town.

The National Industrial Recovery Administration (NIRA) allowed businesses to work together to decide how much of a certain product would be made.

Many unions voiced their opinions through orderly methods like voting.

What other power did that arrangement give big business? By controlling how much of a product was made, big business also controlled the price. The scarcer the product, usually the higher the price. How did this plan match the American ideal of fair competition in buying and selling? It did not.

The National Labor Relations Board, or NLRB, opened the way for another change in business. It allowed workers to form groups called *unions* within companies to bargain with the owners. Before that, workers mostly had to take the wages and the treatment of the employers without question—or quit. Now they could unite and try to force the employers to pay them more or give them safer and cleaner places to work.

Another program was the the Agricultural Adjustment Administration, AAA. By this act, the government paid farmers not to produce as much. Why do you think that was? If there was not as much to sell, the prices would go up. The act also gave the president the right to sell extra American products to other countries. The Farm Credit Administration, the FCA, lent money to farmers at lower rates than banks could.

Many people used food stamps to purchase groceries.

Farmers began to learn about *conservation,* or ways of safely and carefully using natural resources such as water and topsoil. Never again did they want to experience a dust bowl. With new ways of farming and with help from the government, farmers began to recover slowly from the worst of the depression.

These farmers are learning to use their land more efficiently.

Legacies of the New Deal

Although the New Deal did some good for America, it also caused problems. To make the New Deal work, the government became more involved in the people's private lives and businesses. People resented being told where and how to work, what fields to use, and what crops to plant. Some people were sure the government programs were not right. They took the government to court. As a result, some of the programs enacted by the New Deal were declared unconstitutional.

Another problem with the New Deal was that the government could not pay for all the programs. The government had to borrow money. Do you think governments should have different spending habits from individuals? What do you think happened? The debt kept growing, and today it "echoes" as one of America's biggest problems.

Playing Miniature Golf

Golf had long been a highly revered game; some called it "the Royal and Ancient Game." But in 1916, James Barber brought it down to size—

or rather undersize. He had a small version of a large golf course built on his estate, the first miniature golf course.

In ten years, little golf greens were showing up atop New York office buildings. Wall Street businessmen relaxed at lunch by playing "a round" of golf. Other cities offered luxurious indoor miniature golf courses, complete with refreshments and lawn chairs to rest in.

Even after the "crash," the game was popular. Perhaps it was the low admission prices; perhaps it was the illusion of being master of the once snobbish game; perhaps it was the escape into a world where, for a moment, there still were country clubs and exotic places. Whatever the reasons, miniature golf became the "Madness of 1930." The game faded out then, only to return in the 1950s. Today it is still one of America's most popular, and original, pastimes.

During the depression, poor people in Vienna, Austria, searched for food in garbage piles.

Problems in Europe

America was not the only country to suffer from the depression. European countries struggled with high unemployment and slow production levels. Many people thought their governments should do more to help them. Power-hungry men gained rule in several European countries.

Once these men held high political office, they became *dictators,* leaders who had total control. In Germany Adolf Hitler rose to power promising a cure to the country's ills.

In 1936 Hitler and Benito Mussolini, dictator of Italy, agreed to support each other in case of war. Together their countries were called the *Axis* powers. This agreement began the assembling of the countries that would fight against the Allies in the Second World War.

Hitler seemed eager to go to war. He wanted to prove to the world that Germans were better than any other people. He used the German army to take land from smaller, weaker nations around Germany. The people of Britain and France did not like Hitler's actions. However, they did not actively try to stop him. They remembered the horrors of World War I and wanted to avoid another war. They thought that if they let Hitler take a little territory, perhaps he would be satisfied and they would not have to go to war again.

Adolf Hitler at a 1935 rally in Munich, Germany

9

Rulers with Iron Fists

Adolf Hitler

Benito Mussolini

Joseph Stalin

Have you ever played with a bully? A bully is usually someone bigger or stronger than you are. He uses threats to frighten you and force you to do things his way. You might obey a bully, not because you like him or agree with him but because you are afraid he will hurt you if you do not do what he wants.

Imagine that you live in a country that is governed by a bully—one man who has absolute power. Whatever he wants becomes law. All the people in the country must do what this bully wants, whether they agree with his ideas for the country or not. No one is allowed to talk about his own ideas or opinions. If anyone dares to disobey the man in power, that person may be taken away from his family, put in prison, or even executed. Do you think life in such a country would be very happy?

That is what life would be like in a *totalitarian* country. Totalitarianism is a form of government in which the government has total control over the people's lives. Usually governments like these are led by one man, called a *dictator.*

America is a form of *democracy*—a government in which the people work together to make all the important decisions. Americans have freedoms that many other people do not have. Americans can vote for their leaders, express their opinions freely, make decisions about where they live and work, and worship God as they please.

In a totalitarian country, people have very little freedom. They must, at least outwardly, agree with the government about everything. They must go to whatever church the government says is right. They must live wherever the government places them and do whatever work the government wants them to do. Children must study the government's teachings in school. If anyone has free time, he is often required to spend it in some form of community service or government-sponsored activity. Some totalitarian countries have secret police who spy on people to see that they are following orders.

After World War I, several countries were left with weak, indecisive governments. Discouraged people were willing to follow anyone who could make a difference—who could get their country back on its feet again. These countries were easy prey for totalitarian leaders.

People in totalitarian countries are often forbidden to leave their country even for important family events.

Italy: *Il Duce!*

Benito Mussolini was born in the Romagna region of Italy. His father was a blacksmith—tough and strong. He taught young Benito to stand up for himself against the neighborhood bullies. "To win respect," he told Benito, "always carry a sharp knife, and use it when you have to!" Do you think this was good advice?

Benito's mother was a schoolteacher. She was gentle and compassionate, and she often worried about Benito's violent temper. She wanted him to become a teacher. She persuaded his father to send him to the finest schools. As a teenager, Benito was expelled from two different schools. But when he finally made up his mind to work hard, he graduated at the top of his class.

Benito Mussolini did teach school for a time. Then he left Italy and went to Switzerland. For months he went from job to job, even working in a chocolate factory. But nothing satisfied him. He wanted to do something great. He wanted other people to respect him and follow him.

From his boyhood, Mussolini had been interested in politics. Now in Switzerland, he spent most of his evenings in cozy little restaurants called *cafés,* discussing political ideas with other European immigrants. In one of these cafés he met two men and a woman from Russia. The men were named Lenin and Trotsky, and the woman was Angelika Balabanoff. Mussolini listened excitedly to their ideas about government by the ordinary people, the working class, not by a monarch or a privileged upper class. These were the same ideas his father believed in. Ideas like these are part of a philosophy called *socialism.*

Mussolini speaking in the Colosseum

Mussolini returned to Italy and became involved in the Socialist Party. He wrote for a Socialist newspaper. He stirred up workers in revolts and strikes, and once he led a violent mob in a riot through the city streets. He was even put in jail several times. Eventually he became a leader in the Socialist Party.

But when World War I began, Mussolini changed his mind about socialism. The Socialists did not believe Italy should join the war. But Mussolini saw advantages for the nation if they joined the Allies. He lost favor with the Socialists for taking this position. But he stood firm, and when Italy joined the war, he fought on the frontlines.

After the war, Mussolini met with a little band of men in a private room. His eyes scanned the group seated around him—daring men who wanted to change Italy's government. Many of them had been convicted of crimes, and several of them were former soldiers—tough men, accustomed to using violence to reach their goals.

Mussolini explained his thoughts about *fasces (făs' ēz)*. Fasces were bundles of sticks tied with red straps and with an axe blade protruding from the bundle. Fasces were carried in the days of Caesar's Roman Empire by men who walked in front of high government officials. The bundles symbolized the ruler's authority, especially his power to punish wrongdoers. They also symbolized unity. Can you guess why Mussolini wanted to remind his men of these bundles?

Mussolini wanted to use the fasces as a symbol of his new political party. He would be *Il Duce (doo' chā)*— "the leader." The party's flag would be a black banner with a white skull on it. Party members would wear black shirts and a black, flat-topped, coned hat, called a *fez*. They would fight any groups who opposed them. These men would be the first Fascists in Italy.

Mussolini (foreground) stands with Fascist Party members and his friend Adolf Hitler (holding hat).

The Fascists were a terror to the people of Italy. They attacked those who were associated with socialism. Landowners and bankers who hated the Socialists supported Mussolini and his work. Mussolini's Black Shirts were allowed to run wild through the cities, killing and wounding anyone who did not sympathize with Il Duce.

In spite of all this violence, Fascism was gaining more support. Many were dissatisfied with the king; they wanted a stronger leader. Others supported the Fascist Party because they wanted to own land or keep the land they already owned. Some supported Mussolini out of fear.

In 1922 Mussolini and fifty-two thousand Black Shirts marched into Rome. Mussolini forced the king to make him the prime minister of Italy. *"Duce! Duce!"* shouted his followers.

Mussolini did some helpful things for Italy after he came to power. He built roads, schools, factories, and hospitals. He provided land for farmers. He introduced new welfare benefits and sanitation programs. He even improved Italy's railroad system so that the trains ran on time.

Mussolini charmed many Italians with his smile and his confident speeches.

But it did not take long for the Italian people to see what kind of ruler Mussolini was. He wanted total control over industry, education, and the media. "Obey because you must obey," the school children were taught.

He organized his own secret police force whom he called *Cheka* to get rid of his enemies. This force of bodyguards publicly humiliated or killed anyone who criticized Mussolini. They stuffed ballot boxes with votes for Mussolini and threatened people with death if they voted against him.

Il Duce carefully controlled the newspapers so that only good things were printed about him. Do you think anyone dared to say anything against Mussolini?

One man did. He was a leading Socialist named Giacomo Matteotti. He stood up in Parliament and accused Mussolini of his crimes. He had proof that his accusations were true. Then one night, Matteotti was kidnapped by five members of the Cheka and murdered.

All over Italy, people were shocked and angry. Some of them tried to fight against the government. But Mussolini's Black Shirts quickly squelched the uprising. Il Duce's reign of terror continued.

Germany: *Heil, Hitler!*

When Mussolini was at the height of his power, he received a fan letter from a young Austrian man who asked for his photograph. Mussolini brushed off the request. He had more important things to do.

The young Austrian's name was Adolf Hitler. He had admired Mussolini's aggressive takeover of Italy and longed to imitate him.

Hitler was born in a town on the border of Austria and Bavaria. As a boy, he was a poor student. He was lazy and undisciplined, and he did not fit in well with other children. He was often called a dreamer because he preferred drawing, reading, and listening to music above other activities. Both of his parents died before he was twenty.

Hitler went to Vienna at the age of eighteen, hoping to be accepted at the Academy of Fine Arts. But he failed the entrance examinations— twice. For several years he stayed in Vienna, trying to sell his paintings on the streets.

Hitler's triumphal entry into Vienna, March 14, 1938

Hitler was known for his expressive gestures when speaking.

During his years in Vienna, Hitler began to hate the Jews. Perhaps he resented them because many of them were accepted in the social circles of Vienna, while he was not. But his hatred for them kept growing as he read books by other men who hated them. Hitler developed a belief that the only good people in the world were people like himself—people of Germanic ancestry. He called people with fair skin and light eyes *Aryans*—a term that once referred to light-skinned people who invaded India. What do you think of Hitler's belief in one superior race?

Hitler also became interested in politics while he lived in Vienna. He moved to Germany in 1913. After World War I, he joined the German Workers' Party. He used his artistic talent to design advertisements for the party. Then he began to speak at meetings. People enjoyed listening to Hitler. He had a dynamic intensity in his voice that fascinated them. After his speeches, they often cheered, *"Heil* (Hail), *Hitler!"*

In only a few months, membership in the German Workers' Party increased from one hundred to one thousand. Now Hitler wanted to make some changes in the party. He changed the party's name to the National Socialist German Workers' Party (*Nationalsozialistsche*— "Nazi" for short). The flag would now be red with a black hooked cross, or *swastika,* as its emblem. Hitler took complete control of the Nazi Party in 1920.

Hitler borrowed several ideas from his idol, Mussolini. Just as Mussolini had his Black Shirts, Hitler had his own private army called the storm troopers. And he, too, called himself "The Leader"—*der Führer (dêr fyo͞or′ ər)* in German.

One day Hitler and his Nazis tried to take over the government of Germany, but they were arrested. Hitler went to prison for nine months. During his stay in prison, he was made very comfortable and allowed to have as many visitors as he liked. He spent most of that time writing a book called *Mein Kampf,* or *My Struggle.* What do you think his struggle was? The book told about his hatred for the Jews and his desire to rid Germany of all of them. It described his belief in a superior German race as well as his policy about foreign affairs.

Another group Hitler hated were Communists. He did not want the Communist Party to take control of Germany. When Hitler was released from prison, he pulled the weakened Nazi Party back together. In 1932 he ran for president of Germany. He lost the election, but 230 other Nazis won offices in the government. They all voted for Hitler to be the chancellor—second in authority over all of Germany.

The brown-shirted storm troopers were the most unruly but also the most feared of Nazi soldiers.

Just four weeks later, on a cold, snowy night in February, a mysterious thing happened. A fire started in the building where the German government held its meetings. Soon the flames were leaping from the windows, and before the fire was put out, the building was badly damaged. Hitler's message spread through Germany almost as quickly as the fire had spread. "The Communists are responsible for setting the fire," he said.

More than four thousand Communists were arrested after the fire. Hitler sent out his secret police force, the *Gestapo,* to find enemies of the government. Anyone under suspicion was jailed or killed without a trial. Many went to *concentration camps*—places where people were kept as prisoners and forced to do heavy labor. The government seemed to distrust everyone.

Hitler ordered many of his own storm troopers put to death. All the men he could think of who had ever made him angry were killed. Many of them shouted *"Heil, Hitler!"* as they died. They did not know why they were being killed.

Less than a year after the fire, President Hindenburg died. Hitler saw his chance. He became dictator of Germany.

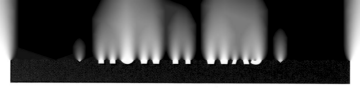

Youth in Hitler's Germany

Hitler wanted to establish a Reich, or empire, that would last for a thousand years. The German people—even the young people—were expected to do everything possible to help him toward this goal.

Hitler Youth rally in Nuremberg

If you had lived in Germany during Hitler's Reich, you would have no such thing as a church youth group. You would join the Hitler Youth or the Society of German Maidens. Your activities in these organizations would take up most of your spare time.

You would wear uniforms and be given strict physical training to make you strong and healthy. If you were a girl, you would be given lessons in child-care and home economics. You would be told your duty was to bear as many healthy children as possible for Germany. If you were a boy, you would learn how to march and shoot guns. Your club leader would be a government official, and he would keep military-style discipline at all times.

Every day you would have to recite this oath: "I promise in the Hitler Youth, to do my duty at all times, in love and faithfulness to the Führer, so help me God."

A meeting of the Society of German Maidens

The sign on this Jewish shop warned Germans not to buy anything there.

Hitler believed that one of the duties of all German people was to hate the Jewish people as much as he did. The Jews were constantly ridiculed, shunned, and sometimes physically harmed by German officials. They lost their positions in the civil service and could no longer attend the universities. The Nazi Party boycotted Jewish shops and other businesses. Many Jews left the country to find a safer place to live.

Then in 1935, Hitler passed the Nuremberg Laws. These laws took away the Jews' freedoms as citizens of Germany. Jews could not vote or hold a public office. Jews could not marry Germans. Jewish children could no longer attend German schools. Jews were forbidden to ride public trains or own telephones. Many Jews were told they could no longer work. Every Jew had to wear a bright yellow Star of David on his clothing so that everyone would know he was Jewish.

> "Now therefore, what have I here, saith the Lord, that my people is taken away for nought? they that rule over them make them to howl, saith the Lord; and my name continually every day is blasphemed."
>
> **Isaiah 52:5**

"By defending myself against the Jews," Hitler wrote in *Mein Kampf*, "I am doing the Lord's work." What do you think about this statement? What do you think the Lord thought about it?

Many concentration camps had this slogan, meaning "Work makes free," on their front gates.

Hitler's Reich would not last a thousand years as he had hoped. After World War II began, Hitler joined forces with Mussolini of Italy. The Axis powers, as they were called, won many early victories in the war.

During the war, Hitler sent Jews from many different European countries to his concentration camps. Most of them were killed in the camps. This one man was responsible for the deaths of nearly two-thirds of the Jews in Europe.

Near the end of the war, Hitler realized defeat was inevitable for Germany. He committed suicide in a bomb shelter in Berlin.

One day earlier, Mussolini had been captured by Communists and shot to death. On the day of Hitler's death, Mussolini's body was taken to a pub-

Hitler and Mussolini ride together on a street in Munich, Germany.

lic square in Milan and hung up by the heels. The crowds no longer shouted, *"Duce!"* and *"Heil, Hitler!"* Instead they cheered because the men who had stolen their freedoms were dead.

Russia: The Man of Steel

Joseph Stalin was born Joseph Vissarionovich Djugashvili in 1879 in a Russian province called Georgia. The name Stalin, which he later adopted, means "man of steel."

Stalin's childhood home

Stalin's childhood was not a happy one. His family was poor, and his father was often drunk. Smallpox left Stalin's face badly scarred, and his left arm was permanently disabled in an accident when he was ten. But despite these setbacks, his mother determined that her son should make something of his life. When he was fifteen, Stalin entered Tiflis Theological Seminary to study religion.

About this time, changes were taking place in Russia. The czar had just died and been succeeded by his son, Nicholas II, a weaker man than his father and less interested in politics. All over the Russian empire, many were unhappy with rule by a czar. They wanted to have more say in how they were governed. Groups of *radicals* began to hold secret meetings to talk of revolution.

Occasionally Stalin stole away from the seminary to attend these meetings. He also read books by men with revolutionary ideas.

One of Stalin's favorite novels was the story of Koba, a romantic hero who led a group of rebels and fought against the czar. He adopted the name for himself, insisting that his classmates call him Koba. How do you think the other seminary students felt about "Koba"?

Some of them liked him. He had strong opinions and daring ideas that fascinated them. Others did not like him. They found him too assertive. When in a group, he never wanted anyone else to take leadership. Sometimes he was defeated in debates or group discussions. Then he would become angry and harbor a grudge against the winner, withdrawing from his friends to pout and plan revenge.

Stalin grew increasingly argumentative and rebellious toward school authorities. He continued to read books that were forbidden by the school. When he was nineteen, he was expelled from the seminary for failing to attend his exams.

Now Stalin was free to do what he really wanted—to become part of the revolutionary movement sweeping across Russia. He became a devoted follower of Lenin, the strongest leader of this movement, and was soon participating in political demonstrations and secret meetings. He published a Socialist newspaper called *Brdzola ("The Struggle")*. Twice he was sent to Siberia as a prisoner because of his illegal political activities.

Toward the end of World War I, Czar Nicholas was forced to resign. Lenin and his followers, who called themselves *Bolsheviks,* saw their

chance to take over. In October of 1917 the Bolshevik Revolution brought Lenin into power in Russia. Stalin, as his faithful supporter, was one of the leaders in the first Soviet government of Russia.

The Bolsheviks renamed themselves Communists. When Lenin died in 1924, Stalin was one of the main candidates for leadership of the Communist Party. He was determined to beat out his rivals. One of these was Leon Trotsky, second only to Lenin in authority. Stalin used the influence of two other

In October 1917 the Bolshevik Party seized control of the government.

Communist leaders to turn public opinion against Trotsky. Trotsky was forced to step down from his position. Stalin eventually *exiled* him, or forced him to leave the country.

Stalin then removed the two leaders who had helped him get rid of Trotsky. One by one, Stalin found ways to get rid of the men who stood in his way. At last he was dictator of Russia.

What do you think the people thought of Stalin now? Some did not like the methods he had used to gain his power, but no one dared to criticize the "man of steel."

Leon Trotsky

Russia relied mostly on farming for its income. But Stalin wanted Russia to become more industrial, to be like the more advanced countries. One of his goals was to increase Russia's industry by a series of Five-Year Plans. He sped up production by forcing people to work harder than ever before. He combined individual farms into large "collective" farms owned by the government.

How do you think the Russian people felt about Stalin's new procedures? Some people were angry. They did not want to work like slaves. They did not want to give up their right to farm independently. Some people opposed Stalin's plans by burning their livestock, grain, and farm equipment. If they could not own their farms, they did not want the government to own them either.

But Stalin paid no attention to what the people wanted. He sent soldiers to the farms and forced the people to surrender at gunpoint. He sent about a million families who had opposed him into exile. Perhaps as many as seven million more died of starvation as a result of Stalin's war on the farmers.

In one sense, Stalin's plans worked. By 1932, three-fifths of all Russian farms were collectives, and industry was increasing at a rate of 14 percent each year. But in another sense, his system was failing. The morale of the people was low. Many had suffered or even died under Stalin's harsh working conditions. And they had no freedom to question anything Stalin ordered.

Another group of people in Russia suffered a different kind of oppression under Stalin. Writers, artists, and composers were not allowed to create what they wanted. Every book had to be *censored,* or examined to make sure its content was in harmony with Stalin's ideas, before it was published. Artists were allowed to paint pictures of only the Bolshevik Revolution or typical Russian life.

Stalin trusted no one. He could not tolerate having anyone disagree with him. In the next several years, he got rid of nearly all the former Bolsheviks in the Communist Party in a deadly purge. He went on to dispose of thousands of other Communists. Anyone who seemed a threat to his authority was imprisoned and usually executed on some false charge. About one and a half million people were killed in four years. Those who were not killed were questioned, tortured, and half-starved in labor camps. People referred to these years as "the Terror."

Stalin expected every person to be a spy. In addition to his own secret police force, he urged neighbors and family members to report to him any "opposition." People lived in constant fear of saying or doing the wrong thing—even in their own homes.

Stalin was one of the three major Allied leaders at the end of World War II.

By the time World War II began, Stalin had purged Russia of all his potential enemies. When Russia defeated Hitler's forces, it emerged as one of the three major Allied powers. Stalin was hailed as a hero all over the world.

But Stalin used his position to spread his influence farther across Europe. He set up Communist governments in Bulgaria, Czechoslovakia, East Germany, Hungary, Poland, and Romania. Russia, or the Union of Soviet Socialist Republics, now dominated Eastern Europe. Stalin cut off the Eastern countries from contact with the Western countries, creating an imaginary dividing line called the *Iron Curtain.* Stalin did not want the people under his control to know about the freedoms enjoyed by the Western countries. Why do you think this was true?

Stalin's health gradually worsened after the war, and in 1953 he had a stroke. Soon afterward he died. After thirty years of oppression, the Russian people had a few more freedoms. How do you think they felt?

The Berlin Wall divided Communist East Berlin from free West Berlin for nearly thirty years.

To Design a Color Map

1. You will need Notebook page 68, tracing paper, tape, and crayons.

2. Study the map on your Notebook page. Color the map red. This land was controlled by the Soviet Union until 1991.

3. Tape the sheet of tracing paper at the edge of the Notebook page. Trace all the boundary lines with your pencil.

4. Label each country to show how the Soviet Union was broken up in 1991.

5. Color the tracing-paper map so that no bordering countries are the same color.

Joseph McCarthy

After World War II, the fear of Communism "echoed" in the United States. Committees were formed in the Senate to find whether Communism had infiltrated the United States government. One senator from Wisconsin, Joseph McCarthy, began to investigate people of whom he was

suspicious. He made lists of the names of his suspects. He boldly accused people in the government of disloyalty to the United States.

Joseph McCarthy reveals his suspicions of Communist sentiments in the U.S. Army.

People listened to McCarthy. When he accused someone, others became suspicious of that person. People McCarthy had accused were *blacklisted* by certain firms, which meant that they could not be hired for work.

Americans felt threatened. They were afraid of saying anything that might sound like criticism of the government. Someone might think they were disloyal and report their names to McCarthy or someone else on one of the committees.

McCarthy lost favor with the American public a few years later. The Senate did not believe he had enough proof to make his accusations. *McCarthyism* came to mean accusing people without sufficient evidence. Although McCarthy was found to be right many years later about some of his accusations, he had violated one of the freedoms of all Americans—the right to free speech, including the freedom of political belief.

Hirohito at age ten

Japan: The Last Emperor-God

For many centuries the people of Japan thought of their emperors as gods. When Hirohito *(hîr′ō • hē′tō)* became emperor of Japan in 1926, he was no exception. The people carried their reverence to such an extreme that they were not even allowed to look at Hirohito in public. Do you think Hirohito liked being thought of in this way?

Hirohito and his family in 1934

Hirohito was a thoughtful and reserved man. He had studied science when he was young, and he soon realized that he was not a descendant of the sun goddess as the people believed. He often expressed a wish to live closer to his people and to see how they lived.

Hirohito wears the ceremonial attire at his formal enthronement in 1928.

Hirohito had a group of advisors who made most of the decisions for the country. Sometimes they would ask for Hirohito's opinion, but he rarely objected to anything they decided. When they decided that Japan should go to war against the United States during World War II, he went along with their decision and signed all the necessary documents.

Nuclear cloud over Nagasaki

Japan was proud of its military tradition. It had never been defeated in a war before. But this war would be different.

The Japanese had high hopes when they first entered World War II. Their attack on American ships in Pearl Harbor was a resounding victory. But defeating the Americans was not as easy as they thought it would be. Japan soon suffered serious defeats. Hirohito knew his people were in danger, but he did not take any decisive action to end the war. He left the military decisions up to his advisors, who refused to surrender and bring disgrace on Japan. If the United States did not act, the war would drag on and many more lives would be lost.

August 6, 1945, is a date Japan will never forget. The Americans dropped the world's first atomic bomb on the city of Hiroshima. Three days later, they dropped another atomic bomb on Nagasaki. Hundreds of thousands of Japanese people were killed.

On August 14, Hirohito met with his war council. In a broken voice, he asked them to surrender. He could not bear to watch his people suffer any longer.

The Americans were generous to Hirohito after the war. They allowed him to keep his position as monarch of Japan, but he could no longer claim to be a god. In the new democratic Japan, the people elected representatives to govern them. Hirohito lived the rest of his life peacefully—touring, spending time with his family, and studying science.

Hirohito and his wife enjoyed a leisurely life after the war ended.

How was Hirohito different from Hitler, Mussolini, and Stalin? He was not a heavy-handed tyrant as they were. But he made the same mistake that they did—he did not use his power for the good of his people.

Hirohito was set so far above his people that he did not understand their needs. He did not see the wounded soldiers lying on the battlefields or the mothers grieving over dead sons. He remained silent when an order from him could have ended the war that took so many Japanese lives.

> *"Lift not up your horn on high:*
> *speak not with a stiff neck.*
> *For promotion cometh neither from the east,*
> *nor from the west, nor from the south.*
> *But God is the judge:*
> *he putteth down one, and setteth up another."*
>
> **Psalm 75:5-7**

10
Never
Such a War

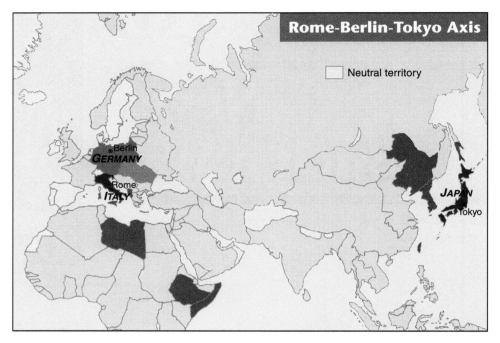

Rome-Berlin-Tokyo Axis

Neutral territory

Berlin
GERMANY
Rome
ITALY
JAPAN
Tokyo

The Gathering Storm

When "the war to end all wars" was over, the victorious were wild to celebrate. And that carefree spirit spilled over into the beginning of the next decade. America grew richer. Europe began to rebuild its cities and heal from years of war. Only a few people were thinking that there could be any more trouble such as the world had just survived.

But just over twenty years later, it was clear that the last war had not ended war at all; rather it had made an even bigger war inevitable. The leaders who would bring on the war were already working together. They were among the most wicked men in history: Adolf Hitler of Germany and Benito Mussolini of Italy. They were responsible for many deaths. Their countries united as the *Axis*.

Later, Italy, Germany, and Japan would become allies in the *Rome-Berlin-Tokyo Axis*. They were all countries that believed that the good of the government was more important than the good of the people. Such powers are called *totalitarian*.

In this cartoon, Hitler has asked the driver to take him to Czechoslovakia.

When Germany demanded some land from Austria and Czechoslovakia, Great Britain and France agreed. Leaders of the world thought it best to give in to Hitler's demands rather than start another war. Besides, they told themselves, Hitler promised that once he got the land in Czechoslovakia, he would be satisfied.

But Hitler was lying. When he had Austria and part of Czechoslovakia, he then wanted Poland. This time *appeasement,* or giving Hitler what he wanted, was out of the question. What do you think happened when Hitler was told he could not have Poland? He ordered his army to take it.

Germany Before World War II

Baltic Sea

LITHUANIA

North Sea

GREAT BRITAIN

NETHERLANDS

BELGIUM

LUXEMBOURG

FRANCE

SWITZERLAND

Berlin ⊛

GERMANY

MEMELAND

POLAND

RUTHENIA

CZECHOSLOVAKIA

AUSTRIA

HUNGARY

RUMANIA

YUGOSLAVIA

Adriatic Sea

Germany in 1933
Remilitarized in 1936
Annexed in 1938 (Austria)
Given through 1938 agreement (Part of Czechoslovakia)
Annexed in 1939 (Memeland)
Became a protectorate in 1939 (Part of Czechoslovakia)

The War Begins

The German forces moved so quickly that people said they fought a *blitzkrieg,* or "lightning war." To weaken Poland, the German air force first dropped bombs on the larger cities, killing many people and filling the others with terror. Then tanks rolled in, followed by huge numbers of German troops marching rank upon rank.

German soldiers advance into Poland.

In September 1939, Germany took over Poland in just eighteen days. In the spring of 1940, Germany defeated Denmark in a day. Norway lasted only about three weeks. Then in May the Germans invaded Belgium, the Netherlands, and France. Britain sent soldiers to help, but they could not hold back the German army.

German armies marched through France, pushing English and French soldiers back. The Germans were so strong that they soon had thousands of soldiers trapped on the northern coast of France. There were not enough ships to take the soldiers across the English Channel. Doom seemed certain for them.

HOW IT WAS

Near Dunkirk, France
Late May Through June 4, 1940

The Germans surprised a force of about four hundred thousand British and French soldiers in northern France, trapping them near the city of Dunkirk. It looked like certain defeat.

The British leaders asked the people of Britain for help. King George VI, the ruler of England, called for a day of prayer for his nation.

The British people responded with courage and determination. Soon thousands of boats, barges, yachts, and even fishing boats started across the English Channel.

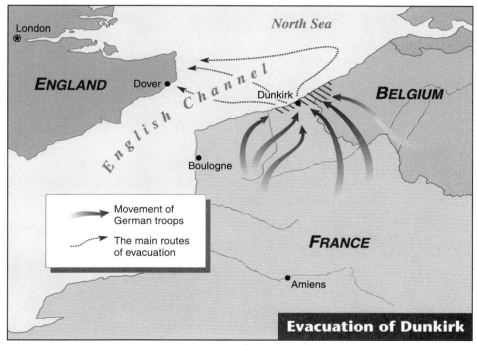

Movement of German troops

The main routes of evacuation

Evacuation of Dunkirk

Winds and waves usually make crossing the Channel difficult. But for nine days the Channel was almost smooth. Clouds and mists covered the harbor so that the German planes could not see where to drop their bombs. The British boats safely made trip after trip until most of the soldiers were rescued.

Winston Churchill, the prime minister of Great Britain, called the rescue at Dunkirk a "miracle of deliverance." Christians recognized it as an answer to prayer.

After the bombing of London, smoke swirls about St. Paul's Cathedral.

Europe Under Hitler

In June 1940, France surrendered. Now Hitler and his allies controlled much of Europe.

Britain stood alone against the German forces. German planes roared across the English Channel to bomb cities in Britain. The Germans also tried to prevent ships from bringing goods to British ports. They set up a blockade and sank ships. But despite death and danger, the British refused to give up.

Many British people in the cities sent their children to live with families in the countryside so that they would be safer. In the cities and countryside alike, the British built bomb shelters underground. When sirens sounded, the people fled into the shelters for safety.

Hitler poses in front of the Eiffel Tower after conquering France.

Winston Churchill
(1874-1965)

After his escape, Churchill became a lieutenant in the South African Light Horse Army.

Winston Churchill, son of a British lord and a beautiful American heiress, showed little promise as a child of becoming one of the greatest statesmen in history. He did poorly in school and was often in trouble.

However, in military school he excelled in the study of tactics and graduated near the top of his 150-member class. He then became a soldier and a war reporter. Captured during the Boer War, he made a daring escape and became a national hero.

When he returned to England, Churchill was elected to Parliament at the age of twenty-six. Shortly before World War I, Churchill saw that war was coming and, as first lord of the Admiralty, prepared the British navy. For many years, he was in and out of popularity—sometimes cheered, many times jeered. At one point he told a friend, "I'm finished."

But Churchill was far from finished. His most important work was still ahead: presiding as prime minister of Great Britain during the next great war. After Dunkirk, Churchill realized that when France fell, England would be Hitler's next target. He rose before the British government and made one of the most famous speeches in history.

> The Battle of Britain is about to begin. . . . The whole fury and
> might of the enemy must very soon be turned on us. . . . Let us
> therefore brace ourselves to our duties, and so bear ourselves,
> that, if the British Empire and its Commonwealth last for a thou-
> sand years, men will say, "This was their finest hour."

The British people proved equal to the awful task. The Royal Air Force, outnumbered and outgunned, managed to protect its country and hold off Hitler's forces. The British people, as Churchill had declared in another famous speech, did not "flag nor fail." And they never surrendered.

Much of the credit for the courage that the British showed in the worst of times goes to Churchill's amazing speeches. But late in his life, the great man of war said that it was many others who had "the lion's heart." It was his privilege, he said, "to give the roar."

In June of 1941, Germany and its allies surprised almost everyone. They attacked the Soviet Union, heading for Moscow, the capital city. But winter came early and hard to the Soviet Union, and the German armies were trapped in that vast land. The Soviets, prepared for the weather, could now fight back. Hitler's lightning attack failed, and the Germans, pinned by snow and cold, lost many soldiers.

Europe in June 1941

The United States Joins the Allies

Since the end of World War I, Americans had wanted to stay out of other countries' problems. Some Americans thought that there was no reason for their men to die in another European war. Others feared that America was unprepared and would be easily defeated. Even so, Americans sent food, weapons, and other manufactured goods to Europe. American men had to register for the *draft,* the system that chose men to go to war.

But late in 1941, something happened that changed the Americans' ideas drastically. It stunned the whole nation—and roused it to rage.

Unlike the Germans, these Russian soldiers were well prepared for winter fighting.

208

Pearl Harbor, Hawaii
Sunday, December 7, 1941

A little before dawn

Pearl Harbor, a large American military base on Oahu Island, Hawaii, held many ships and aircraft.

Over three hundred Japanese bombers suddenly attacked the harbor, sinking or destroying eighteen ships and demolishing two hundred planes.

Thirty-seven hundred Americans died. Over one thousand went down with the battleship USS *Arizona*.

The next day President Franklin D. Roosevelt asked Congress to declare war on Japan. Congress voted to go to war against all the Axis powers.

When America entered the war, its rallying cry was "Remember Pearl Harbor!"

The USS Shaw *bursts into flames.*

A rescue boat helps seamen on the sinking USS West Virginia.

209

A Global War

These Grumman Avengers were American torpedo bombers.

Against the leaders of primarily Germany but also Italy and Japan, the Allies had "The Big Three": Churchill of England, Joseph Stalin of Russia, and Franklin Roosevelt of the United States. These three men met to talk over war plans. The Allies hoped to defeat the Germans in France and push them back to Germany.

Because so many countries were now in the war, it came to be called *World War II*. The Americans fought in the Pacific and in North Africa. And America sent soldiers—and a great leader—to the massive Allied invasion of France.

Allied tanks in North Africa

The Big Three named an American as Allied Commander—General Dwight D. Eisenhower. And they informed him of the daring plan he was to carry out. The Allies worked for months, all in careful secrecy. If the Germans found out what the plan was, nearly all hope would be lost.

Eisenhower encourages paratroopers about to depart on the D-day invasion.

Almost three million men gathered in England. They had thousands of trucks and tons of ammunition, food, and medical supplies. General Eisenhower and his men called the whole plan *Operation Overlord.* It was to be the biggest air and naval invasion in history: the Allies would sail across the English Channel and take France back from Germany. When everything seemed right and ready, General Eisenhower said quietly, "We'll go." And *D-day* began.

Normandy, France
June 6, 1944

A little before dawn

More than twenty-seven hundred ships had sailed during the night from England. They carried 176,000 men and their supplies.

At dawn, the ships opened fire on the beaches of France.

Hundreds of planes flew over the French coast. The planes kept German troops away from the beaches and also bombed German supply factories.

Many soldiers dropped by parachutes behind the Germans.

The fighting was very hard for days, but the Allies won those beaches and began their march across France. Their final goal was to reach Germany.

The Allies now swept across France, pushing the German forces back. French people cheered the Allies and then wept for joy as the German soldiers were run out of their villages and cities. As the Allies marched and fought, they freed prisoners of war.

Churchill walks with French general de Gaulle in newly liberated France.

In America, however, others had been put into a sort of prison— by their own countrymen. More than 110,000 Japanese Americans were put into "camps" for one reason: they were under suspicion because of their Japanese heritage. What do you think of that action?

Many years later, the American government apologized for mistrusting loyal Americans solely because of their Japanese heritage.

Do you think you would like to be placed in a camp as these Japanese Americans were?

The Beginning of the End

By March of 1945, American troops reached the Rhine River. One month later the soldiers reached the Elbe River farther east. There they waited for the arrival of their Soviet allies, who had been fighting their way across Germany from the east.

Hungarian Jews stumble from a freight car upon their arrival at a concentration camp.

The Allies came upon huge prison camps filled with starving people. These were concentration camps that the German leaders had built for anyone who disagreed with their ideas. Because Hitler especially hated the Jews, he ordered them arrested and put in the prison camps. Six million Jews were murdered outright or starved to death.

When the Allies saw the horrors of the concentration camps—the gas chambers and the ovens where bodies of men, women, and children were burned—they were more determined than ever to crush the enemy. They fought both from the east and west, forcing the German army into a smaller and smaller area. By April, it was all but over.

At the end of April 1945, Hitler killed himself. A few days later, on May 7, the defeated Germans surrendered. That day was called *V-E Day,* "Victory in Europe Day."

On V-E Day, the Allies rejoiced. The battle was won—but not yet the war. They still had to defeat Japan.

Dwight David Eisenhower
(1890-1969)

"Opportunity is all about you. Reach out and take it," said Dwight D. Eisenhower, describing some of the values his parents had taught him. Dwight, or "Ike" as he was called from childhood, was born into a poor family in Texas on October 14, 1890. About a year later, the Eisenhower family moved to Abilene, Kansas, where the future president grew up.

Pictured here with his fourth grade class, Dwight is the boy in overalls (front row, second from the left).

Dwight did well in school, though he often got into fights with the other students who ridiculed his shabby clothes. His parents taught him to read the Bible and to live honorably. After high school, he did not have enough money to pay for college tuition, so he worked seven days a week, twelve hours a day, to save for an education. He was accepted at West Point, the United States Military Academy, located in New York. After he graduated from West Point, Eisenhower joined the army and worked at different posts. When World War I broke out, he trained soldiers for battle.

The Eisenhowers on their wedding day

In 1933 Eisenhower served as an aide to General Douglas MacArthur. Almost ten years later, the Allied powers selected him to lead their forces. His success as a five-star general led to his popularity among the American people. When he returned home to the United States, General Eisenhower received a hero's welcome for his leadership in the D-day invasion.

After World War II, General Eisenhower spent some time as the Allied leader of occupied Germany. When he returned once again to the States, he decided he was ready to retire as a military leader and spend time with his family. In 1948 he became the president of Columbia University in New York City.

Eisenhower's time at Columbia University lasted for only two years. President Truman had other plans for this great former general. He wanted Eisenhower to be the leader of a group of Western nations to fight against communism—a group called the North Atlantic Treaty Organization, or NATO. Dwight D. Eisenhower became involved in world affairs once again.

Soon, because of his leadership abilities and his already strong popularity, Eisenhower was encouraged to run in the United States presidential election in 1952. People carried signs and wore buttons that read "I Like Ike." Finally, he agreed to run for the presidency and swept the November elections, defeating his Democratic opponent, Adlai E. Stevenson. Dwight David Eisenhower became the thirty-fourth president of the United States.

In a speech to the Republican National Committee, Eisenhower said, "What counts is not necessarily the size of the dog in the fight—it's the size of the fight in the dog." President Eisenhower proved to be a good fighter and a hard worker throughout his life. Although he faced many difficult decisions and problems during his two terms as president, Eisenhower seized every opportunity to serve his country. He poured his life into the fight to preserve freedom and peace, not only in America but around the world.

Dwight Eisenhower spent his retirement years in a farmhouse near Gettysburg, Pennsylvania. After suffering from several heart attacks and then pneumonia, Dwight D. Eisenhower died on March 28, 1969. Just before he died, he quietly stated his unwavering allegiance to America with the simple, final words, "I've always loved my country."

At one point in the Burma Road, there were twenty-one hairpin curves.

The War in the Pacific

For months after Pearl Harbor, the Japanese seemed to win everywhere they fought. Many islands and countries fell to the Japanese. They took thousands of prisoners and forced them into large concentration camps. There the prisoners lived in terrible conditions, and many were tortured and killed.

The United States had been using a little road across the mountains and jungles of Burma to get supplies to the Chinese army, which was also fighting Japan.

In 1942, British officers surrendered to the Japanese.

The Japanese conquered Burma and closed the supply route. With the road closed, brave American pilots had to fly supplies over the world's highest mountains, the Himalayas.

In the Philippine Islands, the Americans fought hard against the Japanese. In spite of a lack of supplies, they held them back for five months.

The American troops had to eat mules and monkeys because they had no other food. At last they had no choice but to fall back. Their commander, General Douglas MacArthur, promised, "I shall return." But while the Americans were gone, the Japanese tortured and killed many soldiers and Christian missionaries on the islands.

Japanese soldiers hold weapons and flags high after their victory in the Philippines.

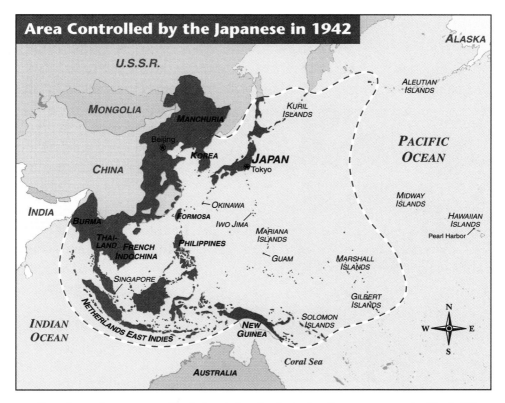

Area Controlled by the Japanese in 1942

Look at the map to find the islands that the Japanese controlled. The Americans knew that it would be hard to capture all the islands. Instead, the United States followed a plan called "island hopping." They decided to retake only the most important islands, with the goal of reaching Tokyo, Japan's capital.

The return of General MacArthur

By January of 1945, the Americans' island hopping landed them in the Philippines again. General MacArthur returned, just as he had promised. He came with six hundred ships and 250,000 men. As he waded ashore, he said, "People of the Philippines, I have returned. . . . Rally to me." He intended to free the islands and to rescue people in the prison camps.

Talking in Code

Radio messages between American ships in the Pacific were often picked up by the Japanese. The Americans tried using different codes, but the Japanese always broke the codes, using lost code books or ones stolen from American radiomen who died in battle.

Navajos Preston and Frank Toledo relay a coded message. In addition to Navajos, Comanches and Choctaws also served as Code Talkers during the War.

One marine, Philip Johnston, who was the son of missionaries and who spoke Navajo, had an idea. Why not, he suggested, let Navajos be the radiomen? They could talk in their own language, not needing a code book. The leaders liked the idea. From 1942 until the end of the war, more than four hundred Navajos were radiomen for the American marines. They used their own language to make up a code that even untrained Navajos could not break. They memorized everything, so there were no code books to get stolen.

There are no words in the Navajo language for such things as airplanes and bombs, for example. So bombers became *jaysho,* "buzzards," and bombs were *ayeshi,* "eggs." The radiomen made up colorful names for countries as well. They called Australia "rolled hat." Can you guess why? The Japanese tried, but they could never break this new secret code. Without the Navajo *Code Talkers,* the marines could not have taken Iwo Jima. In 1982, President Reagan made August 14 "National Code Talkers Day."

To Communicate in Code

1. Either find an existing code or invent one and write it in the boxes above the letters on Notebook page 73.

2. Make up a message and write it in your code on the Notebook page.

3. Let your message fall into "enemy" hands.

4. Intercept an "enemy" message and try to decode it.

The Americans had returned with more men and weapons and fought their way toward Japan. As the U.S. troops got closer and closer to Japan, the fighting became fiercer. It took twenty-five days to take the tiny island of Iwo Jima.

Aerial view of Iwo Jima

Soldiers raise the victory flag on Iwo Jima.

By April, the Americans had only one more island, Okinawa, to take before reaching the Japanese mainland and fighting toward Tokyo. The Japanese military fought back desperately. More than 110,000 Japanese soldiers died. When there were only eleven thousand men left, the Japanese gave up Okinawa. American fighters could now bomb the enemy's factories and cities.

Kamikazes, Japanese suicide pilots, attacked many American ships at Okinawa.

In ten days, American bombs destroyed thirty-two square miles of Japanese industry. Still the Japanese fought on. American bombs fell on cities, setting whole blocks on fire. But the Japanese refused to give up.

Douglas MacArthur
(1880-1964)

Douglas MacArthur was born in 1880 in Arkansas, although he always considered himself a Virginian. His mother's ancestors had lived at the early Jamestown settlement. His uncles from her side of the family

had fought under Generals Robert E. Lee and Stonewall Jackson. MacArthur's father, who became a general himself, fought in both the Civil War and the Spanish-American War.

Douglas MacArthur's parents were his first teachers. Along with regular subjects, they taught him about duty. They told him to do right, no matter what it might cost. "Always our country was to come first," he wrote of those days. There were "two things we must never do: never lie and never tattle."

Douglas was an average student in elementary school. Later he went to a military school near Fort Sam Houston in Texas. He wanted to go to West Point, the United States Military Academy. He studied hard for the entrance tests—and got the highest marks. "It was a lesson I never forgot. Preparedness is the key to success and victory."

MacArthur entered West Point in June 1899. He earned the highest grade average of any West Point cadet in twenty-five years. There were those in his class who were smarter, but MacArthur knew what duties had to come first—his studies—and he did them.

During World War I, MacArthur was wounded twice. He was promoted to the rank of brigadier general for his bravery. In 1919 he became the head of West Point Military Academy. MacArthur attained the rank of general in 1930 and was appointed chief of staff for the whole army, the youngest man ever to have that job. During World War II, MacArthur served in the Pacific.

MacArthur being decorated for bravery in World War I

At the end of the war, he became commander of the American troops sent to Japan as an occupation force. He helped Japan write a new constitution, made the nobles in Japan less influential, and gave Japanese women the right to vote. He invited Christian missionaries to bring the gospel to Japan.

In 1950, when a Communist force from North Korea attacked South Korea, General MacArthur was named commander of the United Nations force assigned to defend South Korea. MacArthur believed the Communists were a deadly enemy and that if they were not defeated in Asia, they would continue to take over lands there. But President Truman would not permit General MacArthur to bomb important bridges, supply centers, or electrical plants needed by the Communists, for fear that such attacks would lead to an even greater war.

General MacArthur in Korea

In his retirement years, MacArthur was called to West Point to receive an award. There he gave one of the most famous speeches in American military history. It began with this theme: "Duty, honor, country; those three hallowed words reverently dictate what you ought to be, what you can be, what you will be."

Victory in Japan

President Franklin D. Roosevelt died in April 1945. The war was concluding, but Harry Truman, who became president after Roosevelt's death, had a big decision to make. Should he use the *atomic bomb*—the new weapon invented by American scientists? President Truman knew that hundreds of thousands of soldiers would be killed and that the war would continue much longer if American forces had to invade Japan. But he also knew that the atomic bomb would be more destructive than any weapon in history—and that it would change forever the way wars were fought.

The United States tried to get Japan to surrender. American planes dropped leaflets on Japan, telling the Japanese people that something terrible would happen if they did not surrender right away. The Japanese refused to surrender. So on August 6, 1945, American airmen dropped the first atomic bomb on Hiroshima, Japan. The bomb killed 140,000 people. Still the Japanese would not give up. Three days later, a second bomb fell on a giant Japanese naval base located at Nagasaki. The next day Japan asked for peace.

On September 2, 1945, General Douglas MacArthur accepted the formal surrender on board the battleship *Missouri* in Tokyo Bay. It was

V-J Day, "Victory in Japan Day"; World War II was over. More than fifty nations had been part of the horror; over fifty-five million people had died. Never before had the world seen such a war.

The atomic bomb caused great destruction in the Japanese city of Nagasaki.

Keeping the Peace

UN Headquarters

After the war, the countries of the world joined together to try to keep the peace. Representatives from nearly fifty nations met in San Francisco, California, to form the United Nations (UN). The UN was designed to listen to international problems and to try to come up with peaceful solutions. Today the United Nations headquarters is in New York City.

Although an organization to keep peace seemed at the time to be a good idea, rarely has the UN been able to stop countries from making war on each other. Until Christ brings peace to men, there will be no lasting peace. On the UN building, where all who enter can see it, appear the words from Isaiah 2:4:

> They shall beat their swords into plowshares, and their spears into pruninghooks: nation shall not lift up sword against nation, neither shall they learn war any more.

Throughout history man has tried unsuccessfully to establish a man-made, one-world government. The fall of many empires throughout the centuries illustrates that any human unity that denies God cannot succeed.

> "Peace I leave with you, my peace I give unto you: not as the world giveth, give I unto you. Let not your heart be troubled, neither let it be afraid."
>
> **John 14:27**

Christians who read the words of Scripture on the UN building know that the promise and hope of those words rests not with those inside that building, but rather with the God of heaven.

11

American Homes
and Customs

No matter what type of structure or where it is, the place where you live is "home" to you. Our homes are places that provide shelter—they keep us safe from winter's chill and summer's heat. Home is a place we can claim as our own. We can go there to eat and sleep and study and relax when we have nowhere else to be. For many people, the home is a place where they can experience the love and closeness of a family.

Look at this map of America. Find the place where your home is today. What type of home might have been there long ago?

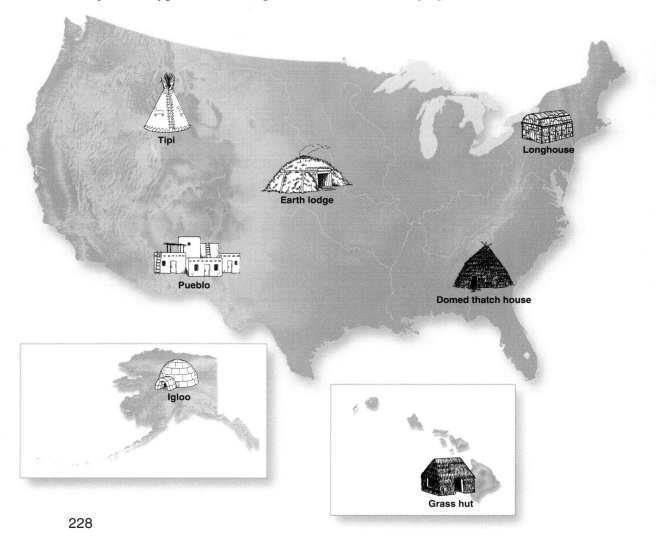

Tipi

Longhouse

Earth lodge

Pueblo

Domed thatch house

Igloo

Grass hut

The Woodland domed thatch house was one of the earliest houses built in America.

Homes of Our Earliest People

Native Americans built the first homes in America. Some of the earliest houses were built by the Mandan people, who lived along the Missouri River. They built cone-shaped frames out of willow branches and covered them with sod. From the outside, their homes looked like mounds of earth. Inside they were warm and dry. Would you like to share a house with all of your aunts, uncles, and cousins? Families of thirty to forty people lived in each Mandan lodge.

How would you like to live in a house made of grass? Many of the Woodland peoples in the southern United States once did. The woven grass they used to build their homes was called *thatch*. They fastened the thatch to a framework of poles with a mixture called *mud wattle*. One type of grass house was the Gothic thatched house. It was shaped like a large dome with a diameter of about thirty feet. A house like this could be built in just two days.

The Anasazi made their homes in high places. They liked the secure feeling of living where no one could approach them without being seen. They built their homes in the walls of canyons and farmed on the plains below. The villages themselves were called *pueblos,* which means "town" in Spanish.

Anasazi cliff dwellings

Anasazi homes were built like apartment buildings, one home on top of another. Each room was made from sandstone blocks and mud, and from the outside they looked like little square caves cut into the cliffs. Most of the ground-level rooms had no windows or doors. Families used ladders to climb to the upper levels. For protection at night, the ladders were pulled inside. What if someone came home after his ladder had been pulled in? He might be able to climb the cliff. Some families cut secret footholds into the cliff walls.

The Anasazi abandoned their cliff dwellings around A.D. 1300. People can still visit the homes the Anasazi left behind.

The Plains people traveled often, following the buffalo herds that roamed the prairies. They needed homes that could be taken apart, moved, and reassembled easily. The Sioux, Blackfoot, Cheyenne, and other peoples made their homes out of buffalo skins wrapped around upright poles. These homes were called *tipis*. The word comes from the Sioux words *ti,* meaning "to dwell," and *pi,* meaning "used for."

Tipis were ideal for many kinds of weather. They were lightweight, but they held heat well in winter. They stayed dry in rain and secure in high winds. Which members of the family do you think built the tipi? The men killed the buffalos, but the women did all the rest. They tanned, cut, and sewed together the hides; peeled the bark from the sapling poles; arranged the poles in a cone shape for the tipi frame; and fit the covering around the tipi.

An Iroquois longhouse

The Iroquois people, who once lived where New York State is today, had homes called *longhouses.* Several related families lived together in one longhouse. Each family had its own little booth for sleeping and cooking. Often all the families would gather in the central hallway to talk. Longhouses could be more than one hundred feet long.

Many Native Americans lived in tipis like this one.

What went on inside Native American homes? Probably many of the same things that go on in ours. People told stories and sang songs and cooked meals. Children played games. At night the families slept.

Cooking was simple in Native American homes. Fire was the main source of heat. Some homes had *pit ovens,* or holes in the ground lined with hot stones. Most homes had either a chimney or an opening in the ceiling where smoke could escape. These openings could be closed during rain so that the homes would stay dry.

What kind of beds do you think Native Americans slept on? Plains Indians slept on pallets made from buffalo hides. Other peoples had furnishings of furs, mats woven from thin branches, and decorative storage boxes or pouches made from rawhide.

Homes of the Colonists

The very first settlers came to America from Spain in the 1500s. They founded a colony in what is now Florida. Their homes were small one-room huts made of wood and palmetto fronds like the huts of the Seminoles living in the area.

A colonist's wigwam home

The first settlers in Jamestown, Virginia, in the early 1600s lived in primitive homes. They needed shelter immediately. At first some settlers lived in holes in the ground. They dug pits and lined them with bark. Later many constructed wigwams—an arched frame of poles covered with animal skins or bark—like those of the Native Americans. A combination of poor shelter, undernourishment, and disease brought death to many settlers during those first few years.

Plymouth home

As new groups of colonists came to America, they built homes like those they had known in the Old World. When the next group of English colonists came to Jamestown, they built English cottages with thatched roofs. Since Plymouth was farther north, the weather there was colder than the weather in Jamestown.

Plymouth colonists nailed smooth oak boards called *clapboards* to the walls to keep out the chilling winds. All the homes had huge stone fireplaces for cooking and heat. Since glass was scarce in the New England area, most homes had oiled paper in their windows. Oiled paper was similar to our waxed paper today—it let light in, but people could not see through it clearly. Some windows had shutters to keep out the cold. Most Jamestown homes had two small chimneys at either end of the house instead of a large, central fireplace.

Many later colonists built their homes of brick. Why didn't the Plymouth colonists build their homes from stone or brick? They needed *lime* to make the mortar used for holding the bricks together, and lime was not available in Massachusetts.

Jamestown homes

In the state of New York, Dutch settlers built houses like those in Holland. One feature of Dutch homes was a weathervane at the top of the roof. Weathervanes were often shaped like animals, such as roosters, lions, horses, or fish. Many Dutch homes also had wide metal gutters overhanging the front and rear entrances of the house. The gutters protected the stone walls and

Dutch roofs were often shaped like the one on this hospital in the Netherlands.

mud mortar from rain, but on rainy days they often sent showers of water down on the heads of passersby.

Along the Delaware River, Swedish settlers built the first log cabins in America. They fit the logs together by cutting notches in the ends of each log and stacking them. The roofs were made out of shingles cut from logs. Because log cabins saved the expense of nails and could be built quickly, their popularity spread. As Americans settled farther and farther west, the log cabin became the most common frontier home. Five of America's presidents, including Abraham Lincoln, were born in log cabins.

This log cabin was the birthplace of the 16th president, Abraham Lincoln.

Homes with a Past

Since people from different countries settled in different places, we can still see differences in styles of homes around America today. In learning to recognize architectural styles from other countries, you will find "echoes" of the long-ago settlers of a place.

The land around Louisiana was settled primarily by French colonists. What styles of homes would you expect to find there? If you go to New Orleans today, where many people still speak French, you will see homes built in the colonial French style. Sloping tile roofs and sturdy posts along the outside of the house point to a French influence.

The Southwest and Florida were home to many of the first Spanish colonists. If you visit any of the large cities in these regions, you may hear Spanish being spoken and see Spanish-style homes. Do you know what to look for? Whitewashed stucco or adobe walls, wide verandas, and small courtyards are clues that the homes were built like those in Spain.

A Georgian house

Homes of the Aristocrats

In the eighteenth century, the *Georgian* house became a symbol of the aristocratic family in America. It was a large, square, two-story house with a symmetrical appearance. It was named after the kings of England who ruled between 1714 and 1830. Most Georgian homes had several steps leading up to a decorative front door.

Thomas Jefferson, the third president of the United States, was also an accomplished architect. He designed his famous home, Monticello, after the Roman style he had often seen during his travels to Europe. It has a central dome and a wide front porch with six columns. Above the columns is a triangular section called a pediment. Inside the pediment is a small window in the shape of a semicircle.

Thomas Jefferson's house, Monticello

In the early 1800s, people built mansions and public buildings that looked more like Greek temples than houses. Tall white columns graced every front porch and often surrounded the building as well. Some columns were even built inside homes, along the sides of a room. The bases and tops of these columns were ornately carved in classic Greek patterns.

The Lincoln Memorial is based on Greek architecture.

After the American Civil War, people were ready for a new style of home. In the 1860s, the Victorian house rose to popularity in America. The home was named for the era in which Queen Victoria ruled England.

Victorian homes are often called "gingerbread houses" today. Why do you think this is so? Victorian houses usually have many pretty details on the outside, like intricately-carved wooden posts or decorative trim under the eaves. Many also have balconies, gables, towers, and turrets. Some look almost like castles.

The people of the Victorian age liked to decorate the insides of their houses too. Do you like to save things? Victorians were *sentimental*— they saved things that held a special meaning for them. They liked to display souvenirs, dried flowers, and photographs everywhere. They also liked rich-looking things—dark wood furniture, heavy curtains, oriental rugs, and statues.

The interior of a Victorian home

Making Homes Beautiful

Most people want their homes to be comfortable, safe, and pleasant. In what ways do we add beauty to our homes? Does your home have

A leaded glass window

wallpaper, pictures on the walls, or curtains at the windows? Are there plants inside your home or trees growing in the yard?

Native Americans cared about the look of their homes too. The poles of their tipis were always arranged to look even and neat. Some tipis were decorated with colorful drawings. The chief's tipi usually had an emblem such as a horse's tail hanging above the entrance flap.

English colonists often filled in their windows with many small, diamond-shaped panes of glass. Smaller windowpanes broke less easily than the large ones. The panes were held in place by criss-crossed pieces of lead, forming a pretty pattern. Many homes in medieval England had this type of window. Windows like these are called *leaded windows*. Some homes have them today. Have you ever seen them?

During the Victorian age, Americans wanted so many beautiful things in their homes that often the rooms looked cluttered and disorganized. What kinds of things would you add to a home to make it beautiful and unique?

Flowers are a popular way to make one's home beautiful.

239

A solar home

Homes of Today

Today people live in many different kinds of homes. Some people live in apartments. Apartment buildings never used to be more than four or five stories high. But during the Victorian age, the elevator was invented. Elevators and a steel building frame made it possible to make apartment buildings many stories high. Today in some big cities, people live in skyscraper apartment buildings.

Other people live in houses. Houses come in all different shapes and sizes. A *ranch* house is a rectangular, one-story home. A *split-level* house has rooms on different levels, separated by about half a story. Other homes are *two-story* houses, with a staircase to the second story. Do you live in one of these types of homes?

In the late 1900s, some architects began experimenting with new ideas for building houses. The *solar home* was one of their ideas. Solar homes are designed to store heat energy from the sun. Most solar homes have several large windows facing south that trap the sun's heat. Air or water in the home is heated as it passes through *collectors,* tubes or metal plates beneath the windows.

The *earth-sheltered* home was probably borrowed from the building practices of the earliest Americans. It is built completely below ground or in the side of a hill or mound of earth. Since the temperature underground is almost always about 55° Fahrenheit, the home stays cool in summer and warm in winter.

When designing an earth-sheltered home, the architect begins by drawing a sketch, like this one by Malcolm Wells.

Would you like to live in a house that is right next to the ocean?

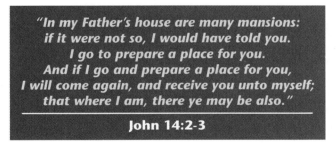

Some houses are not for people to live in, but for children to play in.

Some people today do not live in houses at all. Some people travel often, taking along a mobile home. Some military people live for months and months on ships or submarines. Some people live with many other people in special shelters, nursing homes, orphanages, or dormitories.

What changes will the future bring to homes? Scientists have even researched the possibility of building homes in space. What do you think of this idea? Would you like to be one of the first to try out a space home?

"In my Father's house are many mansions: if it were not so, I would have told you. I go to prepare a place for you. And if I go and prepare a place for you, I will come again, and receive you unto myself; that where I am, there ye may be also."

John 14:2-3

Each home is different because each home has different people living in it. The people in a home and the things those people believe create the home's *atmosphere.* What can you contribute to your home today to improve its atmosphere?

Christians can look forward to a perfect, eternal home with Christ in heaven. Nothing is more important than knowing where your eternal home will be. Jesus Christ deeply desires that you join Him someday in this perfect home. Do you know for sure that He is preparing a place for you?

To Make a Cross-sectional Diagram

1. Get Notebook page 80 and a pencil.

2. Pretend that the drawing on the Notebook page is a diagram of your room at home with one of its walls missing so that people can look directly into it, as they would a room in a dollhouse. What would they be able to see?

3. Label important features of your room, such as your bed, your closet, your dresser, and so on.

4. Exchange papers with another student and examine his diagram. How is his room similar to yours? How is it different?

Traditions and Celebrations

What would it be like to live in a country that had no birthday cakes? What if no one told bedtime stories or played baseball in the spring? What if no one gave wedding presents or decorated trees at Christmas?

That is what life would be like in America without *traditions*. Traditions are things that people do again and again—like exploding fireworks every Fourth of July or going on hayrides every autumn.

Traditions are an important part of culture. They are partly what makes one culture different from another. Traditions are often passed down from generation to generation. Some of America's traditions come from other countries. They were brought across the ocean by immigrants. And some traditions come from Native Americans, who have lived in America longer than any other people.

Traditions of Taste

Have you ever thought that when you eat a hot dog, you are really eating a variation on a German sausage? Or that when you bite into a slice of pizza, you are sampling an old Italian tradition?

When settlers came to America from foreign countries, each group brought with them their traditional ways of cooking. The Dutch made sweet little cakes called *koekjes,* from which we get the word *cookies.* The Chinese brought the technique of stir-frying. Many of America's citrus fruits were first introduced by the Spanish. And the Native Americans were the first to grow corn in America.

Certain states and regions of America have traditional foods. The South is famous for black-eyed peas and okra, two foods that came to America from Africa with the slaves. Grits, a uniquely southern dish, originated with Native Americans who taught colonists how to make hominy from dried corn kernels. Southerners ground up the hominy and added butter and milk to create the creamy grits of today.

In the Northeast, seafood is traditional fare. Lobster and clams are popular, and the New England states are especially known for their clam chowder. Pennsylvania Dutch recipes include cheesecake, waffles, and noodles. People in the Southwest cook with tortillas and season with chili peppers, borrowing from their southern neighbors in Mexico.

Many people consider lobster a favorite seafood dish.

People who like spicy food flavor some dishes with a hot chili pepper.

Lemons originated in India and were brought to America by Christopher Columbus.

To Make a Regional Food

1. Listen as your teacher reads to you about bizcochitos. Read the recipe from Notebook page 81. Answer your teacher's questions about the recipe.

2. Help your teacher set up the equipment for cutting out the cookies.

3. Watch as your teacher rolls out the dough. Take turns using the cookie cutters and sprinkling the sugar on top of the cookies.

4. Bake the cookies, let them cool, and then taste them. What flavor do you taste in the cookies? Which ingredient gives them this flavor?

Special Occasions

Does your family celebrate your birthday? In most American families, some kind of birthday feasting takes place. Many families make special birthday cakes with candles. They sing "Happy Birthday" to the person celebrating.

The tradition of the birthday cake with candles came from Germany. Germans often eat *napfkuchen,* a butter cake dusted with powdered sugar, or a rich fruit-and-nut cake called *stollen.* They place lighted candles around the edge of the cake plate.

The custom of singing to someone on his birthday is practiced in many different parts of the world. In places like Mexico, the birthday person is serenaded from the street in the early hours of the morning. Do you think the United States should adopt this tradition?

The United States Marine Band has played for every president except George Washington. John Philip Sousa is shown here conducting the band.

Music is a part of many American traditions. Carols are sung at Christmas and special hymns at Easter. Patriotic songs are heard on the Fourth of July. Often people sing praise songs at Thanksgiving. And Americans sing their national anthem at the beginning of sporting events and concerts. Each state has its own traditional song. What is your state's song?

Have you ever heard this song?

Steal away, steal away,
Steal away to Jesus!
Steal away, steal away home,
I ain't got long to stay here.

My Lord, He calls me,
He calls me by the thunder,
The trumpet sounds within-a my soul,
I ain't got long to stay here.

"Steal Away" is a *spiritual*—a traditional song of the African American slaves. Slaves often sang spirituals as they worked in the fields. Some spirituals were fast and rhythmic while others were slow and hauntingly beautiful. Spirituals focused on the religious beliefs of the slaves. Many slaves were true believers in Jesus Christ.

Today spirituals are sung all over America by many different races. The African American dialect is kept in most traditional spirituals. Can you find traces of it in "Steal Away"? Often the words to spirituals centered on the theme of heaven. Can you understand why the hope of heaven was so important to slaves?

The wedding ring is also a traditional marriage symbol.

A bride wearing the traditional white gown and veil

Traditions are often based on *symbolism.* A symbol is an object or observance that has a deeper meaning. It represents something other than itself.

Most brides wear white at weddings. The color white is a symbol of purity. A custom popular in the past has been for the bride to wear orange blossoms, small white flowers, in her hair or on her clothing. Orange blossoms symbolized both her purity and her desire to have children. Do you know the symbolism of the ring? The pure gold band symbolizes love's purity; and its shape, a perfect circle, symbolizes the eternal nature of love.

The Jewish marriage ceremony takes place beneath a canopy, called a *huppah,* which represents the bridal chamber spoken of in Psalm 19:5. Sometimes a veil covering the bride's face takes the place of an actual canopy.

At a Jewish wedding reception, someone always smashes a glass under his foot. Not everyone agrees about what this tradition symbolizes. Some say that it reminds everyone present that marriage is a solemn occasion to be treated with respect. Some say it is a symbol of the destruction of the temple.

Seasonal Celebrations

Many families set up *crèches* at Christmas. *Crèche* is a French word meaning *crib* or *nursery*. A crèche, or a Nativity scene, is a representation of the birth of Christ using figures of the stable, the manger, the characters, and the animals. Many people feel that having a crèche in their homes helps them focus on the true meaning of Christmas.

Legend says that the custom of the crèche was begun by Francis of Assisi, a monk in Italy centuries ago. Out walking one December evening, Francis came upon some shepherds asleep under the moon. They reminded him of the shepherds who saw the baby Jesus on that first Christmas night. So Francis asked for their help.

He set up a manger, borrowed some sheep, and found a man, a woman, and a baby to dress up in costumes. He invited people from the nearby town of Greccio to come to the Nativity scene on Christmas Eve. People sang and listened to Francis read the Christmas story from the Bible. Some churches today still have living Nativity scenes.

The crèche, or Nativity scene, is the most popular way to remind Christians of the true meaning of Christmas.

In Germany in the 1400s, people liked to perform plays at Christmastime, using evergreen trees hung with fruit to represent the trees in the Garden of Eden. Later, peasants took trees into their homes and hung fruit, candles, and cookies on them. Some say these were the first Christmas trees. Others say that Martin Luther decorated the first Christmas tree. He placed lighted candles on a pine to show his children what the forest trees looked like in the moonlight.

German soldiers took the tradition to America during the War for Independence. But the Christmas tree gained widespread popularity in 1841 when Prince Albert gave one to Queen Victoria as a Christmas surprise.

Some colonial Christmas traditions are no longer in practice today. One was the burning of the yule log. A member from each household went out and cut down a large tree for this celebration time. During the time that the yule log was burning, no work was done as people celebrated Christmas. Often slaves sent for the yule log chose the thickest, greenest log they could find. Do you know why they did this?

Another favorite tradition of Colonial school children was "barring out the schoolmaster." Near Christmastime, the students in the one-room schoolhouse would lock their teacher out of the schoolhouse until he promised to give each of them a small gift.

The Crow Fair in Montana

Some seasonal traditions are kept only by certain groups of Americans. *Powwows* are a Native American tradition from long ago. French explorers heard natives use a word to describe people gathering together to trade. The word sounded to them like "powwow." Now the word refers to any kind of special meeting.

Native Americans still hold powwows today. The Crow Fair, held in Montana every summer, is the largest powwow in North America. Lakota, Ojibwa, Cheyenne, Crow, Cree, Blackfoot, and Fox people come from miles away to dress in native clothing and participate in different types of Native American dances and songs.

Ideas to Uphold

Sometimes one person's idea can become a tradition for an entire nation. When Julius Sterling Morton moved from Detroit, Michigan, to the Nebraska Territory in 1854, he noticed that there were hardly any trees in Nebraska. Morton wrote for the newspaper and spoke about the need for orchards and forests.

In 1872 the entire state of Nebraska made April 10 a special day for planting trees. Prizes were given to those who planted the most. The Nebraskans planted over one million trees.

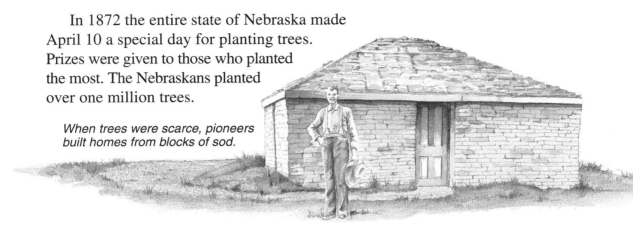

When trees were scarce, pioneers built homes from blocks of sod.

Soon the idea spread to other states. Today almost every state has Arbor Day. Most celebrate it in the month of April. Nebraska's Arbor Day is now April 22, Morton's birthday. Have you ever celebrated Arbor Day by planting a tree?

America has special days to honor parents. Mother's Day is the second Sunday in May each year, and Father's Day is the third Sunday in June. Does your family keep special traditions for either of these two days?

Some families plan specific times to get together with other relatives outside their immediate family. These occasions are usually called *reunions.* Reunions are also times for remembering. The family you were born into determines many of the traditions you will have as you grow up. Have you ever thought that the Lord put you into your particular family for a special reason?

A family reunion

James Naismith

Games and Rhymes

In 1891 James Naismith was a physical-education teacher at the School for Christian Workers in Massachusetts. He had just been asked to invent a new game— a team sport that could be played indoors during winter. He found two peach baskets and attached them to the balcony railing on either end of the gym, about ten feet above the floor. He taught the rules of his new game to his P.E. class. Then he divided the class into two teams. Using a soccer ball, the class played the first basketball game in December of 1891.

Much about the game has changed since 1891. Basketball is played on playgrounds, as well as on the college and professional levels. There are even some fancy plays with names such as *alley oop* and *slam dunk*. But the excitement of that first game is still the same.

A basketball game in 1892

253

Did you have a favorite game when you were younger or a favorite book that you wanted someone to read to you again and again? See whether the following poem sounds familiar to you:

Ring-a-ring o' roses,
A pocket full of posies,
A-tishoo! A-tishoo!
We all fall down.

This chant began as a nursery rhyme. Some people say the words refer to the bubonic plague, which swept through Europe and Asia in the 1300s. Some of the symptoms of the plague were a rosy rash and sneezing. People often carried herbs in their pockets, hoping to protect themselves. Most children today use the words "Ashes, ashes" in place of the sneezing sounds. Can you see some connections between the children's game and the plague?

Did you ever wonder who Little Miss Muffet was? She might have been Patience Muffet, daughter of Dr. Thomas Muffet. Dr. Muffet, who lived in the late 1500s, was an *entomologist,* a scientist who studies insects. History tells us he was especially fascinated with spiders; he even wrote a scientific work about them called *Silkworms and their flies.*

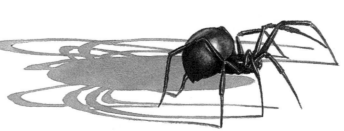

Nursery Rhymes

Little Jack Horner
Sat in the corner
Eating his Christmas pie.
He put in his thumb
And pulled out a plum
And said, "What a good boy am I!"

This famous nursery rhyme has a legend behind it. An abbot in Glastonbury, England, had a steward whose last name was Horner. At Christmastime the abbot sent his steward to England with a gift for the king, hoping to gain his favor. The gift was a pie, and baked inside were the title deeds to twelve manors. According to the story, Horner pulled out the deed to the Manor of Mells. A man named Thomas Horner moved into the Manor of Mells shortly afterwards, and his family has lived in the manor ever since.

255

Hot Cross Buns,
Hot Cross Buns,
One-a-penny, two-a-penny
Hot Cross Buns!

This chant is an "echo" of a street cry in England. Hot cross buns, golden pastries marked with a cross in white icing, were sold and eaten for breakfast on Good Friday. The cry became a folksong and later a popular nursery rhyme. Many Americans still serve hot cross buns at Easter.

American Ways

What a land of diversity America is! But yet in a sense, Americans are all one culture. America is like a mulligan stew: none of the ingredients loses its flavor; all the flavors simply combine to make the overall taste stronger. Diversity is America—one wonderful country spiced with traditions from many lands.

What about you? You will have your own family someday. What traditions will you keep—or what new ones will you begin?

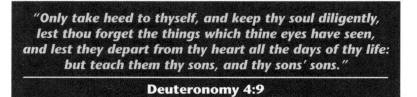

"Only take heed to thyself, and keep thy soul diligently, lest thou forget the things which thine eyes have seen, and lest they depart from thy heart all the days of thy life: but teach them thy sons, and thy sons' sons."

Deuteronomy 4:9

12

Changing the Boundaries

After the War

The years between World War II and the end of the twentieth century were marked by great changes in the American way of life. Technology advanced the fields of aerospace, medicine, communication, and transportation. Black Americans struggled to achieve equal rights under the law. And a new enemy, Communism, grew to dominance in Asia, Eastern Europe, and Africa, threatening democracy worldwide.

The Fifties— A Time of Optimism and Struggle

Harry S Truman

America greeted the end of World War II with celebrations. But peace did not prevail for long. In 1950 the Korean War erupted. Communist North Korea hoped to conquer democratic South Korea. Truman chose General Douglas MacArthur to lead the United Nations forces in Korea. By October most of Korea was under United Nations control. Then thousands of soldiers from Communist China poured over the Chinese border into Korea, pushing MacArthur's forces back into South Korea. General MacArthur thought that the battle should be carried into Manchuria (in China). President Truman, worried that expanding the war might lead to World War III, wanted to keep the war in Korea. When MacArthur made public comments criticizing the president's policy, President Truman called MacArthur home.

During the 1950s, President Truman said that the United States would help any nation that was struggling against a Communist takeover. His statement became known as the Truman Doctrine.

This railway depot in Florida had segregated waiting rooms.

Dwight David Eisenhower

During Eisenhower's administration the nation became increasingly concerned with the issue of civil rights, the right of all people to be treated equally. Across America black citizens struggled to live under "Jim Crow" laws, laws that said whites could do one thing but blacks must do something else. These laws determined where children could go to school, where people could sit in restaurants, which motels they could stay in, and where they could sit on buses.

Then, just before Christmas in 1955, Rosa Parks, a black seamstress, boarded a bus in Montgomery, Alabama. The "Blacks Only" section at the back of the bus was filled. Mrs. Parks sat in one of the middle rows. Soon a white passenger boarded the bus. There were no seats in the "Whites Only" section at the front of the bus. The bus driver told Mrs. Parks to give her seat to the white man. She refused. What do you

think happened to Mrs. Parks for refusing to move? She was arrested and put in jail. Mrs. Parks had had a long day. She was tired and thirsty. But the jailer would not let her get a drink. The jail's drinking fountain was marked "Whites Only."

Rosa Parks is fingerprinted for participating in a bus boycott.

Civil rights leader,
Martin Luther King Jr.

To protest the arrest of Mrs. Parks, Martin Luther King Jr. organized a boycott of the Montgomery bus system. Black citizens decided not to ride the bus until the buses were *desegregated,* or available for people of all races. For over a year black Americans boycotted the Montgomery buses. At last the Supreme Court of the United States ruled that Montgomery's bus laws were unconstitutional.

The "space race" took off in 1957 when the Soviet Union announced that *Sputnik,* the world's first manmade satellite, had orbited the earth. *Sputnik II,* launched later, carried a dog named Laika.

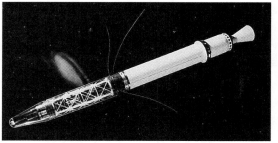

The satellite Explorer I *was launched from Cape Canaveral on January 31, 1958.*

The United States was embarrassed to be behind the Soviets in space travel. Within a few months the United States launched the satellite Explorer I. And in schools everywhere, teachers emphasized science and mathematics. Technology continued to advance. In response to the need for small equipment to take on space missions, computer scientists began the quest to make the huge room-sized computers of the late 1940s and early 1950s smaller.

Imagine using a computer that fills an entire room!

It was not just the space race that strained relations between the United States and the Soviet Union. The Soviets continued to work to make countries Communist while the United States sent money and help to nations trying to stay free. This struggle between Communism and democracy was called the Cold War because a hot, or fighting, war did not develop between the United States and the Soviet Union.

The United States, with other United Nations countries, continued to fight alongside South Korea in its war against Communist North Korea until a truce was signed between the two countries in 1953. Neither side had been able to conquer the other. North Korea remained Communist, and South Korea remained democratic.

Another spot in the Cold War began to get hot in 1954. North Vietnam, a Communist country, decided to take over South Vietnam, which was anti-Communist. The United States offered to help South Vietnam by sending military advisors.

Many Americans were afraid of Communism, but Senator Joseph McCarthy declared that there were Communists within the American government and military. Senator McCarthy accused people of being secret Communists. Some of the people he accused lost friends and jobs when they were thought to be Communists. Others were treated rudely. At last the Senate held investigations. They determined that McCarthy had been accusing people without sufficient evidence.

In 1959 Alaska and Hawaii joined the Union as the forty-ninth and fiftieth states.

John and Jacqueline Kennedy on the night of the presidential election

The Sixties— A Time of Progress and Uncertainty

John Fitzgerald Kennedy

John Kennedy and his popular wife represented a new, forward-looking America. At forty-three, Kennedy was the youngest man ever elected president. He was the first Catholic president and the first president to be born in the 1900s. Kennedy faced an increasing Communist presence around the world, which threatened the security of the United States.

Communism continued to expand from the Soviet Union into other parts of the world. In Berlin, Germany, the Communists erected a wall to keep the people of East Berlin (Communist) away from West Berlin (democratic). People died trying to escape from East Berlin.

President Kennedy addresses the threat of Communism at a press conference.

Most of these were shot to death by East German border guards.

Cuba became Communist in 1959 when Fidel Castro came to power. In 1961 some Cubans who had immigrated to the United States invaded Cuba in an attempt to take the government from the Communists. The invasion failed. President Kennedy told the country that the United States had trained and supplied the invading troops.

Fidel Castro (foreground)

The Cuban Missile Crisis

Carol Jean ran home from her friend Donna's house as fast as she could. Her heart was pounding. She slammed the front door.

"Mom, the Russians are coming!" Carol Jean heard no answer. "Mom," she called again. Carol Jean found her parents and older brother in the family room staring at the television. Their faces were stern. Mom looked worried.

Carol Jean sat down next to her mother and listened. What she'd heard was true then. There really were missiles in Cuba aimed at the United States. There really might be war between the Soviet Union and America.

When the station broke for a commercial, Carol Jean asked her father, "Daddy, will we be bombed?"

"I don't know, honey," he said. "We'll just pray and trust the Lord to take care of our country."

President John F. Kennedy had learned that the Soviet Union had placed nuclear missiles in Cuba, about one hundred miles off the coast of Florida.

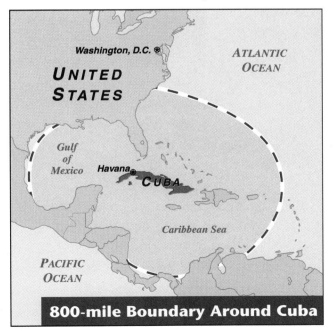

800-mile Boundary Around Cuba

If these missiles were launched against American cities, many people would die and the United States would retaliate by launching nuclear missiles against the Soviet Union. World War III would begin. President Kennedy determined that he would stand strong for America. He declared that any Soviet ship carrying weapons would be turned back eight hundred miles from Cuba. Any ship attempting to run the blockade would be attacked.

263

Many Soviet citizens as well as Americans were afraid. World War II started twenty-two years after World War I, and now it looked as though World War III would break out just twenty-three years after World War II.

Soviet ships approached the eight-hundred-mile mark. A Soviet submarine stationed itself between the Soviet cargo ships and the American aircraft carrier. The situation was tense. President Kennedy urged President Khrushchev to turn his ship around. President Khrushchev told President Kennedy to lift the blockade. President Kennedy refused. He declared that the blockade would not be lifted until the missile sites in Cuba were dismantled and removed.

"Ye that fear the Lord, trust in the Lord: he is their help and their shield."

Psalm 115:11

For thirteen days, no one knew what would happen. Many people, like Carol Jean, expected war. Many Americans built bomb shelters in their yards or basements. Russian government officials moved their families out of Moscow. As last, President Khrushchev ordered his troops in Cuba to take down the missile launching pads, dismantle them, and return them to the Soviet Union. The crisis was over. People could relax and enjoy life again.

Playing with Toys

Children have always played with toys. Look at these toys from the last decades of the twentieth century. Some toys remain popular for many years. Do you have any of these toys?

The fifties

The sixties

The seventies

The eighties

The nineties

Meredith had to endure rude comments from his fellow students nearly every day.

Civil rights remained a tense issue through the 1960s. Although the Supreme Court had ordered the schools to desegregate "with all deliberate speed," local governments in many areas refused to comply. When James Meredith tried to become the first African American to register at the University of Mississippi, the governor of Mississippi personally stood in his way. Thousands of federal troops were sent to protect Meredith while he registered for classes. President Kennedy said, "The time has come for the Congress of the United States . . . [to make] it clear to all that race has no place in American life or law."

The space race intensified when President Kennedy announced his goal for the country to send a man to the moon and bring him back safely by the end of the 1960s. In May 1961, Alan Shepard was the first American astronaut to go into outer space. In early 1962, John Glenn became the first American to orbit the earth.

Then came November 22, 1963. From inside their open limousine, President and Mrs. Kennedy waved to crowds that lined the streets of Dallas, Texas. The president was on his way to make a speech. Suddenly shots rang out. The president slumped over in his seat. The limousine raced to the hospital, but it was too late. President Kennedy died of gunshot wounds to the head. The

The Kennedys arriving in Dallas

death of the handsome young president was a great blow to the country. Lyndon Johnson called Kennedy's death "a loss that cannot be weighed."

Johnson took his oath of office on board the plane that had brought Kennedy to Dallas.

Lyndon Baines Johnson

Lyndon Johnson was sworn in as president on the afternoon of President Kennedy's death. As he flew back to Washington, D.C., Johnson knew his task as president would not be easy. Halfway around the world, in Vietnam, more than sixteen thousand military advisors helped the South Vietnamese in their fight against Communism. At home, more and more people took sides over civil rights.

Soldiers in a rice paddy in Vietnam

By the time Johnson left office in 1969, more than five hundred thousand American troops were in Vietnam. Most of them had been drafted into the military service. As brave men and women gave their lives fighting for the freedom of South Vietnam, many people at home wondered whether the United States should even be involved in the war. Some men who were drafted burned their draft cards and refused to go to war. Some went to Canada to avoid going into military service.

Blacks made some progress in civil rights during Johnson's administration. The Civil Rights Act of 1964 opened all hotels, motels, restaurants, and other businesses to people of all races. Poll taxes—money people had to pay in order to vote—and literacy tests for voting were outlawed. Before this time, black people in some states were required to prove they could read and write at a certain level before being allowed to vote. In

Why is no one eating at this lunch counter? Many nonviolent sit-ins like this one occurred throughout the U.S.

some places, blacks were made to answer "Thirty Questions" in order to vote. Some of the questions were so difficult that even the people asking the questions did not know the answers.

Martin Luther King Jr. (front row, left) poses with U.S. political leaders.

But though the government could change the laws, it could not erase prejudice or hatred from people's hearts. In 1968, Dr. Martin Luther King Jr. was shot to death by a white man. Up until King's death most of the protests, marches, and sit-ins by black people had been nonviolent. However, after Dr. King's murder, riots broke out in over one hundred cities across the country.

Richard Milhous Nixon

Perhaps the accomplishment President Richard Nixon was most proud of was the improved relations between the United States and China. Nixon was the first president to visit Communist China, where he opened trade with this huge country.

President Nixon stands on the Great Wall during his visit to China.

On July 16, 1969, the world watched in fascination as *Apollo 11,* perched atop a huge *Saturn 5* rocket, lifted off from Florida's Cape Kennedy. Traveling at 15,400 miles per hour, *Apollo 11* moved into Earth orbit. The astronauts checked the systems of the spacecraft and then fired the engines to achieve 23,300 miles per hour, the speed needed to escape Earth's gravity. *Apollo 11* was headed to the moon!

Saturn 5; *inset*—Apollo 11 *crew (Neil Armstrong, Michael Collins, and Edwin Aldrin)*

Four days later, on July 20, Americans were thrilled to hear Mission Control in Texas speak to the astronauts. "We copy you down, *Eagle,*" Mission Control said. Then, from 240,000 miles away, the answer came through, "Tranquility Base here. The *Eagle* has landed." Americans were on the moon! Six hours after landing, astronaut Neil Armstrong stepped onto the moon and said, "That's one small step for a man, one giant leap for mankind."

The astronauts left an American flag and a plaque on the moon. Inscribed on the plaque were the names of the *Apollo 11* astronauts and President Nixon as well as the statement "We came in peace for all mankind."

Armstrong and Aldrin plant the American flag on the moon; Aldrin sets up equipment for studying the moon's surface.

270

People who opposed the Vietnam War often held peace demonstrations in the 1960s.

The Seventies— A Time of Unrest and Change

The war in Vietnam continued to expand during Nixon's presidency, but in 1973 the president ended American troop involvement, leaving only military advisors and weapons. Prisoners of war were exchanged. Men who had spent years in North Vietnamese prison camps returned to America as heroes. Other veterans, though, found that they were not welcomed as heroes. Many of them experienced angry receptions from people who felt America's involvement in Vietnam was unjust.

Richard Nixon's final years in office were marred by scandal. His vice president, Spiro Agnew, was forced to resign because of charges of tax evasion. And in 1972 several employees of Nixon's re-election campaign broke into the Democratic Party's headquarters at the Watergate Hotel in Washington, D.C. Evidence showed that President Nixon was deeply involved in the attempt to cover up the break-in, that is, make it seem unimportant and uninteresting so that people would forget about it. Nixon won the election of 1972, but concern about his part in Watergate grew among the American people. At last it became clear that Congress intended to *impeach* the president, or accuse him of crimes. Nixon resigned rather than face being removed from office.

Nixon bids farewell to his supporters as he leaves office.

271

In one of his foreign diplomacy efforts, President Ford meets with President Anwar Sadat of Egypt.

Gerald Rudolph Ford

Gerald Ford was the only president who was not elected by the American people. He was appointed vice president when Spiro Agnew resigned. Then when President Nixon resigned, Ford became president.

Ford meets with the National Security Council near the end of the Vietnam War.

Ford was president during one of the saddest occasions in American history. In 1975, the last Americans left South Vietnam. South Vietnam quickly fell to the Communist North Vietnamese. The Vietnam War was the longest war America had ever fought and the only war it had lost. More than fifty-eight thousand Americans died trying to keep the people of South Vietnam free. Today Vietnam is a united country under a Communist government.

"Boat People"

Over one hundred thousand South Vietnamese left their country at the end of the Vietnam War to escape the Communism they knew would soon overrun their country. Other Vietnamese people followed, traveling to America any way they could. Some escaped Vietnam on rafts or in small boats. These refugees were called "boat people." Vietnamese immigrants settled in cities all over America, many of them on the West Coast. Today Vietnamese people live and work all over the United States, their contributions "echoing" in America.

After Watergate and the end of the Vietnam War, Americans needed something happy to celebrate. That something happened in 1976, the two hundredth anniversary of the founding of the American nation. All over the country people celebrated. On July 4, 1976, President Ford watched as tall ships sailed into New York Harbor for a grand national birthday party.

James Earl Carter Jr.

Jimmy Carter called his years in office "a time to heal." After Watergate, many Americans were glad to elect an "outsider," someone who had not been involved in Washington politics.

President Carter had stood for equal rights for black Americans for years. As a businessman in Georgia he had refused to join a community

group that stood for racial segregation. When his church voted on a resolution to exclude African Americans from attending, only the Carters and one other family voted against it. When Jimmy Carter became governor of Georgia, he announced in his inaugural address that "the time for racial discrimination is over." Carter appointed many qualified women and people of minority ethnic groups to government posts.

Jimmy Carter (left) takes a stroll with Vice President Walter Mondale.

During his administration, Carter hosted peace talks with President Sadat (left) and Prime Minister Begin (right) of Israel.

For a while it looked as though relations between the United States and the Soviet Union were getting better. President Carter and Soviet President Leonid Brezhnev signed an agreement that would reduce

Carter and Brezhnev sign the SALT II agreements in Vienna, Austria.

nuclear weapons in both countries. However, when the Soviet army invaded the country of Afghanistan, tension between the United States and the Soviet Union increased, and the Senate refused to *ratify,* or approve, the agreement.

In 1980 the Olympic Games were held in Moscow, the capital city of the Soviet Union. President Carter made the decision that no American athlete would compete at the Moscow Olympics to protest the Afghanistan invasion. Fifty-five other nations also boycotted the 1980 Olympic Games.

Iran, a large country in the Middle East, had been ruled for many years by Shah Mohammed Reza Pahlavi. A revolution in Iran in 1979 removed the shah from power. It seemed that no country wanted to take him in. Finally he came to the United States for medical treatment.

Representatives from the U.S. military greet the shah (right) during one of his visits to the U.S.

Carter welcomes a released hostage.

Some Iranians were angry with the United States for allowing the shah to come. One angry group of Iranian revolutionaries took sixty-one Americans hostage at the American embassy in Teheran, the capital of Iran. Nine of the hostages were soon released, but fifty-two Americans remained in custody for over four hundred days. President Carter authorized a rescue mission, but the mission failed. Carter took responsibility for the lives that were lost during the rescue mission. As his term of office came to a close, Carter spent all his time negotiating for the return of the hostages. Finally, on the last morning of his administration, the hostages were released.

President Reagan greets Margaret Thatcher, Prime Minister of Britain.

The Eighties— A Time of Strength and Challenge

Ronald Wilson Reagan

During the 1980s President Ronald Reagan took a strong anti-Communist stance. To counter the continued threat of Soviet power, Reagan oversaw a massive increase in America's military might. These increases cost billions of dollars, and America's national debt soared to several trillion dollars. Reagan proposed a defense system that would destroy any missiles directed at the United States. This system, called the Strategic Defense Initiative, was commonly known as "Star Wars."

President Reagan visited West Germany in 1987. While there, he spoke to a crowd gathered at the Berlin Wall. Speaking of Mikhail Gorbachev, the president of the Soviet Union, Reagan said, "Mr. Gorbachev, tear down this wall."

President Reagan's administration saw trouble in the Middle East. Two hundred forty-one American marines were killed when the Marine Corps Headquarters in Beirut, Lebanon, was bombed. In response to the Beirut bombing, Reagan ordered U.S. troops to move from the city of Beirut into ships stationed a short distance from Lebanon. Reagan also sent troops to Grenada, a small island country in the Caribbean Sea, when the lives of American students were in danger.

During the Reagan years, great progress was made in medicine and technology. A man named Barney Clark received the world's first artificial heart. The heart kept Clark alive for 112 days. Also during the eighties many homes and schools obtained their first personal computers.

Vietnam War Memorial

In 1982, the Vietnam War Memorial was dedicated in Washington, D.C. The names of the fifty-eight thousand Americans killed during the war were engraved on the granite wall. Veterans, family members, and friends visited "The Wall" to remember their experiences and to honor the memory of those who gave their lives for their country.

January 28, 1986, dawned clear and cold. Seven astronauts waved at cheering crowds as they walked out to

Crew of the space shuttle Challenger

board the space shuttle *Challenger*. One of the astronauts was Christa McAuliffe, a schoolteacher from New Hampshire who had been selected as the first teacher to ride a shuttle. Then, just seventy-three seconds after liftoff, the shuttle disintegrated. All seven astronauts were killed. Many people thought this tragedy would be the end of the American space program. However, about a year and a half later, the shuttle *Discovery* carried out a successful mission.

Ronald Reagan appointed Sandra Day O'Connor to the Supreme Court of the United States. Mrs. O'Connor was the first woman to serve as a Supreme Court justice.

The swearing-in ceremony of Sandra Day O'Connor

The Zero Factor

Since 1840 every American president elected during a year ending with zero had died in office: Harrison—1840, Lincoln—1860, Garfield—1880, McKinley—1900, Harding—1920, Franklin Roosevelt—1940, and Kennedy—1960. When Ronald Reagan was elected in 1980, many people feared he would not live out his term of office because of the "Zero Factor." During his first term he was shot in the chest during an assassination attempt, but he fully recovered. He also survived his second term in office.

Reagan talks with Soviet Premier Mikhail Gorbachev in Red Square.

Gorbachev and Reagan sign an agreement to reduce nuclear arms.

The Nineties— A Time of Power and Hope

George Herbert Walker Bush

George Bush was elected president in 1988 after serving as Reagan's vice president for eight years. Under Reagan the military power of the United States had been built up to immense proportions but at a huge cost. Bush inherited a national debt of over three trillion dollars. However, America's military might stood her in good stead as she faced war in the Middle East and the crumbling of the massive Soviet Union.

The situation in the Middle East grew hot as the situation in the Soviet Union became increasingly uncertain. The Persian Gulf War climaxed George Bush's presidency. The country of Iraq, under President Saddam Hussein, invaded the small oil-producing country of Kuwait and announced that Kuwait was now part of Iraq. Iraqi troops then gathered along the Saudi Arabian border. Many people feared that Iraq would attack Saudi Arabia next.

The United States relied on Kuwaiti and Saudi Arabian oil exports. So when Iraq threatened to take control of this oil, President Bush, along with thirty-eight other United Nations leaders, launched an attack on Iraq. Technology helped the Allies win the Persian Gulf War. Computerized guided missiles were launched with deadly accuracy from ships in the Persian Gulf. The war lasted from the middle of January to the end of February 1991, ending in an Allied victory. Iraq pulled out of Kuwait.

Americans were proud of General Colin Powell, the first African American to hold the post of chairman of the Joint Chiefs of Staff, Amer-

Bush (center) and Powell at a Pentagon briefing before Desert Storm

ica's highest military post. Powell, along with General H. Norman Schwarzkopf, led the United Nations forces during the Persian Gulf War. Like Colin Powell, other African Americans held important government posts, such as cabinet secretary, Supreme Court justice, and congressman, marking progress in the quest for civil rights.

Countries surrounding the Soviet Union had been ruled by Communist governments for many years. Many citizens of these countries wanted to be free. In 1989, Communist governments fell in many countries of Eastern Europe. Perhaps the most dramatic moment in the fall of Communism was the destruction of the Berlin Wall. The wall had been a symbol of Communist oppression since it was built in 1961.

Soviet citizens were unhappy with Communism too. Several of the fifteen Soviet republics began talking about declaring independence. In 1991 President Bush announced that the United States now recognized Latvia, Estonia, and Lithuania (three of the republics of the Soviet Union) as independent nations. On Christmas Day 1991, Mikhail Gorbachev, the general secretary of the Commu-

Lamplight shines through holes in the Berlin Wall as it is being torn down.

nist Party, resigned. The Soviet Union was dissolved. President Bush announced, "Our adversary of forty-five years, the one nation that posed a worldwide threat to freedom and peace, is now seeking to join the community of free nations."

William Jefferson Clinton

With the end of the Cold War, many Americans turned their focus toward home. Now that they did not need to worry about Communists taking over America, they wanted a president who would work to make life in the United States easier. And so, in 1992, Bill Clinton was elected president. Every president since 1952 had been a veteran of World War II, but Clinton had not even been born until after that war ended. President Clinton hoped to improve the nation's economy and provide health insurance for all Americans. Winning the election again in 1996, Bill Clinton promised to "build a bridge to the future."

President Clinton introduces Russian president Boris Yeltsin.

Computer technology continued to progress as the nation moved toward the twenty-first century. Electronic mail—called e-mail—could be sent from a home computer in the United States to another computer anywhere in the world in a matter of seconds. Instead of waiting for several days to get a letter or document in the mail, businesses and families purchased fax machines, which transmitted copies of documents using telephone lines. Filmmakers now use computer graphics to create scenes and even entire films. Composers use computers to write music; artists use them to draw. Students use the Internet, a huge information resource, to do research on almost any subject right from home.

To Write a Newspaper Article

1. Listen as your teacher reads several newspaper articles.

2. Choose an event that is described in this chapter. Research the event.

3. Imagine that you were a journalist when the event occurred. Write a newspaper article reporting the event. Answer the questions who, what, where, when, why, and how in your article.

4. Write an appropriate headline at the top of your story.

"Some trust in chariots, and some in horses: but we will remember the name of the Lord our God."

Psalm 20:7

Yes, there has been progress in people's lives and advances in technology, but what will tomorrow bring? Americans look forward to the future and changes to come. And the decisions of America's leaders will affect those under them—every citizen—even you. But whether the United States of America declines or prospers, the Christian's hope remains only in God, the everlasting King. Americans walk into the twenty-first century knowing that their leader's heart "is in the hand of the Lord" and that He "turneth it whithersoever he will" (Proverbs 21:1). Have you prayed for your country's leaders today?

Resource Treasury

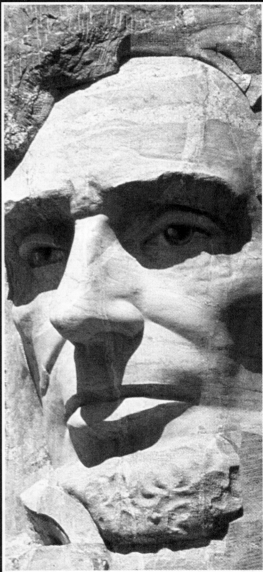

Presidents

	President	Vice President	In Office	Political Party
1.	George Washington	John Adams	1789-97	None
2.	John Adams	Thomas Jefferson	1797-1801	Federalist
3.	Thomas Jefferson	Aaron Burr George Clinton	1801-9	Democratic-Republican
4.	James Madison	George Clinton Elbridge Gerry	1809-17	Democratic-Republican
5.	James Monroe	Daniel Tompkins	1817-25	Democratic-Republican
6.	John Quincy Adams	John C. Calhoun	1825-29	Democratic-Republican
7.	Andrew Jackson	John C. Calhoun Martin Van Buren	1829-37	Democratic
8.	Martin Van Buren	Richard M. Johnson	1837-41	Democratic
9.	William H. Harrison	John Tyler	1841	Whig
10.	John Tyler		1841-45	Whig
11.	James K. Polk	George M. Dallas	1845-49	Democratic
12.	Zachary Taylor	Millard Fillmore	1849-50	Whig
13.	Millard Fillmore		1850-53	Whig
14.	Franklin Pierce	William R. King	1853-57	Democratic
15.	James Buchanan	John C. Breckinridge	1857-61	Democratic
16.	Abraham Lincoln	Hannibal Hamlin Andrew Johnson	1861-65	Republican, Union
17.	Andrew Johnson		1865-69	Union
18.	Ulysses S. Grant	Schuyler Colfax Henry Wilson	1869-77	Republican
19.	Rutherford B. Hayes	William A. Wheeler	1877-81	Republican
20.	James A. Garfield	Chester A. Arthur	1881	Republican
21.	Chester A. Arthur		1881-85	Republican
22.	Grover Cleveland	Thomas A. Hendricks	1885-89	Democratic
23.	Benjamin Harrison	Levi P. Morton	1889-93	Republican
24.	Grover Cleveland	Adlai E. Stevenson	1893-97	Democratic
25.	William McKinley	Garret A. Hobart Theodore Roosevelt	1897-1901	Republican
26.	Theodore Roosevelt	Charles W. Fairbanks	1901-9	Republican
27.	William H. Taft	James S. Sherman	1909-13	Republican

	President	Vice President	In Office	Political Party
28.	Woodrow Wilson	Thomas R. Marshall	1913-21	Democratic
29.	Warren G. Harding	Calvin Coolidge	1921-23	Republican
30.	Calvin Coolidge	Charles G. Dawes	1923-29	Republican
31.	Herbert Hoover	Charles Curtis	1929-33	Republican
32.	Franklin D. Roosevelt	John N. Garner Henry A. Wallace Harry S Truman	1933-45	Democratic
33.	Harry S Truman	Alben W. Barkley	1945-53	Democratic
34.	Dwight D. Eisenhower	Richard M. Nixon	1953-61	Republican
35.	John F. Kennedy	Lyndon B. Johnson	1961-63	Democratic
36.	Lyndon B. Johnson	Hubert H. Humphrey	1963-69	Democratic
37.	Richard M. Nixon	Spiro Agnew Gerald Ford	1969-74	Republican
38.	Gerald Ford	Nelson Rockefeller	1974-77	Republican
39.	Jimmy Carter	Walter Mondale	1977-81	Democratic
40.	Ronald Reagan	George Bush	1981-89	Republican
41.	George Bush	Dan Quayle	1989-93	Republican
42.	Bill Clinton	Al Gore	1993-	Democratic

George Washington

1

1789-97

Born:
Feb. 22, 1732

Died:
Dec. 14, 1799

Place of birth:
Westmoreland County, Virginia

Little-known fact:
He ran a ferry service across the Potomac River during his first year as president.

John Adams

2

1797-1801

Born:
Oct. 30, 1735

Died:
July 4, 1826

Place of birth:
Braintree, Massachusetts

Little-known fact:
He acted as lawyer for British soldiers charged with firing into an angry mob in prewar Boston.

Thomas Jefferson

3

1801-9

Born:
Apr. 13, 1743
Died:
July 4, 1826

Place of birth:
Shadwell, Virginia

Little-known fact:
He was an excellent violinist.

James Madison

4

1809-17

Born:
Mar. 16, 1751
Died:
June 28, 1836

Place of birth:
Port Conway, Virginia

Little-known fact:
He wrote nine of the ten amendments that make up the Bill of Rights.

James Monroe

5

1817-25

Born:
Apr. 28, 1758
Died:
July 4, 1831

Place of birth:
Westmoreland County, Virginia

Little-known fact:
He was the first president to sail on a steamboat.

John Quincy Adams

6

1825-29

Born:
July 11, 1767
Died:
Feb. 23, 1848

Place of birth:
Braintree, Massachusetts

Little-known fact:
He was a published poet.

Andrew Jackson

7

1829-37

Born:
Mar. 15, 1767

Died:
June 8, 1845

Place of birth:
Waxhaw, South Carolina

Little-known fact:
He survived the first assassination attempt in America's history.

Martin Van Buren

8

1837-41

Born:
Dec. 5, 1782

Died:
July 24, 1862

Place of birth:
Kinderhook, New York

Little-known fact:
In his autobiography he never mentioned his wife, to whom he was married for twelve years.

William Henry Harrison

9

Mar. 4, 1841-Apr. 4, 1841

Born:
Feb. 9, 1773

Died:
Apr. 4, 1841

Place of birth:
Berkeley, Virginia

Little-known fact:
His wife and his children were never present at the White House during his short time in office.

John Tyler

10

1841-45

Born:
Mar. 29, 1790

Died:
Jan. 18, 1862

Place of birth:
Greenway, Virginia

Little-known fact:
He was born within twelve miles of William Henry Harrison's birthplace.

James Knox Polk

11

1845-49

Born:
Nov. 2, 1795

Died:
June 15, 1849

Place of birth:
Mecklenburg County,
North Carolina

Little-known fact:
He and Warren G. Harding had the same birthday: November 2.

Zachary Taylor

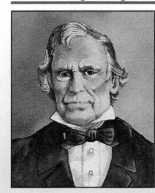

12

**Mar. 4, 1849-
July 9, 1850**

Born:
Nov. 24, 1784

Died:
July 9, 1850

Place of birth:
Orange County, Virginia

Little-known fact:
Because of his refusal to be sworn in on a Sunday, another man was president for a day.

Millard Fillmore

13

1850-53

Born:
Jan. 7, 1800

Died:
Mar. 8, 1874

Place of birth:
Locke, New York

Little-known fact:
Both of his children died unmarried; therefore, he has no descendants.

Franklin Pierce

14

1853-57

Born:
Nov. 23, 1804

Died:
Oct. 8, 1869

Place of birth:
Hillsborough, New Hampshire

Little-known fact:
He had the first furnace put in the White House.

James Buchanan

15

1857-61

Born:
Apr. 23, 1791
Died:
June 1, 1868

Place of birth:
Cove Gap, Pennsylvania

Little-known fact:
He had one nearsighted eye and one farsighted eye; he tilted his head when he talked to adjust his vision.

Abraham Lincoln

16

1861-65

Born:
Feb. 12, 1809
Died:
Apr. 15, 1865

Place of birth:
Hardin County, Kentucky

Little-known fact:
He lost eight elections before he won the presidential election in 1860.

Andrew Johnson

17

1865-69

Born:
Dec. 29, 1808
Died:
July 31, 1875

Place of birth:
Raleigh, North Carolina

Little-known fact:
After he left the White House, he became a U.S. Senator.

Ulysses Simpson Grant

18

1869-77

Born:
Apr. 27, 1822
Died:
July 23, 1885

Place of birth:
Point Pleasant, Ohio

Little-known fact:
He once commended an officer who arrested him for speeding in his presidential carriage.

Rutherford Birchard Hayes

19

1877-81

Born:
Oct. 4, 1822

Died:
Jan. 17, 1893

Place of birth:
Delaware, Ohio

Little-known fact:
His wife, Lucy, was the first First Lady who had graduated from college.

James Abram Garfield

20

Mar. 4, 1881-
Sept. 19, 1881

Born:
Nov. 19, 1831

Died:
Sept. 19, 1881

Place of birth:
Orange, Ohio

Little-known fact:
He was the last president to be born in a log cabin.

Chester Alan Arthur

21

1881-85

Born:
Oct. 5, 1829

Died:
Nov. 18, 1886

Place of birth:
Fairfield, Vermont

Little-known fact:
He employed a French chef and often took two or three hours for dinner.

Grover Cleveland

22

1885-89

Born:
Mar. 18, 1837

Died:
June 24, 1908

Place of birth:
Caldwell, New Jersey

Little-known fact:
He enjoyed hunting and named his shotgun "Death and Destruction."

Benjamin Harrison

23

1889-93

Born:
Aug. 20, 1833
Died:
Mar. 13, 1901

Place of birth:
North Bend, Ohio

Little-known fact:
He had electricity installed in the White House.

Grover Cleveland

24

1893-97

Born:
Mar. 18, 1837
Died:
June 24, 1908

Place of birth:
Caldwell, New Jersey

Little-known fact:
He banished his wife's pet mockingbird to a remote part of the White House.

William McKinley

25

**Mar. 4, 1897-
Sept. 14, 1901**

Born:
Jan. 29, 1843
Died:
Sept. 14, 1901

Place of birth:
Niles, Ohio

Little-known fact:
He refused to be photographed with his cigars to avoid being a bad example to children.

Theodore Roosevelt

26

1901-9

Born:
Oct. 27, 1858
Died:
Jan. 6, 1919

Place of birth:
New York, New York

Little-known fact:
Everyone in his family owned a pair of wooden stilts.

William Howard Taft

27

1909-13

Born:
Sept. 15, 1857
Died:
Mar. 8, 1930

Place of birth:
Cincinnati, Ohio

Little-known fact:
He began the tradition of the president throwing out the first baseball of the season.

Woodrow Wilson

28

1913-21

Born:
Dec. 28, 1856
Died:
Feb. 3, 1924

Place of birth:
Staunton, Virginia

Little-known fact:
He was the first president with a Ph.D.

Warren Gamaliel Harding

29

**Mar. 4, 1921-
Aug. 2, 1923**

Born:
Nov. 2, 1865
Died:
Aug. 2, 1923

Place of birth:
Corsica, Ohio

Little-known fact:
He was the first president to have a radio in the White House.

Calvin Coolidge

30

1923-29

Born:
July 4, 1872
Died:
Jan. 5, 1933

Place of birth:
Plymouth, Vermont

Little-known fact:
He had a pet raccoon that he walked on a leash.

Herbert Clark Hoover

31

1929-33

Born:
Aug. 10, 1874

Died:
Oct. 20, 1964

Place of birth:
West Branch, Iowa

Little-known fact:
"The Star-Spangled Banner" became the national anthem of the United States while he was president.

Franklin Delano Roosevelt

32

1933-45

Born:
Jan. 30, 1882

Died:
Apr. 12, 1945

Place of birth:
Hyde Park, New York

Little-known fact:
He was the first president to appear on television.

Harry S Truman

33

1945-53

Born:
May 8, 1884

Died:
Dec. 26, 1972

Place of birth:
Lamar, Missouri

Little-known fact:
He had read every book in the public library in Independence, Missouri, by the time he was fourteen.

Dwight David Eisenhower

34

1953-61

Born:
Oct. 14, 1890

Died:
Mar. 28, 1969

Place of birth:
Denison, Texas

Little-known fact:
He was the first president to go underwater in an atomic submarine.

John Fitzgerald Kennedy

35

1961-63

Born:
May 29, 1917

Died:
Nov. 22, 1963

Place of birth:
Brookline, Massachusetts

Little-known fact:
Kennedy could read two thousand words a minute with almost total comprehension.

Lyndon Baines Johnson

36

1963-69

Born:
Aug. 27, 1908

Died:
Jan. 22, 1973

Place of birth:
Stonewall, Texas

Little-known fact:
His wife, Lady Bird, and his daughters, Lynda Bird and Luci Baines, all shared his initials: "LBJ."

Richard Milhous Nixon

37

1969-74

Born:
Jan. 9, 1913

Died:
Apr. 22, 1994

Place of birth:
Yorba Linda, California

Little-known fact:
He was named after King Richard the Lion-Hearted of England.

Gerald Rudolph Ford

38

1974-77

Born:
July 14, 1913

Died:
—

Place of birth:
Omaha, Nebraska

Little-known fact:
Cottage cheese topped with catsup was his favorite lunch.

James Earl Carter

39

1977-81

Born:
Oct. 1, 1924

Died:
—

Place of birth:
Plains, Georgia

Little-known fact:
A giant helium-filled peanut, honoring his peanut-farming background, graced his Inauguration Day parade.

Ronald Wilson Reagan

40

1981-89

Born:
Feb. 6, 1911

Died:
—

Place of birth:
Tampico, Illinois

Little-known fact:
He appointed the first female U.S. Supreme Court Justice, Sandra Day O'Connor.

George Herbert Walker Bush

41

1989-93

Born:
June 12, 1924

Died:
—

Place of birth:
Milton, Massachusetts

Little-known fact:
He joined the navy immediately after high school and was World War II's youngest navy pilot for a time.

William Jefferson Clinton

42

1993-

Born:
Aug. 19, 1946

Died:
—

Place of birth:
Hope, Arkansas

Little-known fact:
He resembles his father, who was killed in a car accident three months before Bill was born.

Definition of terms

community, social, and personal services: every type of work in which individuals help others without growing, mining, manufacturing, or distributing goods

government: refers to all people employed in running the state and in overseeing money spent by the state

wholesale and retail trade:
wholesale trade—sale of goods in large quantities for lower prices

retail trade—sale of goods or commodities in small quantities directly to consumers

finance, insurance, and real estate:
finance—refers to banking

insurance—buying and selling of insurance policies

real estate—buying and selling of land, including all natural resources and permanent buildings on it

---

Alabama December 14, 1819

22

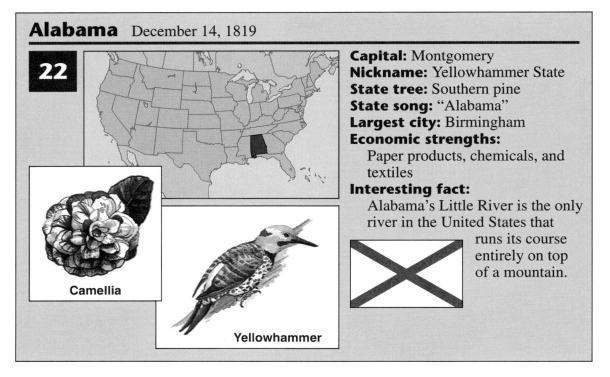

Capital: Montgomery
Nickname: Yellowhammer State
State tree: Southern pine
State song: "Alabama"
Largest city: Birmingham
Economic strengths:
  Paper products, chemicals, and textiles
Interesting fact:
  Alabama's Little River is the only river in the United States that runs its course entirely on top of a mountain.

Camellia

Yellowhammer

Alaska   January 3, 1959

49

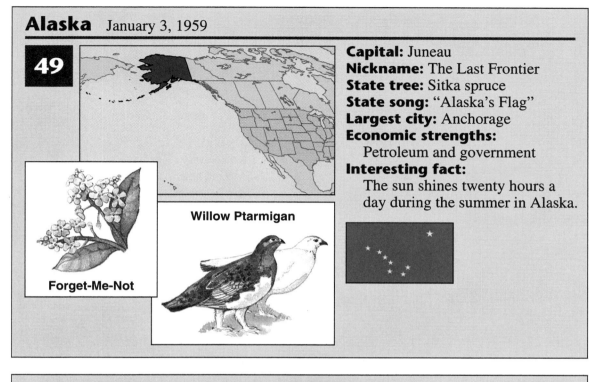

Capital: Juneau
Nickname: The Last Frontier
State tree: Sitka spruce
State song: "Alaska's Flag"
Largest city: Anchorage
Economic strengths:
  Petroleum and government
Interesting fact:
  The sun shines twenty hours a
  day during the summer in Alaska.

Forget-Me-Not

Willow Ptarmigan

Arizona   February 14, 1912

48

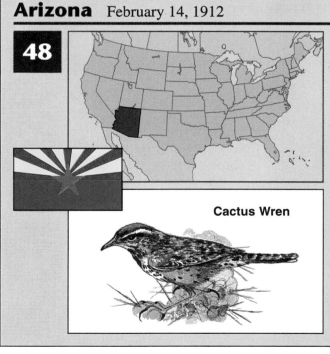

**Saguaro
Cactus Flower**

Capital: Phoenix
Nickname: Grand Canyon State
State tree: Palo verde
State song: "Arizona"
Largest city: Phoenix
Economic strengths:
  Trade; community, social, and
  personal services; government
Interesting fact:
  Oraibi, a Hopi reservation, has
  been inhabited longer than any
  other place in the United States—
  over eight hundred years.

Cactus Wren

Arkansas June 15, 1836

25

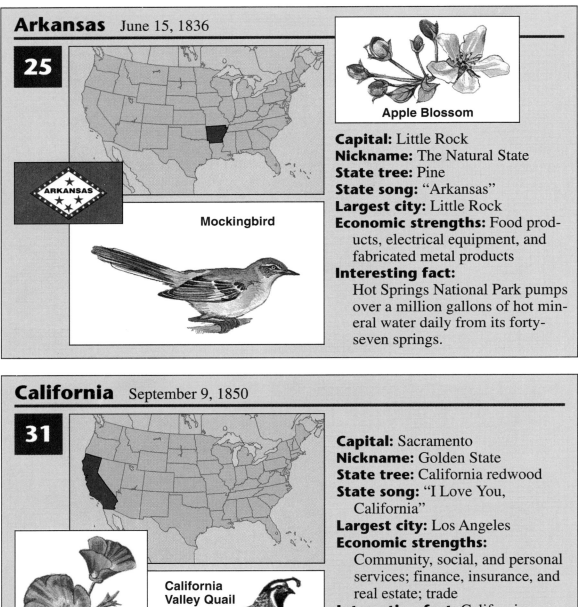

Apple Blossom

Mockingbird

Capital: Little Rock
Nickname: The Natural State
State tree: Pine
State song: "Arkansas"
Largest city: Little Rock
Economic strengths: Food products, electrical equipment, and fabricated metal products
Interesting fact:
Hot Springs National Park pumps over a million gallons of hot mineral water daily from its forty-seven springs.

California September 9, 1850

31

Capital: Sacramento
Nickname: Golden State
State tree: California redwood
State song: "I Love You, California"
Largest city: Los Angeles
Economic strengths:
Community, social, and personal services; finance, insurance, and real estate; trade
Interesting fact: California grows almost all of the U.S. market of almonds, walnuts, dates, figs, olives, and pomegranates.

California Valley Quail

Golden Poppy

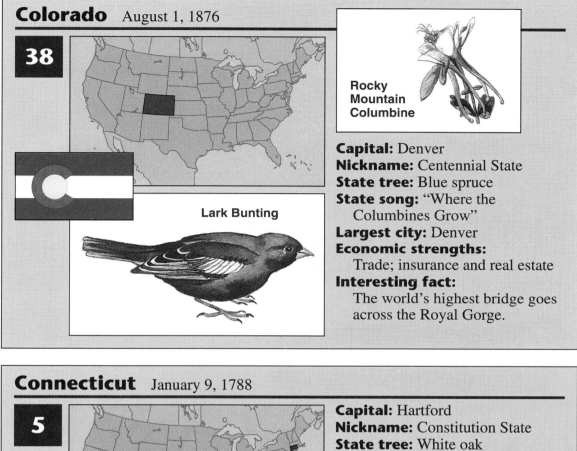

Colorado   August 1, 1876

38

Rocky
Mountain
Columbine

Capital: Denver
Nickname: Centennial State
State tree: Blue spruce
State song: "Where the
   Columbines Grow"
Largest city: Denver
Economic strengths:
   Trade; insurance and real estate
Interesting fact:
   The world's highest bridge goes
   across the Royal Gorge.

Lark Bunting

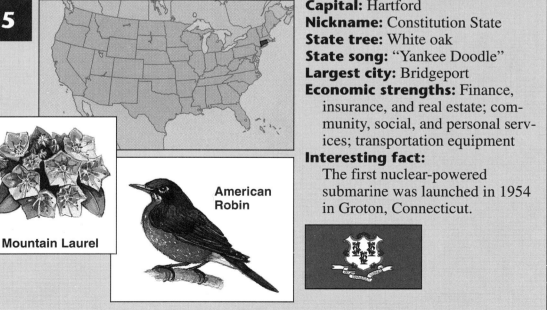

Connecticut   January 9, 1788

5

Capital: Hartford
Nickname: Constitution State
State tree: White oak
State song: "Yankee Doodle"
Largest city: Bridgeport
Economic strengths: Finance,
   insurance, and real estate; com-
   munity, social, and personal serv-
   ices; transportation equipment
Interesting fact:
   The first nuclear-powered
   submarine was launched in 1954
   in Groton, Connecticut.

Mountain Laurel

American
Robin

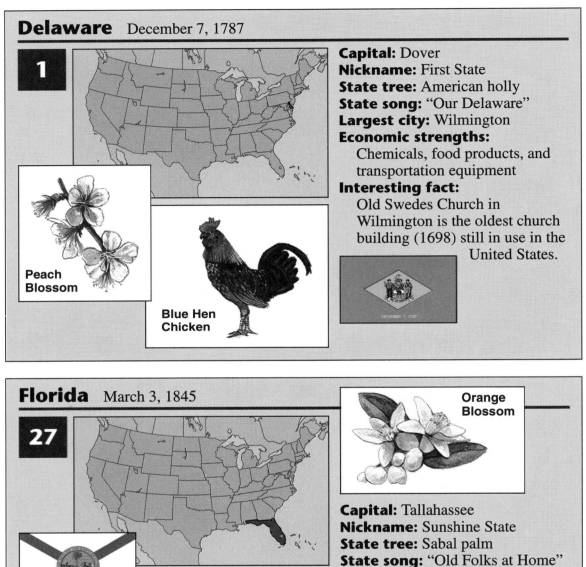

Delaware December 7, 1787

1

Capital: Dover
Nickname: First State
State tree: American holly
State song: "Our Delaware"
Largest city: Wilmington
Economic strengths:
Chemicals, food products, and transportation equipment
Interesting fact:
Old Swedes Church in Wilmington is the oldest church building (1698) still in use in the United States.

Peach Blossom

Blue Hen Chicken

Florida March 3, 1845

27

Orange Blossom

Capital: Tallahassee
Nickname: Sunshine State
State tree: Sabal palm
State song: "Old Folks at Home"
Largest city: Jacksonville
Economic strengths:
Community, social, and personal services; trade; finance, insurance, and real estate
Interesting fact:
The Kennedy Space Center at Cape Canaveral is the launch site for the U.S. space program.

Mockingbird

Georgia January 2, 1788

4

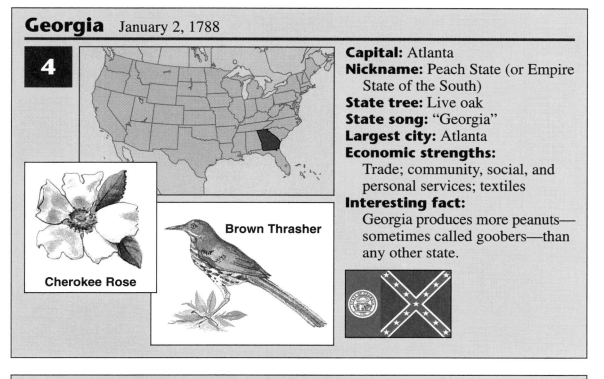

Cherokee Rose

Brown Thrasher

Capital: Atlanta
Nickname: Peach State (or Empire State of the South)
State tree: Live oak
State song: "Georgia"
Largest city: Atlanta
Economic strengths:
Trade; community, social, and personal services; textiles
Interesting fact:
Georgia produces more peanuts—sometimes called goobers—than any other state.

Hawaii August 21, 1959

50

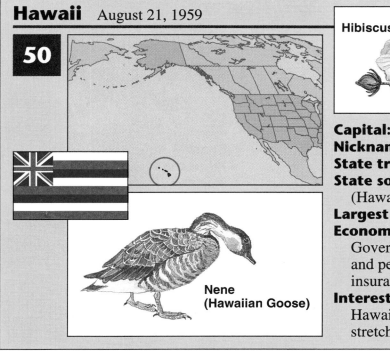

Hibiscus

Nene (Hawaiian Goose)

Capital: Honolulu
Nickname: Aloha State
State tree: Kukui (Candlenut)
State song: "Hawaii Ponoi" (Hawaii's Own)
Largest city: Honolulu
Economic strengths:
Government; community, social, and personal services; finance, insurance, and real estate
Interesting fact:
Hawaii's chain of 132 islands stretches for 1,523 miles.

303

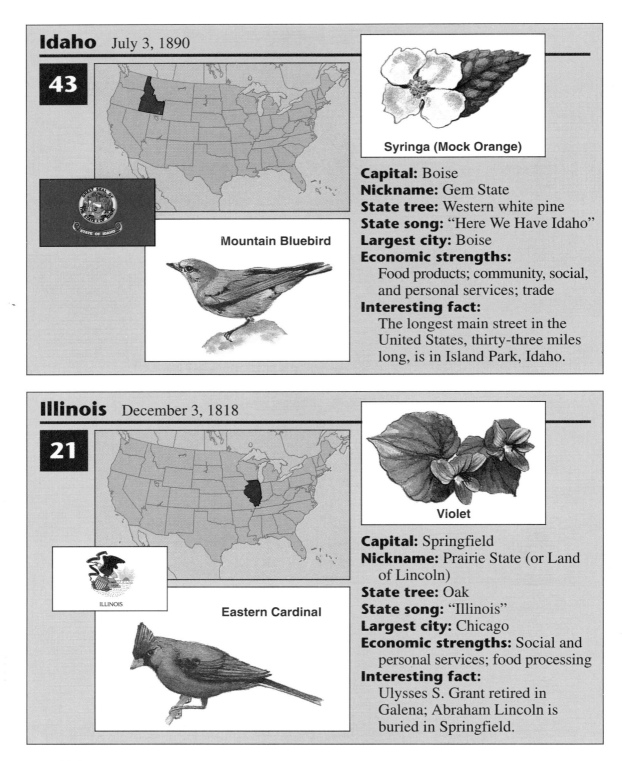

Idaho   July 3, 1890

43

Syringa (Mock Orange)

Capital: Boise
Nickname: Gem State
State tree: Western white pine
State song: "Here We Have Idaho"
Largest city: Boise
Economic strengths:
Food products; community, social, and personal services; trade
Interesting fact:
The longest main street in the United States, thirty-three miles long, is in Island Park, Idaho.

Mountain Bluebird

STATE OF IDAHO

Illinois   December 3, 1818

21

Violet

Capital: Springfield
Nickname: Prairie State (or Land of Lincoln)
State tree: Oak
State song: "Illinois"
Largest city: Chicago
Economic strengths: Social and personal services; food processing
Interesting fact:
Ulysses S. Grant retired in Galena; Abraham Lincoln is buried in Springfield.

ILLINOIS

Eastern Cardinal

Indiana   December 11, 1816

19

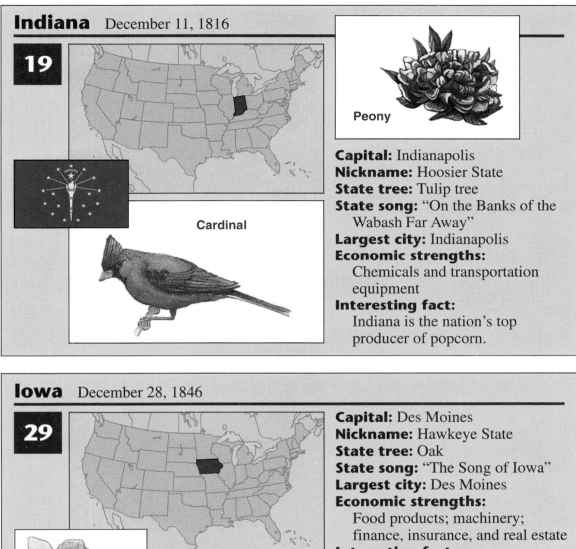

Peony

Cardinal

Capital: Indianapolis
Nickname: Hoosier State
State tree: Tulip tree
State song: "On the Banks of the Wabash Far Away"
Largest city: Indianapolis
Economic strengths:
Chemicals and transportation equipment
Interesting fact:
Indiana is the nation's top producer of popcorn.

Iowa   December 28, 1846

29

Capital: Des Moines
Nickname: Hawkeye State
State tree: Oak
State song: "The Song of Iowa"
Largest city: Des Moines
Economic strengths:
Food products; machinery; finance, insurance, and real estate
Interesting fact:
Effigy Mounds, a thousand-year-old Indian cemetery, is in Iowa.

Wild Rose

Goldfinch

IOWA

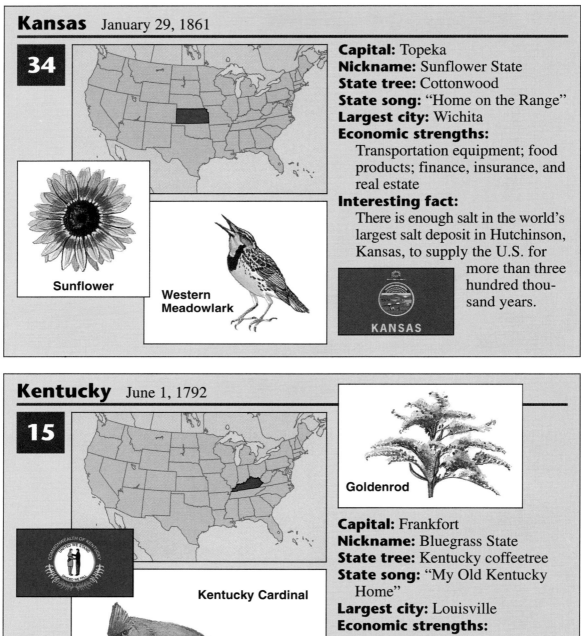

Kansas January 29, 1861

34

Capital: Topeka
Nickname: Sunflower State
State tree: Cottonwood
State song: "Home on the Range"
Largest city: Wichita
Economic strengths:
  Transportation equipment; food products; finance, insurance, and real estate
Interesting fact:
  There is enough salt in the world's largest salt deposit in Hutchinson, Kansas, to supply the U.S. for more than three hundred thousand years.

Sunflower

Western Meadowlark

KANSAS

Kentucky June 1, 1792

15

Goldenrod

Kentucky Cardinal

Capital: Frankfort
Nickname: Bluegrass State
State tree: Kentucky coffeetree
State song: "My Old Kentucky Home"
Largest city: Louisville
Economic strengths:
  Transportation equipment, chemicals, and machinery
Interesting fact:
  Fort Knox contains more than six billion dollars in gold bullion.

Louisiana April 30, 1812

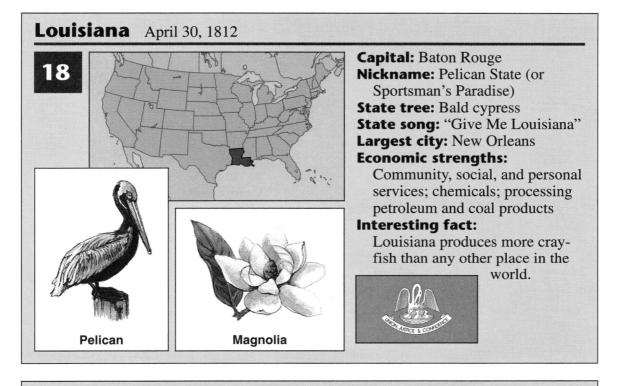

18

Capital: Baton Rouge
Nickname: Pelican State (or Sportsman's Paradise)
State tree: Bald cypress
State song: "Give Me Louisiana"
Largest city: New Orleans
Economic strengths:
Community, social, and personal services; chemicals; processing petroleum and coal products
Interesting fact:
Louisiana produces more crayfish than any other place in the world.

Pelican

Magnolia

Maine March 15, 1820

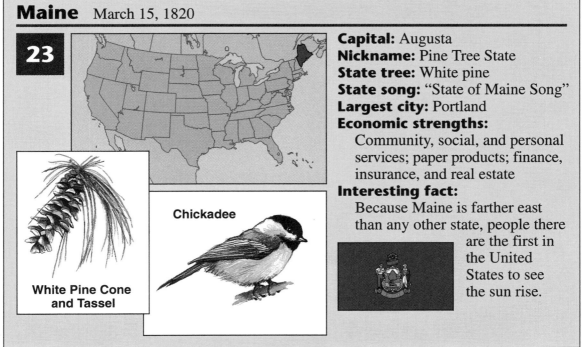

23

Capital: Augusta
Nickname: Pine Tree State
State tree: White pine
State song: "State of Maine Song"
Largest city: Portland
Economic strengths:
Community, social, and personal services; paper products; finance, insurance, and real estate
Interesting fact:
Because Maine is farther east than any other state, people there are the first in the United States to see the sun rise.

White Pine Cone and Tassel

Chickadee

307

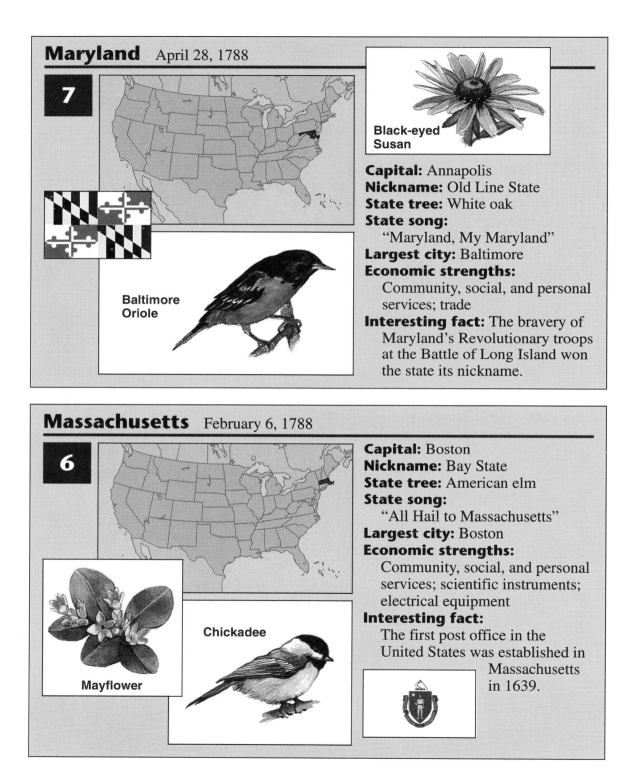

Maryland   April 28, 1788

7

Black-eyed Susan

Capital: Annapolis
Nickname: Old Line State
State tree: White oak
State song:
   "Maryland, My Maryland"
Largest city: Baltimore
Economic strengths:
   Community, social, and personal
   services; trade
Interesting fact: The bravery of
   Maryland's Revolutionary troops
   at the Battle of Long Island won
   the state its nickname.

Baltimore Oriole

Massachusetts   February 6, 1788

6

Capital: Boston
Nickname: Bay State
State tree: American elm
State song:
   "All Hail to Massachusetts"
Largest city: Boston
Economic strengths:
   Community, social, and personal
   services; scientific instruments;
   electrical equipment
Interesting fact:
   The first post office in the
   United States was established in
                  Massachusetts
                  in 1639.

Chickadee

Mayflower

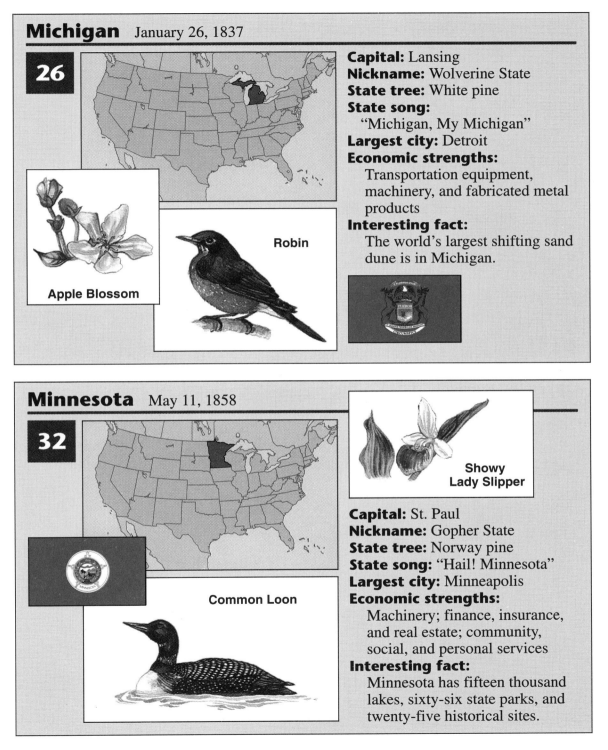

Michigan   January 26, 1837

26

Capital: Lansing
Nickname: Wolverine State
State tree: White pine
State song:
   "Michigan, My Michigan"
Largest city: Detroit
Economic strengths:
   Transportation equipment,
   machinery, and fabricated metal
   products
Interesting fact:
   The world's largest shifting sand
   dune is in Michigan.

Apple Blossom

Robin

Minnesota   May 11, 1858

32

Showy
Lady Slipper

Common Loon

Capital: St. Paul
Nickname: Gopher State
State tree: Norway pine
State song: "Hail! Minnesota"
Largest city: Minneapolis
Economic strengths:
   Machinery; finance, insurance,
   and real estate; community,
   social, and personal services
Interesting fact:
   Minnesota has fifteen thousand
   lakes, sixty-six state parks, and
   twenty-five historical sites.

Mississippi December 10, 1817

20

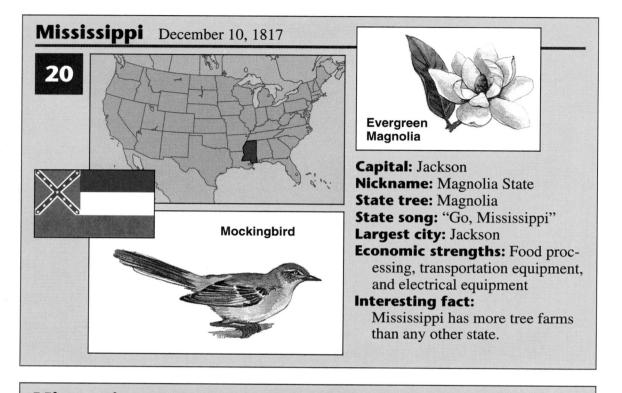

Evergreen Magnolia

Mockingbird

Capital: Jackson
Nickname: Magnolia State
State tree: Magnolia
State song: "Go, Mississippi"
Largest city: Jackson
Economic strengths: Food processing, transportation equipment, and electrical equipment
Interesting fact:
Mississippi has more tree farms than any other state.

Missouri August 10, 1821

24

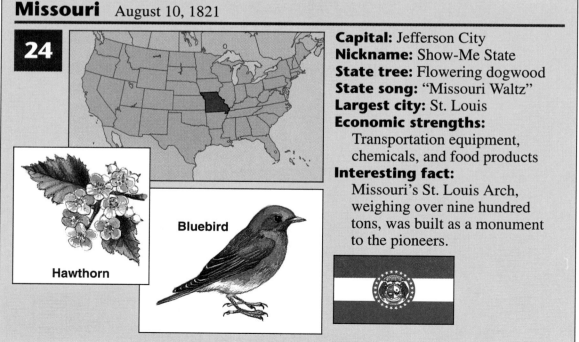

Hawthorn

Bluebird

Capital: Jefferson City
Nickname: Show-Me State
State tree: Flowering dogwood
State song: "Missouri Waltz"
Largest city: St. Louis
Economic strengths:
Transportation equipment, chemicals, and food products
Interesting fact:
Missouri's St. Louis Arch, weighing over nine hundred tons, was built as a monument to the pioneers.

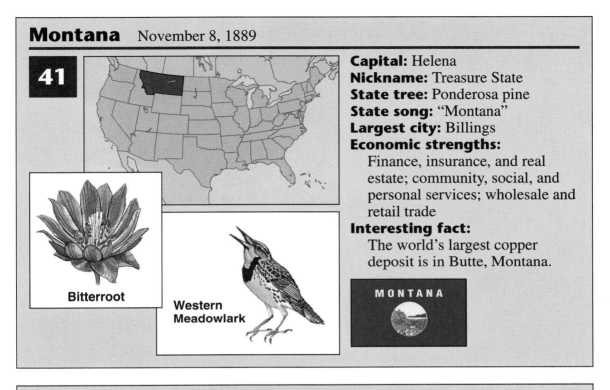

Montana   November 8, 1889

41

Capital: Helena
Nickname: Treasure State
State tree: Ponderosa pine
State song: "Montana"
Largest city: Billings
Economic strengths:
Finance, insurance, and real estate; community, social, and personal services; wholesale and retail trade
Interesting fact:
The world's largest copper deposit is in Butte, Montana.

Bitterroot

Western Meadowlark

MONTANA

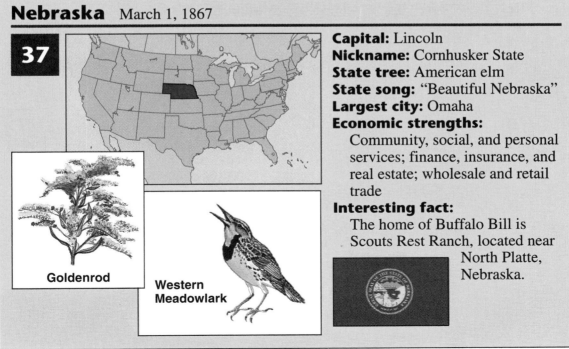

Nebraska   March 1, 1867

37

Capital: Lincoln
Nickname: Cornhusker State
State tree: American elm
State song: "Beautiful Nebraska"
Largest city: Omaha
Economic strengths:
Community, social, and personal services; finance, insurance, and real estate; wholesale and retail trade
Interesting fact:
The home of Buffalo Bill is Scouts Rest Ranch, located near North Platte, Nebraska.

Goldenrod

Western Meadowlark

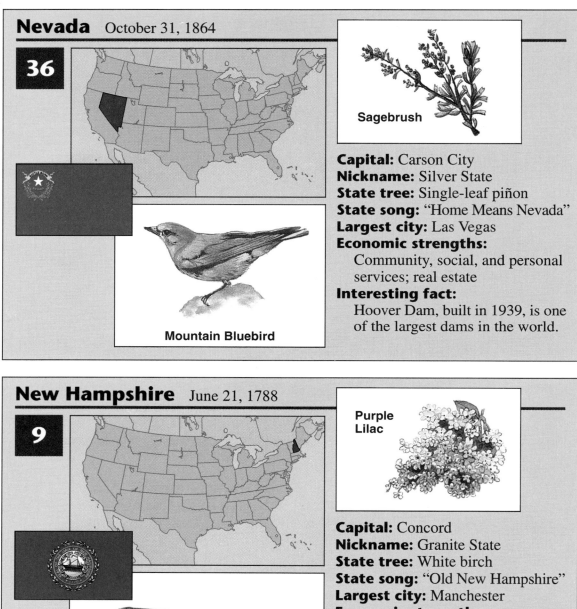

Nevada   October 31, 1864

36

Sagebrush

Capital: Carson City
Nickname: Silver State
State tree: Single-leaf piñon
State song: "Home Means Nevada"
Largest city: Las Vegas
Economic strengths:
  Community, social, and personal
  services; real estate
Interesting fact:
  Hoover Dam, built in 1939, is one
  of the largest dams in the world.

Mountain Bluebird

New Hampshire   June 21, 1788

9

Purple Lilac

Capital: Concord
Nickname: Granite State
State tree: White birch
State song: "Old New Hampshire"
Largest city: Manchester
Economic strengths:
  Machinery; finance, insurance,
  and real estate
Interesting fact:
  Mount Washington is the highest
  peak in the Northeast.

Purple Finch

New Jersey   December 18, 1787

3

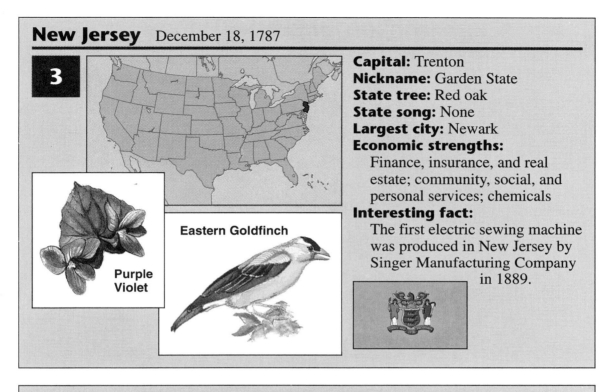

Capital: Trenton
Nickname: Garden State
State tree: Red oak
State song: None
Largest city: Newark
Economic strengths:
Finance, insurance, and real estate; community, social, and personal services; chemicals
Interesting fact:
The first electric sewing machine was produced in New Jersey by Singer Manufacturing Company in 1889.

Purple Violet

Eastern Goldfinch

New Mexico   January 6, 1912

47

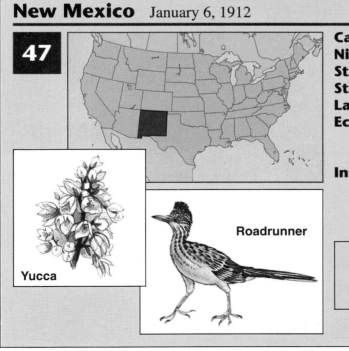

Capital: Santa Fe
Nickname: Land of Enchantment
State tree: Piñon
State song: "O, Fair New Mexico"
Largest city: Albuquerque
Economic strengths:
Community, social, and personal services; government; trade
Interesting fact:
Carlsbad Caverns has the largest natural cave "room" in the world— 1,500 feet × 300 feet × 300 feet.

Yucca

Roadrunner

New York July 26, 1788

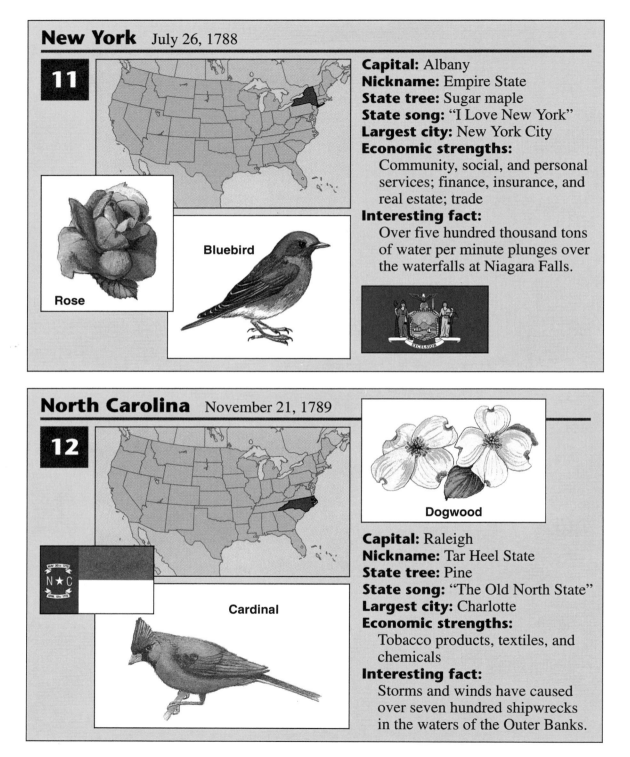

11

Capital: Albany
Nickname: Empire State
State tree: Sugar maple
State song: "I Love New York"
Largest city: New York City
Economic strengths:
Community, social, and personal services; finance, insurance, and real estate; trade
Interesting fact:
Over five hundred thousand tons of water per minute plunges over the waterfalls at Niagara Falls.

Rose

Bluebird

North Carolina November 21, 1789

12

Dogwood

Cardinal

Capital: Raleigh
Nickname: Tar Heel State
State tree: Pine
State song: "The Old North State"
Largest city: Charlotte
Economic strengths:
Tobacco products, textiles, and chemicals
Interesting fact:
Storms and winds have caused over seven hundred shipwrecks in the waters of the Outer Banks.

North Dakota   November 2, 1889

39

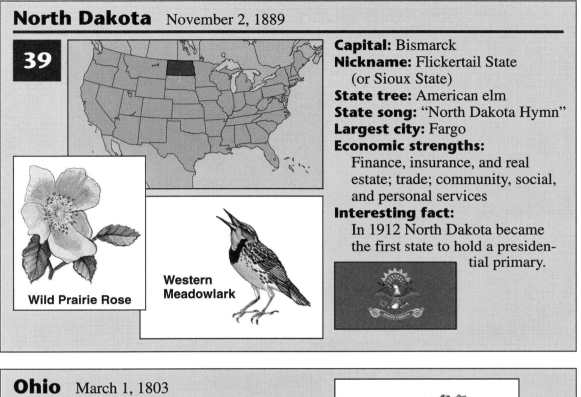

Capital: Bismarck
Nickname: Flickertail State
(or Sioux State)
State tree: American elm
State song: "North Dakota Hymn"
Largest city: Fargo
Economic strengths:
Finance, insurance, and real estate; trade; community, social, and personal services
Interesting fact:
In 1912 North Dakota became the first state to hold a presidential primary.

Wild Prairie Rose

Western Meadowlark

Ohio   March 1, 1803

17

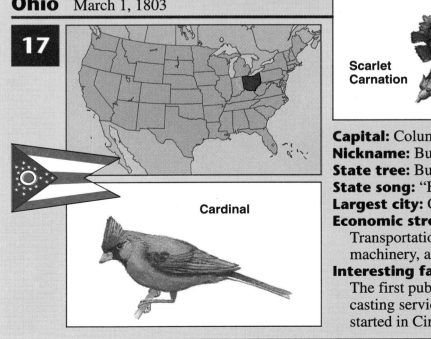

Scarlet Carnation

Cardinal

Capital: Columbus
Nickname: Buckeye State
State tree: Buckeye
State song: "Beautiful Ohio"
Largest city: Cleveland
Economic strengths:
Transportation equipment, machinery, and food products
Interesting fact:
The first public weather forecasting service in the U.S. was started in Cincinnati in 1869.

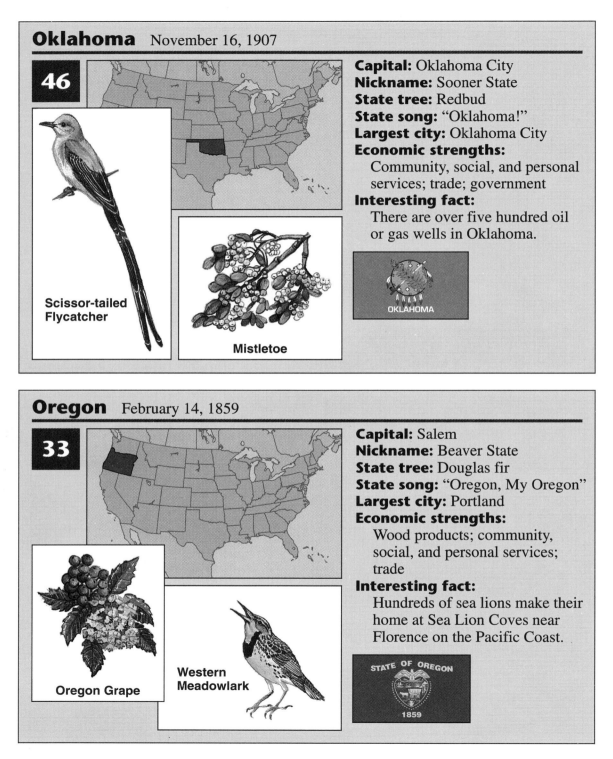

Oklahoma November 16, 1907

46

Capital: Oklahoma City
Nickname: Sooner State
State tree: Redbud
State song: "Oklahoma!"
Largest city: Oklahoma City
Economic strengths:
Community, social, and personal services; trade; government
Interesting fact:
There are over five hundred oil or gas wells in Oklahoma.

Scissor-tailed Flycatcher

Mistletoe

OKLAHOMA

Oregon February 14, 1859

33

Capital: Salem
Nickname: Beaver State
State tree: Douglas fir
State song: "Oregon, My Oregon"
Largest city: Portland
Economic strengths:
Wood products; community, social, and personal services; trade
Interesting fact:
Hundreds of sea lions make their home at Sea Lion Coves near Florence on the Pacific Coast.

Oregon Grape

Western Meadowlark

STATE OF OREGON
1859

316

Pennsylvania   December 12, 1787

2

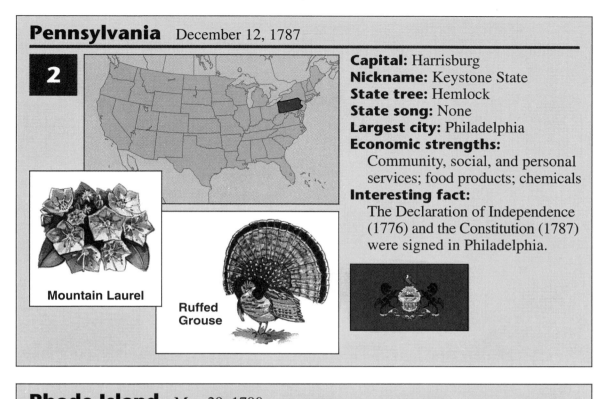

Capital: Harrisburg
Nickname: Keystone State
State tree: Hemlock
State song: None
Largest city: Philadelphia
Economic strengths:
   Community, social, and personal services; food products; chemicals
Interesting fact:
   The Declaration of Independence (1776) and the Constitution (1787) were signed in Philadelphia.

Mountain Laurel

Ruffed Grouse

Rhode Island   May 29, 1790

13

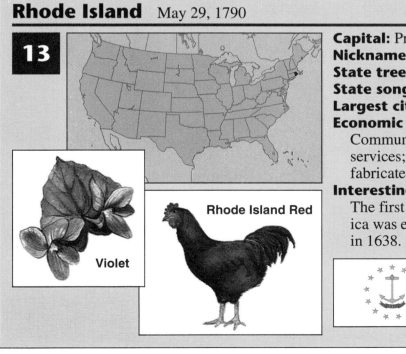

Capital: Providence
Nickname: The Ocean State
State tree: Red maple
State song: "Rhode Island"
Largest city: Providence
Economic strengths:
   Community, social, and personal services; jewelry and silverware; fabricated metal products
Interesting fact:
   The first Baptist church in America was established in Providence in 1638.

Violet

Rhode Island Red

South Carolina May 23, 1788

8

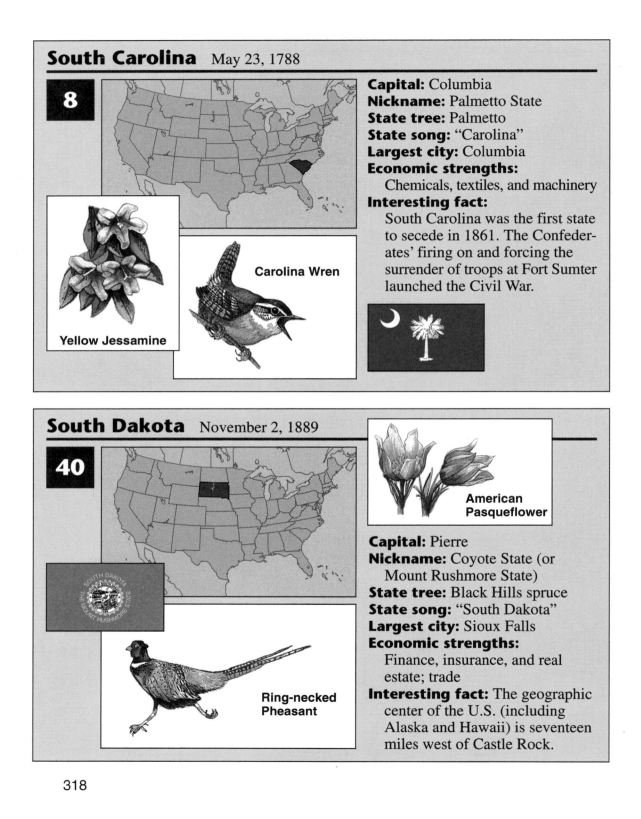

Capital: Columbia
Nickname: Palmetto State
State tree: Palmetto
State song: "Carolina"
Largest city: Columbia
Economic strengths:
Chemicals, textiles, and machinery
Interesting fact:
South Carolina was the first state to secede in 1861. The Confederates' firing on and forcing the surrender of troops at Fort Sumter launched the Civil War.

Yellow Jessamine

Carolina Wren

South Dakota November 2, 1889

40

American Pasqueflower

Capital: Pierre
Nickname: Coyote State (or Mount Rushmore State)
State tree: Black Hills spruce
State song: "South Dakota"
Largest city: Sioux Falls
Economic strengths:
Finance, insurance, and real estate; trade
Interesting fact: The geographic center of the U.S. (including Alaska and Hawaii) is seventeen miles west of Castle Rock.

Ring-necked Pheasant

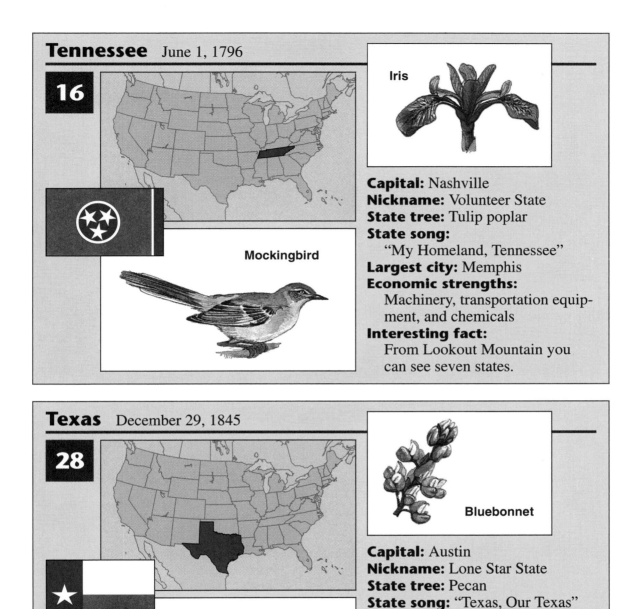

Tennessee June 1, 1796

16

Iris

Capital: Nashville
Nickname: Volunteer State
State tree: Tulip poplar
State song:
    "My Homeland, Tennessee"
Largest city: Memphis
Economic strengths:
    Machinery, transportation equipment, and chemicals
Interesting fact:
    From Lookout Mountain you can see seven states.

Mockingbird

Texas December 29, 1845

28

Bluebonnet

Capital: Austin
Nickname: Lone Star State
State tree: Pecan
State song: "Texas, Our Texas"
Largest city: Houston
Economic strengths:
    Community, social, and personal services; chemicals; food processing
Interesting fact:
    One-third of the U.S. supply of petroleum is found in Texas.

Mockingbird

Utah   January 4, 1896

45

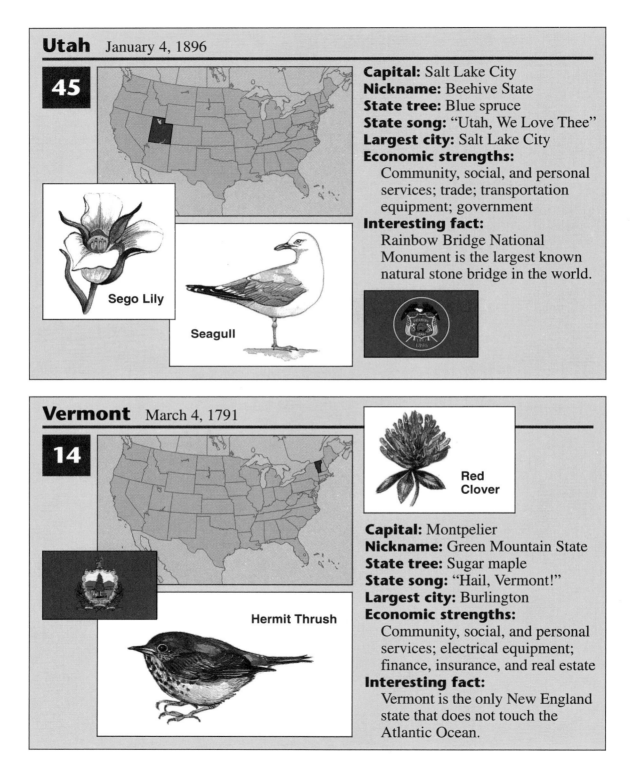

Capital: Salt Lake City
Nickname: Beehive State
State tree: Blue spruce
State song: "Utah, We Love Thee"
Largest city: Salt Lake City
Economic strengths:
Community, social, and personal services; trade; transportation equipment; government
Interesting fact:
Rainbow Bridge National Monument is the largest known natural stone bridge in the world.

Sego Lily

Seagull

Vermont   March 4, 1791

14

Red Clover

Capital: Montpelier
Nickname: Green Mountain State
State tree: Sugar maple
State song: "Hail, Vermont!"
Largest city: Burlington
Economic strengths:
Community, social, and personal services; electrical equipment; finance, insurance, and real estate
Interesting fact:
Vermont is the only New England state that does not touch the Atlantic Ocean.

Hermit Thrush

Virginia   June 25, 1788

10

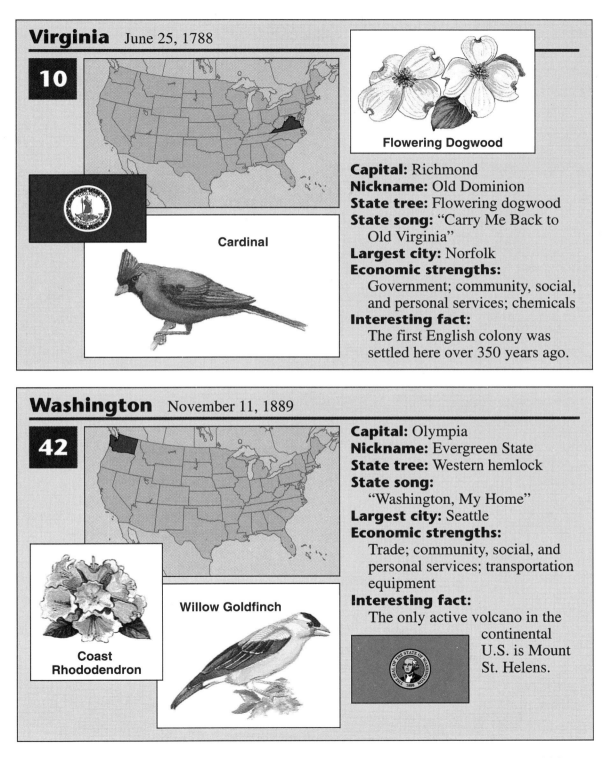

Flowering Dogwood

Cardinal

Capital: Richmond
Nickname: Old Dominion
State tree: Flowering dogwood
State song: "Carry Me Back to Old Virginia"
Largest city: Norfolk
Economic strengths:
Government; community, social, and personal services; chemicals
Interesting fact:
The first English colony was settled here over 350 years ago.

Washington   November 11, 1889

42

Capital: Olympia
Nickname: Evergreen State
State tree: Western hemlock
State song:
"Washington, My Home"
Largest city: Seattle
Economic strengths:
Trade; community, social, and personal services; transportation equipment
Interesting fact:
The only active volcano in the continental U.S. is Mount St. Helens.

Coast Rhododendron

Willow Goldfinch

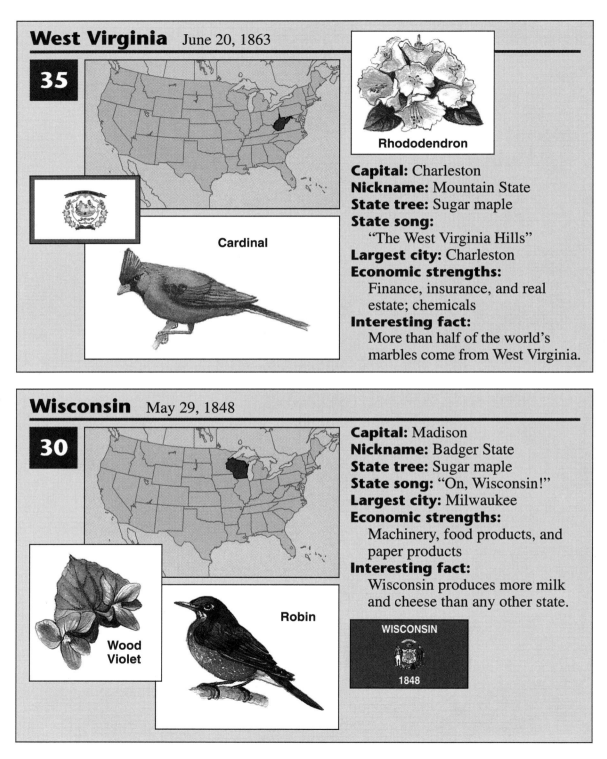

West Virginia June 20, 1863

35

Rhododendron

Cardinal

Capital: Charleston
Nickname: Mountain State
State tree: Sugar maple
State song:
 "The West Virginia Hills"
Largest city: Charleston
Economic strengths:
 Finance, insurance, and real
 estate; chemicals
Interesting fact:
 More than half of the world's
 marbles come from West Virginia.

Wisconsin May 29, 1848

30

Capital: Madison
Nickname: Badger State
State tree: Sugar maple
State song: "On, Wisconsin!"
Largest city: Milwaukee
Economic strengths:
 Machinery, food products, and
 paper products
Interesting fact:
 Wisconsin produces more milk
 and cheese than any other state.

Robin

Wood
Violet

WISCONSIN
1848

Wyoming July 10, 1890

44

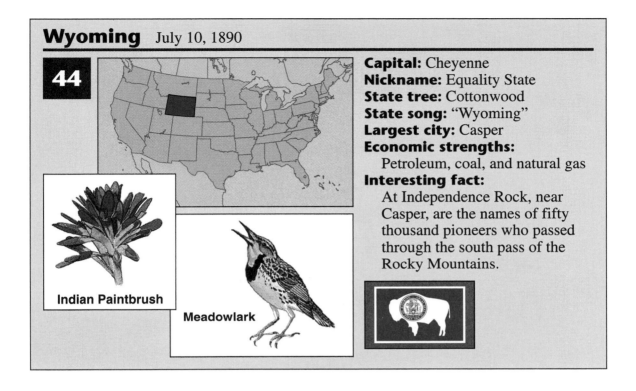

Indian Paintbrush

Meadowlark

Capital: Cheyenne
Nickname: Equality State
State tree: Cottonwood
State song: "Wyoming"
Largest city: Casper
Economic strengths:
  Petroleum, coal, and natural gas
Interesting fact:
  At Independence Rock, near Casper, are the names of fifty thousand pioneers who passed through the south pass of the Rocky Mountains.

Signs of Freedom

Mount Rushmore

The Mount Rushmore National Memorial in South Dakota is a lasting tribute to four of America's most influential presidents. The faces of George Washington, Thomas Jefferson, Abraham Lincoln, and Theodore Roosevelt are sculpted into the granite of Mount Rushmore, with each face being around sixty feet tall.

Above: Borglum (right) and another workman suspended beside Jefferson's face

Left: Mount Rushmore near its completion

The monument was designed by American sculptor Gutzon Borglum. The actual sculpting work took about six and a half years, but it took over fourteen years to complete the entire project. Unfortunately, Gutzon Borglum died before the final face was completed, but the work was carried on by his son Lincoln. The project, begun in 1927, was completed in 1941. The site had already been established as a National Memorial on October 1, 1925.

Tomb of the Unknown Soldier

A marble monument adjoins a huge field of white crosses. It is the Tomb of the Unknown Soldier in Arlington National Cemetery near Washington, D.C.

The tomb honors those who died in World War I, World War II, the Korean War, and the Vietnam War and who were not able to be

identified. One soldier from World War I lies under the white marble monument. One soldier from each of the other three wars is buried in a crypt at the head of the tomb.

The inscription on the tomb reads "Here rests in honored glory an American soldier known but to God."

Special Days

Mother's Day

Anna Jarvis of Philadelphia is credited with the idea of having a holiday to honor mothers. In 1907 she started a letter-writing campaign to thousands of influential people, urging them to support a "mother's day." Her effort was soon rewarded; the first observance of Mother's Day in the United States was on May 10, 1908, in Grafton,

Anna Jarvis

West Virginia, and in Philadelphia, Pennsylvania. By 1911 Mother's Day was being celebrated in every state in the United States as well as in six foreign countries. In 1914 President Woodrow Wilson declared that every second Sunday in May would be set aside to honor mothers.

Father's Day

Father's Day was not officially celebrated until several years after Mother's Day. It was first observed in 1909, when June Bruce Dodd persuaded the Ministerial Society of Spokane, Washington, to have special church services to honor fathers. This special celebration for fathers steadily gained recognition, and in 1924, President Calvin Coolidge recommended that all states set aside the third Sunday in June as the day to honor fathers. Father's Day did not become a national holiday until 1972.

Veterans Day

First celebrated in 1919, Veterans Day was originally a holiday known as Armistice Day—the anniversary of the ending of World War I. In 1954 President Dwight D. Eisenhower changed the name of the holi- day to Veterans Day when he signed an act of Congress "to honor veterans on the eleventh day of November of each year . . . a day dedicated to world peace."

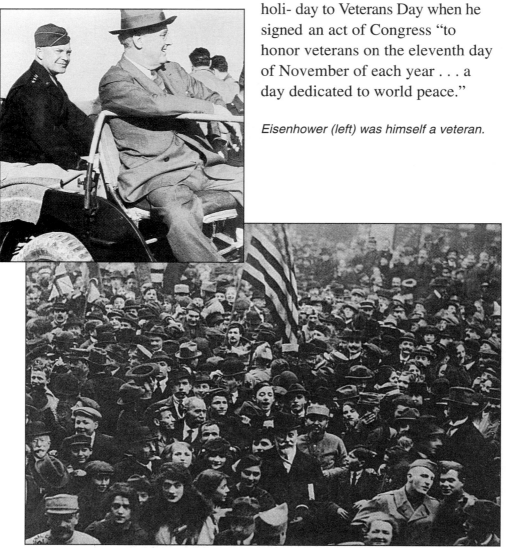

Eisenhower (left) was himself a veteran.

An armistice celebration in Paris

Armed Forces Day

In 1949 Armed Forces Day was created to replace three separate days: Army Day, Navy Day, and Air Force Day. It was aimed at promoting unity in the honoring of the Armed Forces. Armed Forces Day is observed on the second Saturday in May. Each year a special prayer is prepared by the Chaplains' Board to be used by all the military chaplains on this day.

Presidents' Day

Presidents' Day, also referred to as Washington-Lincoln Day, is celebrated on the third Monday in February. In 1968 a law went into effect which provided workers with a three-day holiday for several federal holidays. This "Monday holiday law" provided for a day to honor George Washington and Abraham Lincoln, both of whom were born in February. Today, most states recognize this holiday and extend it to honoring other presidents.

John Trumbull, Surrender of Lord Cornwallis, *Architect of the Capitol*

Maps

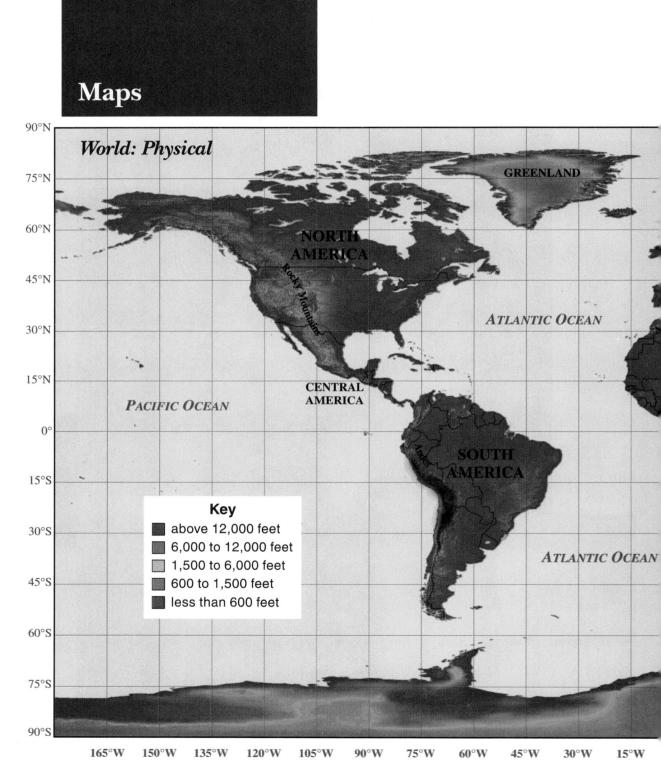

World: Physical

Key
- above 12,000 feet
- 6,000 to 12,000 feet
- 1,500 to 6,000 feet
- 600 to 1,500 feet
- less than 600 feet

GREENLAND

NORTH AMERICA

Rocky Mountains

ATLANTIC OCEAN

PACIFIC OCEAN

CENTRAL AMERICA

Andes

SOUTH AMERICA

ATLANTIC OCEAN

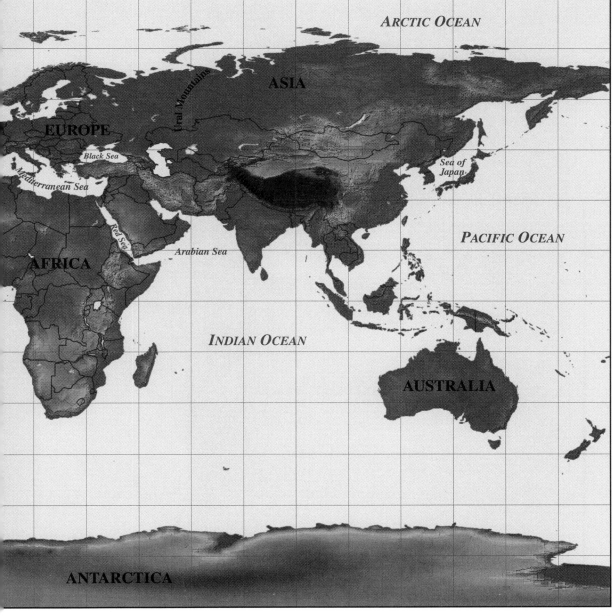

ARCTIC OCEAN

ASIA

Ural Mountains

EUROPE

Black Sea

Mediterranean Sea

Red Sea

Arabian Sea

Sea of
Japan

PACIFIC OCEAN

AFRICA

INDIAN OCEAN

AUSTRALIA

ANTARCTICA

| 15°E | 30°E | 45°E | 60°E | 75°E | 90°E | 105°E | 120°E | 135°E | 150°E | 165°E | 180° |

World: Political

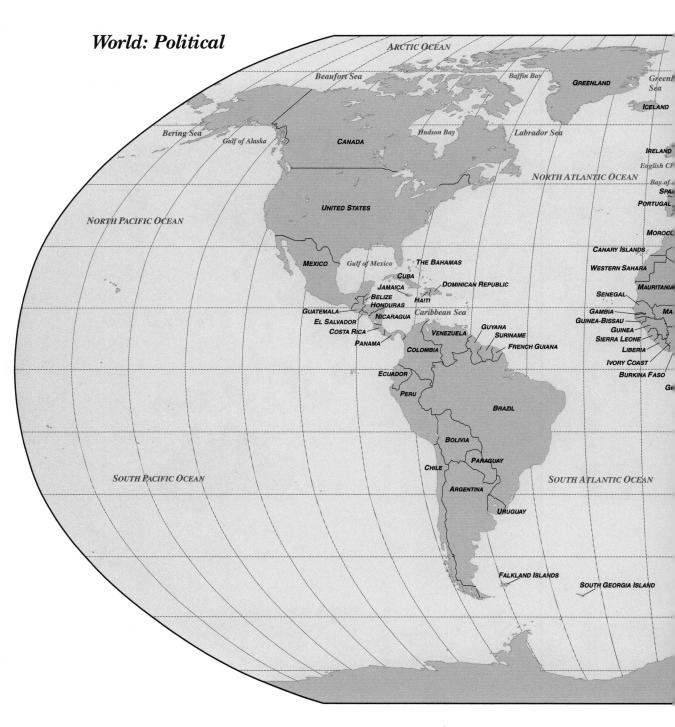

ARCTIC OCEAN

Beaufort Sea

Baffin Bay

GREENLAND

Green
Sea

ICELAND

Bering Sea

Gulf of Alaska

CANADA

Hudson Bay

Labrador Sea

IRELAND

English Ch

NORTH ATLANTIC OCEAN

Bay of

NORTH PACIFIC OCEAN

UNITED STATES

SPA

PORTUGAL

MOROCC

CANARY ISLANDS

MEXICO

Gulf of Mexico

THE BAHAMAS

WESTERN SAHARA

CUBA

DOMINICAN REPUBLIC

MAURITANIA

JAMAICA

BELIZE

HAITI

SENEGAL

HONDURAS

Caribbean Sea

GAMBIA

MA

GUATEMALA

NICARAGUA

GUINEA-BISSAU

EL SALVADOR

GUYANA

GUINEA

COSTA RICA

VENEZUELA

SURINAME

SIERRA LEONE

PANAMA

COLOMBIA

FRENCH GUIANA

LIBERIA

IVORY COAST

ECUADOR

BURKINA FASO

PERU

G

BRAZIL

BOLIVIA

PARAGUAY

CHILE

SOUTH ATLANTIC OCEAN

SOUTH PACIFIC OCEAN

ARGENTINA

URUGUAY

FALKLAND ISLANDS

SOUTH GEORGIA ISLAND

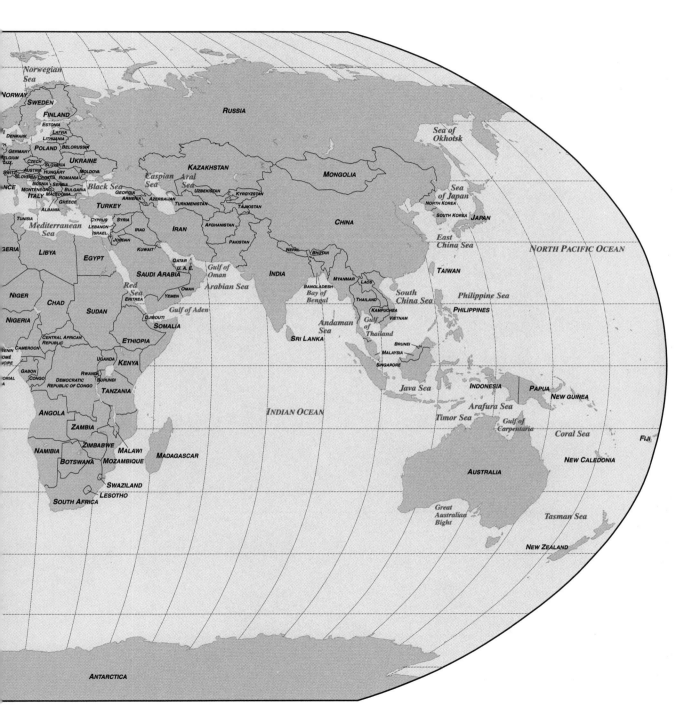

Norwegian
Sea

NORWAY
SWEDEN
FINLAND
Estonia
Latvia
DENMARK
LITHUANIA
GERMANY
POLAND
BELORUSSIA
CZECH
SLOVAKIA
UKRAINE
AUSTRIA
HUNGARY
MOLDOVA
SWITZ.
SLOVENIA
CROATIA
ROMANIA
NCE
ITALY
BOSNIA & SERBIA
MONTENEGRO
BULGARIA
MACEDONIA
GREECE
ALBANIA
Black Sea
TURKEY
GEORGIA
ARMENIA
AZERBAIJAN
TUNISIA
CYPRUS
SYRIA
LEBANON
ISRAEL
Mediterranean
Sea
GERIA
LIBYA
EGYPT
IRAQ
JORDAN
KUWAIT
QATAR
U. A. E.
SAUDI ARABIA
OMAN
YEMEN
NIGER
CHAD
SUDAN
Red
Sea
ERITREA
DJIBOUTI
SOMALIA
NIGERIA
CENTRAL AFRICAN
Republic
BENIN
CAMEROON
OMÉ
ICIPE
GABON
CONGO
UGANDA
RWANDA
KENYA
SURUNDI
ORIAL
A
DEMOCRATIC
REPUBLIC OF CONGO
TANZANIA
ANGOLA
ZAMBIA
NAMIBIA
ZIMBABWE
MALAWI
BOTSWANA
MOZAMBIQUE
MADAGASCAR
SWAZILAND
LESOTHO
SOUTH AFRICA

RUSSIA

KAZAKHSTAN

Caspian
Sea
Aral
Sea
UZBEKISTAN
KYRGYZSTAN
TURKMENISTAN
TAJIKISTAN
AFGHANISTAN
IRAN
PAKISTAN

MONGOLIA

CHINA

NEPAL
BHUTAN
INDIA
BANGLADESH
Bay of
Bengal
MYANMAR
LAOS
THAILAND
KAMPUCHEA
VIETNAM
Gulf of
Oman
Arabian Sea
Andaman
Sea
Gulf
of
Thailand
SRI LANKA
MALAYSIA
BRUNEI
SINGAPORE

Sea of
Okhotsk

Sea
of Japan
NORTH KOREA
SOUTH KOREA
JAPAN

East
China Sea
NORTH PACIFIC OCEAN

TAIWAN

South
China Sea
Philippine Sea
PHILIPPINES

Java Sea
INDONESIA
PAPUA
NEW GUINEA

INDIAN OCEAN

Timor Sea
Arafura Sea
Gulf of
Carpentaria
Coral Sea
FIJI
NEW CALEDONIA

AUSTRALIA

Great
Australian
Bight
Tasman Sea

NEW ZEALAND

ANTARCTICA

The United States: Physical

PACIFIC OCEAN

WASHINGTON
Olympia ▲ Mt. Rainier
▲ Mt. St. Helens
Salem

OREGON

Boise

IDAHO

NEVADA

Carson City

Sacramento

UTAH

Salt Lake City

CALIFORNIA

Grand Canyon

ARIZONA

Phoenix

Helena

MONTANA

Rocky Mountains

WYOMING

Cheyenne

Denver
Pikes Peak

COLORADO

Santa Fe

NEW MEXICO

NORTH DAKOTA
Bismarck

Badlands

SOUTH DAKOTA
Pierre

Black Hills

NEBRASKA

Platte River

Linco

KANSAS

Arkansas River

OKLAHOMA

Oklahoma City

Red River

TEXAS

Austin

Honolulu

HAWAII

same scale as large map

ALASKA

Yukon River

Juneau

0 100 200 300 400 500

scale in miles

336

MINNESOTA

Lake Superior

MICHIGAN

Lake Huron

WISCONSIN

St. Paul •

Lake Michigan

MICHIGAN

• Madison

• Lansing

L. Ontario

NEW YORK

MAINE

Green Mtns.

Augusta •

White
Mtns.

Montpelier •

NEW HAMPSHIRE

Concord •

VERMONT

Albany • Boston •

MASSACHUSETTS

Providence •

Hartford •

RHODE ISLAND

IOWA

Des Moines •

ILLINOIS

INDIANA

Lake Erie

OHIO

PENNSYLVANIA

Harrisburg •

Trenton •

CONNECTICUT

NEW JERSEY

• Indianapolis

Columbus •

Dover •

Annapolis •

DELAWARE

peka

Jefferson City •

Springfield •

Ohio River

Frankfort •

WEST
VIRGINIA

Charleston •

Appalachian Mountains

Washington,
D.C.

Richmond •

MARYLAND

Missouri River

MISSOURI

KENTUCKY

VIRGINIA

Raleigh •

ATLANTIC
OCEAN

ARKANSAS

• Nashville

TENNESSEE

Great Smoky Mtns.

NORTH CAROLINA

SOUTH
CAROLINA

Little Rock •

• Atlanta

Columbia •

Mississippi River

GEORGIA

N

W   E

S

Montgomery •

ALABAMA

• Jackson

MISSISSIPPI

Baton Rouge •

LOUISIANA

• Tallahassee

FEET

12,000

9,000

5,000

2,000
1,000
500
0

Gulf of Mexico

FLORIDA

0   100   200   300   400   500

scale in miles

337

The United States: Political

Olympia

WASHINGTON

Salem

OREGON

Boise

IDAHO

Helena

MONTANA

NORTH DAKOTA

Bismarck

SOUTH DAKOTA

Pierre

WYOMING

Cheyenne

NEBRASKA

Lincoln

Sacramento

Carson City

NEVADA

Salt Lake City

UTAH

Denver

COLORADO

Topeka

KANSAS

CALIFORNIA

ARIZONA

Phoenix

NEW MEXICO

Santa Fe

OKLAHOMA

Oklahoma City

TEXAS

Austin

ALASKA

Juneau

NEW HAMPSHIRE

VERMONT

MAINE

Augusta

MINNESOTA

MICHIGAN

Montpelier

Concord

MASSACHUSETTS

Boston

Paul

WISCONSIN

Albany

Providence

Lansing

NEW YORK

RHODE ISLAND

Madison

Hartford

CONNECTICUT

PENNSYLVANIA

Trenton

OWA

OHIO

Harrisburg

NEW JERSEY

Des Moines

Columbus

Dover

DELAWARE

ILLINOIS

INDIANA

Indianapolis

W.

Annapolis

MISSOURI

Springfield

VIRGINIA

Richmond

MARYLAND

Jefferson City

Charleston

VIRGINIA

Frankfort

KENTUCKY

Raleigh

ARKANSAS

Nashville

N. CAROLINA

TENNESSEE

Little Rock

Columbia

ALABAMA

Atlanta

S. CAROLINA

Jackson

Montgomery

GEORGIA

LOUISIANA

Tallahassee

N

Baton Rouge

MISSISSIPPI

FLORIDA

W   E

S

Honolulu

HAWAII

339

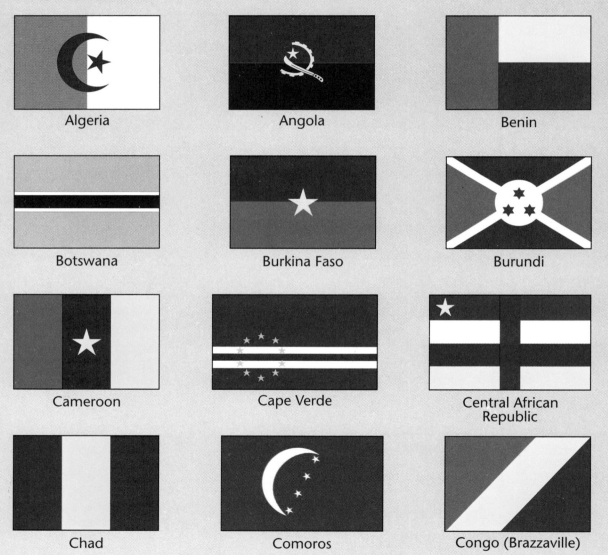

Flags of the Nations

Flags of Africa

Algeria

Angola

Benin

Botswana

Burkina Faso

Burundi

Cameroon

Cape Verde

Central African
Republic

Chad

Comoros

Congo (Brazzaville)

Democratic Republic
of Congo*

Djibouti

Egypt

Equatorial Guinea

Eritrea

Ethiopia

Gabon

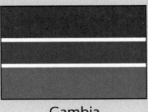

Gambia

Ghana

Guinea

Guinea-Bissau

Ivory Coast
(Cote d'Ivoire)

Kenya

Lesotho

Liberia

*formerly Zaire

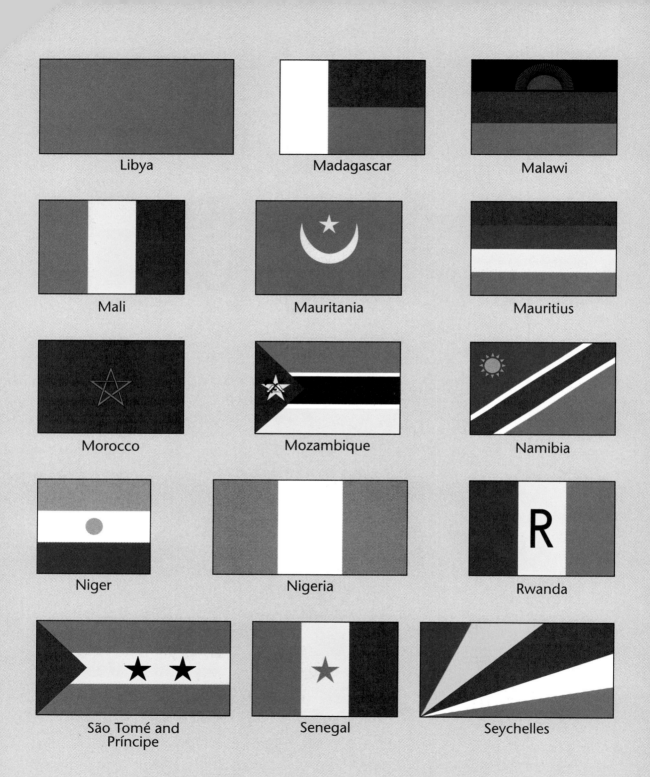

Libya

Madagascar

Malawi

Mali

Mauritania

Mauritius

Morocco

Mozambique

Namibia

Niger

Nigeria

Rwanda

São Tomé and
Príncipe

Senegal

Seychelles

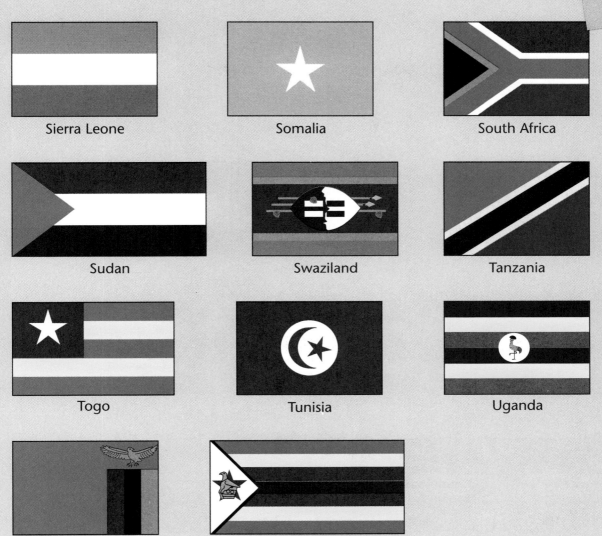

Sierra Leone

Somalia

South Africa

Sudan

Swaziland

Tanzania

Togo

Tunisia

Uganda

Zambia

Zimbabwe

Flags of the Americas

Antigua and Barbuda

Argentina

Bahamas

Barbados

Belize

Bolivia

Brazil

Canada

Chile

Colombia

Costa Rica

Cuba

Dominica

Dominican Republic

Ecuador

El Salvador

Grenada

Guatemala

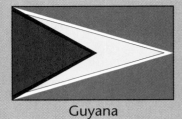

Guyana

Haiti

Honduras

Jamaica

Mexico

Nicaragua

Panama

Paraguay

Peru

St. Kitts and Nevis

St. Lucia

St. Vincent and the Grenadines

Suriname

Trinidad and Tobago

United States

Uruguay

Venezuela

Flags of Asia and the Pacific

Afghanistan

Armenia

Australia

Azerbaijan

Bahrain

Bangladesh

Bhutan

Brunei

Cambodia

China

Cyprus

Fiji

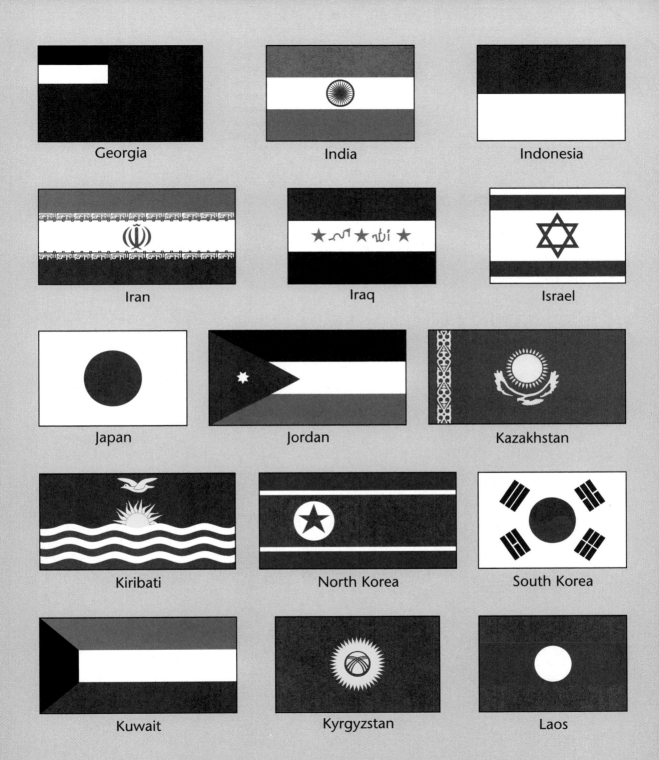

Georgia

India

Indonesia

Iran

Iraq

Israel

Japan

Jordan

Kazakhstan

Kiribati

North Korea

South Korea

Kuwait

Kyrgyzstan

Laos

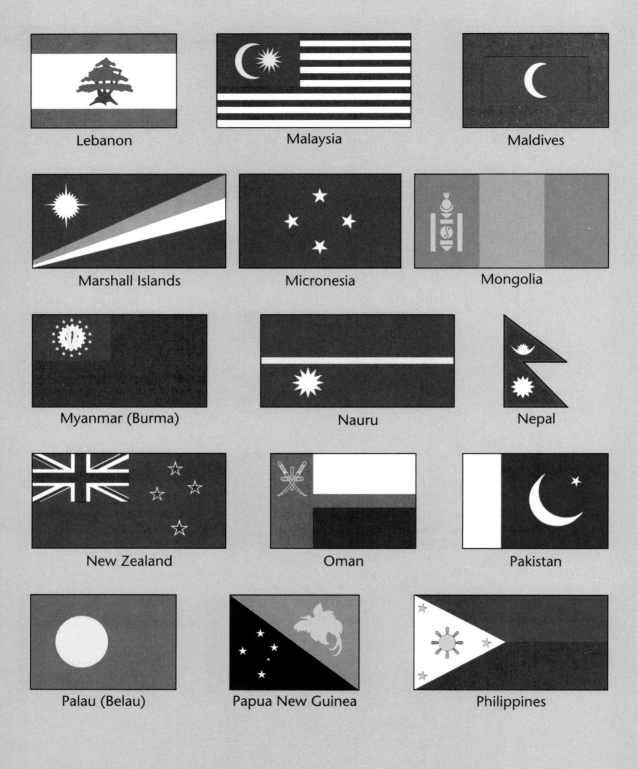

Lebanon

Malaysia

Maldives

Marshall Islands

Micronesia

Mongolia

Myanmar (Burma)

Nauru

Nepal

New Zealand

Oman

Pakistan

Palau (Belau)

Papua New Guinea

Philippines

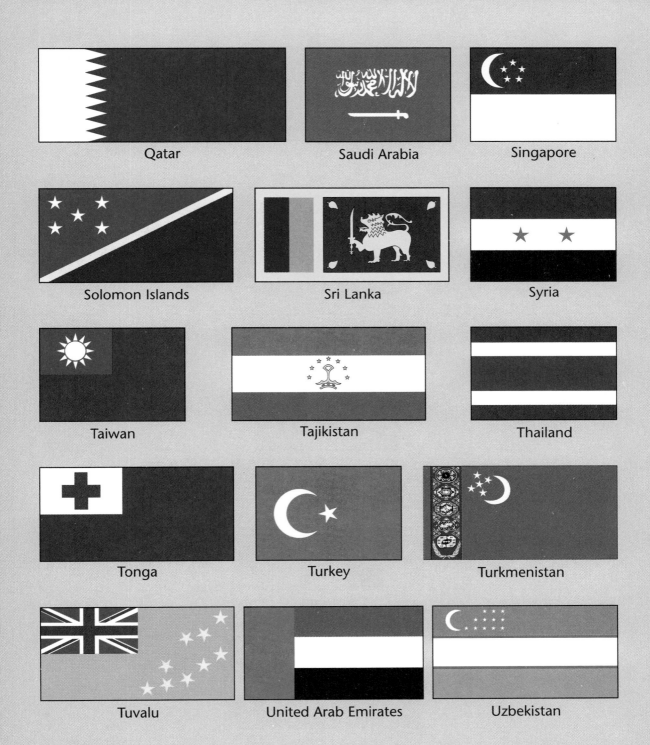

Qatar

Saudi Arabia

Singapore

Solomon Islands

Sri Lanka

Syria

Taiwan

Tajikistan

Thailand

Tonga

Turkey

Turkmenistan

Tuvalu

United Arab Emirates

Uzbekistan

349

Vanuatu

Vietnam

Western Samoa

Yemen

Flags of Europe

Albania

Andorra

Austria

Belarus

Belgium

Bosnia-Herzegovina

Bulgaria

Croatia

Czech Republic

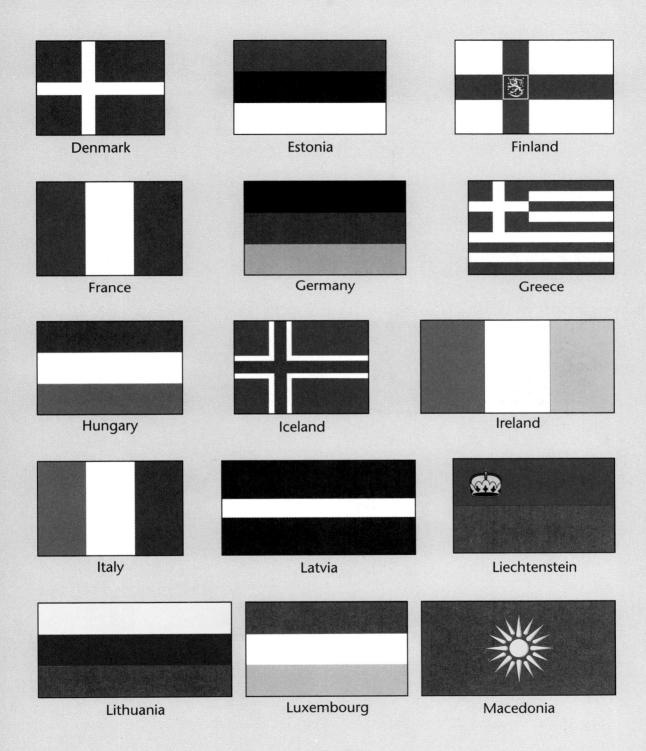

Denmark

Estonia

Finland

France

Germany

Greece

Hungary

Iceland

Ireland

Italy

Latvia

Liechtenstein

Lithuania

Luxembourg

Macedonia

351

Malta

Moldova

Monaco

Netherlands

Norway

Poland

Portugal

Romania

Russia

San Marino

Slovakia

Slovenia

Spain

Sweden

Switzerland

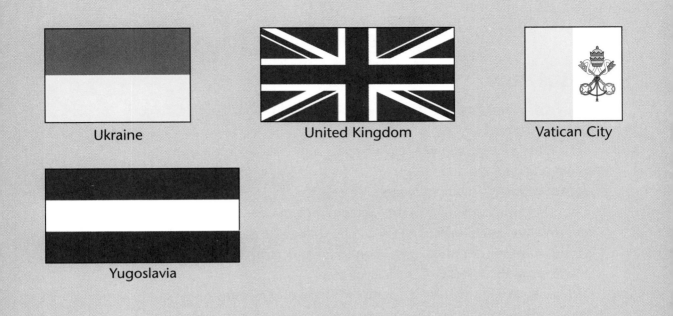

Ukraine

United Kingdom

Vatican City

Yugoslavia

Glossary

alliance an agreement between individuals or groups to side with each other on a particular issue

archaeologists people who excavate ancient sites, searching for clues about ancient civilizations

artifacts objects made by people

assembly line a line of workers and equipment assembling products step-by-step, each worker and machine doing one part of the job

atomic bomb an explosive weapon of great destruction that derives its power from the release of nuclear energy

blitzkrieg "lightning war" or quick military movement

Bolshevik a member of the left-wing party of the Russian Social Democratic Workers' Party (early to mid-1900s); later called *Communist*

boycott refusal to buy or use a product or to go to a certain place as a way of protesting something that the consumer does not like

budget a plan that determines how money will be spent

capitalism an economic system characterized by private and corporate ownership and by distribution of the production of goods

cartography the making of maps or charts

consumer a person who buys a product

continent one of the seven largest areas of land on the earth

credit an arrangement to acquire an item through partial payment with a plan to pay the balance through installments

culture the way of life of the people who live in a certain place

D-day the day designated to carry out Operation Overlord

democracy a government by the people

draft a system of selecting men for enrollment in the armed forces

Eastern Hemisphere the part of the earth that is east of the prime meridian

economy the way a country handles its money and resources

equator an imaginary line halfway between the North and South Poles, dividing the earth into two half spheres; measured as 0° latitude

geography the study of a place—the land, climate, natural resources, and the way all these things influence the people

Harlem Renaissance the artistic movement among black people of Harlem in the 1920s

history a record of activities and events in the lives of all the people who have ever lived

inflation the rising of prices when the demand for a product is greater than the supply

Iron Curtain an imaginary dividing line between the Eastern European countries (called the Soviet bloc) and the Western European countries from 1945 to 1990

latitude the distance north or south of the earth's equator, measured in degrees on a map or globe

longhouse a long house for several families, especially of the Iroquois, typically built of poles and bark with a central corridor leading to family compartments

manufacturer a person or company that makes products

meridians imaginary longitudinal lines that run from north to south on a map or globe

nationalism extreme patriotic feelings for a nation

Northern Hemisphere the part of the earth above the equator

North Pole the northernmost point on the earth

primary sources first-person accounts of events

prime meridian an imaginary line on a map or globe running from the North Pole to the South Pole, passing through England and the Atlantic Ocean; measured as 0° longitude

ratify to agree to or approve

resources materials, such as raw materials and labor, available to a company or country for production and profit

socialism a social system characterized by the collective ownership of the production and distribution of goods with political power being held by the community

Southern Hemisphere the part of the earth below the equator

South Pole the southernmost point on the earth

stock a fund that a corporation raises by selling shares to individuals, entitling the stockholders to dividends and other rights of ownership in the company

stock market the buying and selling of stocks at the stock exchange

suffrage the right to vote

time zone any of the twenty-four longitudinal divisions of the earth in which standard time is kept; each time zone observing one hour earlier than the zone immediately to the east

tipi a Native American home made of buffalo skins wrapped around upright poles

topography land features of a region, such as rivers, lakes, mountains, canyons, caves, valleys, and so on

totalitarianism a form of government in which the government controls all aspects of its citizens' lives

tradition a practice or belief that is handed down from generation to generation

union an alliance of workers within a company for mutual interests and benefits

V-E Day "Victory in Europe Day"

V-J Day "Victory in Japan Day"

Western Hemisphere the part of the earth west of the prime meridian

Index

A

Alabama, 94, 298
Alaska, 106, 261, 299
Anasazi. *See* Native Americans
Apollo 11, 269-70
Appomattox Court House, 92
Arbor Day, 252
archaeologists, 73
Arizona, 100, 299
Arkansas, 94, 300
Armed Forces Day, 329
Armistice Day, 328
Armstrong, Neil, 42, 270
artifacts, 72-74
assembly line, 29-30, 113
Axis powers, 172, 187, 200, 208-9, 213

B

Berlin Wall, 262, 277, 281
Blackfoot. *See* Native Americans
Black Hawk, chief of the Sauk and the Fox, 96
Bleeding Kansas, 98
blitzkrieg, 202
Boer War, 206
Bolsheviks, 63, 190, 192
Boone, Daniel, 94
boycott, 129, 260, 275
Bradford, William, 133
Brezhnev, Leonid, 275
Brown, John, 98
Bush, George, 280-81

C

California, 107, 300
capitalism, 133-35
Carnegie Foundation, 124

Carter, James Earl, 274-76
cartography, 5, 77
Central Powers, 49, 56, 59, 66-67
Challenger, 278
Chanute, Octave, 34-35
Cherokee. *See* Native Americans
Cheyenne. *See* Native Americans
Chickasaw. *See* Native Americans
Choctaw. *See* Native Americans
Christmas, 243, 246, 249-50
Churchill, Winston, 193, 204, 206-7, 210
civil rights, 259, 267-68, 281
Civil War (American), 91-93, 99, 103, 223. *See also* War Between the States
Clark, William, 107
Clemenceau, Georges, 67
Clinton, Bill, 282
Cold War, 261, 282
Colorado, 105, 301
Columbus, Christopher, 4
Communism, 132, 134, 216, 224, 258, 261-62, 272, 281-82
concentration camps, 184, 187, 214, 217
Connecticut, 90, 301
Constitution, 88, 111
consumer, 128-29, 134-38, 147
Coolidge, Calvin, 113, 163, 165, 287, 294
Coronado, Francisco Vásquez de, 101
credit, 115, 150-51, 163
Cree. *See* Native Americans
Creek. *See* Native Americans
Crow. *See* Native Americans

Khrushchev, Nikita, 264
King, Martin Luther, Jr., 260, 268
Kitty Hawk, 36-38, 42
Korean War, 258

L
Lakota. *See* Native Americans
La Salle, Robert, 93
latitude, 8-9, 17
law of supply and demand, 129, 131, 140, 143, 145, 147
L'Enfant, Pierre Charles, 78
Lenin, Vladimir Ilich, 63, 177, 189-90
Lewis, Meriwether, 107
Lilienthal, Otto, 33-34
Lincoln, Abraham, 79, 235, 279
Lindbergh, Charles, 122-23
longitude, 8-9, 17
Louisiana, 93, 236, 307
Louisiana Purchase, 12, 96
Lusitania, 55-56
Luther, Martin, 250

M
MacArthur, Douglas, 215, 218-19, 223-25, 258
Madison, James, 286, 288
Magellan, Ferdinand, 4
Maine, 90, 307
manufacturers, 128-29, 135, 140
Maryland, 78, 88, 308
Massachusetts, 88, 253, 308
Mexican War, 100
Michigan, 23, 28, 97, 309
Minnesota, 99, 122, 309
Mississippi, 93, 310
Missouri, 97, 107, 310
Missouri Compromise, 97

Model T, 25-26, 28-30, 113
Monroe, James, 286, 288
Montana, 104, 251, 311
Mother's Day, 252
Mussolini, Benito, 172, 176-81, 183, 187, 198, 200

N
Nagasaki, 197, 225
Narragansett. *See* Native Americans
nationalism, 45
Native Americans
    Anasazi, 101, 230
    Blackfoot, 231, 251
    Cherokee, 100
    Cheyenne, 104, 231, 251
    Chickasaw, 100
    Choctaw, 100
    Cree, 251
    Creek, 100
    Crow, 251
    Fox, 96, 251
    Hupa, 107
    Iroquois, 231
    Lakota, 251
    Narragansett, 89
    Navajo, 220
    Nez Perce, 104
    Ojibwa, 251
    Plains, 231
    Sauk, 96
    Seminole, 100, 233
    Sioux, 98, 104, 231
natural boundaries, 16, 76
natural resources, 75, 137, 169
Navajo. *See* Native Americans
Nazi Party, 182-83
Nebraska, 99, 251-52, 311
Nevada, 105, 312

New Deal, 164, 167-70
New Hampshire, 90, 312
New Jersey, 90, 313
New Mexico, 101, 313
New York, 89, 122, 124, 171,
    235, 274, 314
New York Stock Exchange, 156
Nez Perce. *See* Native Americans
Nicholas II, czar of Russia, 63,
    188, 190
Nixon, Richard Milhous, 269-71
North America, 314
North Carolina, 94
North Dakota, 99, 315
Northern Hemisphere, 7
North Pole, 7-8
Nuremberg Laws, 186

O
O'Connor, Sandra Day, 278
Ohio, 99, 315
Ojibwa. *See* Native Americans
Oklahoma, 100, 316
Operation Overlord, 211
Oregon, 107, 316
Oregon Trail, 107

P
Parks, Rosa, 259-60
Pearl Harbor, 106, 197, 217
Pennsylvania, 88, 317
Persian Gulf War, 280-81
Plains. *See* Native Americans
Plymouth Colony, 133, 234
political boundary, 12
political map, 12
Ponce de León, Juan, 94
Powell, Colin, 281
primary sources, 74
prime meridian, 8

profit, 129, 136, 154, 156
Prohibition, 111, 117-18
pueblo, 230
Puritan, 102

R
Reagan, Ronald Wilson, 220,
    277-78, 280
Rhode Island, 89, 317
Roosevelt, Franklin D., 164, 166,
    193, 209-10, 225, 279
Roosevelt, Theodore, 286, 293

S
Sauk. *See* Native Americans
Schomburg, Arthur, 124
Schwarzkopf, Norman, 281
Scott, Dred, 97
secondary sources, 74
Second Continental Congress, 88
Seminole. *See* Native Americans
shares, 115, 125
Sioux. *See* Native Americans
Sitting Bull, 98
Smith, John, 133
Smithsonian Institution, 34-35
socialism, 177, 189
South Carolina, 92, 318
South Dakota, 98, 318
Southern Hemisphere, 7
South Pole, 7
Soviet Union, 190, 193-94, 208,
    260-64, 275, 277, 280-81
Spalding, Eliza, 105
Spirit of St. Louis, 122
Sputnik, 260
Sputnik II, 260
Stalin, Joseph, 188-93, 198, 210
Statue of Liberty, 89

Photograph Credits

The following agencies and individuals have furnished materials to meet the photographic needs of this textbook. We wish to express our gratitude to them for their important contribution.

Linda Abrams
Alaska Division of Tourism
Suzanne R. Altizer
American Automobile Manufacturers Association
Dr. Ward Andersen
Aramco World Magazine
Architect of the Capitol
Basketball Hall of Fame
Belgium Tourism
Robert & Jan Brantley
B. W. Carper
Stephen Christopher
George R. Collins
Conservation & Renewable Energy Inquiry & Referral Service
Consulate General of Japan
Manda Cooper
Corbis-Bettmann
Corel Corporation
Terry M. Davenport
Tim Davis
Defense Audiovisual Agency
Detroit Public Library
Dwight D. Eisenhower Library
Eastman Chemicals Division
Ewing Galloway
Gene Fisher
Florida State Archives
Ford Motor Company
Franklin D. Roosevelt Library
George Bush Presidential Materials Project
Gerald R. Ford Library

German Information Center
Peggy E. Hargis
Grace Collins Hargis
Harry S. Truman Library
Hawaii Visitors and Convention Bureau
Henry Ford Museum
Hogan Jazz Archive
Honda of America Manufacturing, Inc.
Hoover Institution Archives
Illinois Historic Preservation Agency
Imperial War Museum, London
Jimmy Carter Library
John F. Kennedy Library
Brian D. Johnson
Tim Keesee
Library of Congress
Louisiana Office of Tourism
MacArthur Memorial
Mayo Foundation
Daniel McGrath
Metropolitan Museum of Art
Joan Mulfinger
National Aeronautics and Space Administration (NASA)
National Archives
National Baseball Hall of Fame
National Baseball Library
National Gallery of Art
National Park Service
National Portrait Gallery
Nebraska State Historical Society
New York Public Library

New York State Department of Economic Development
Burton Pretty on Top
R. J. Reynolds Industries, Inc.
Ted Rich
Ed Richards
Rise Studio
Dr. Ella Sekatau
The Senate Historical Office
Smithsonian Institution
Tennessee State Library
Texas State Library
Tonto National Monument
U.S. Energy Department & Resources Administration
U.S. Holocaust Memorial Museum
United Nations
United States Army
United States Air Force (USAF)
United States Department of Agriculture (USDA)
United States Marine Band
United States Marine Corps
United States Mint
University of Washington Libraries
Unusual Films
Virginia State Travel Service
Dawn L. Watkins
The White House
Woolaroc Museum
Wright State University
Dr. William Yost
Young America's Foundation
Greg Zeman

Cover
NASA (left); George R. Collins (top right); Franklin D. Roosevelt Library (bottom right)

Title Page
Suzanne R. Altizer

Chapter 1
Grace Collins Hargis 1; Unusual Films 2 (bottom), 3 (bottom), 9, 20; NASA 2-3 (top), 4 (right);

New York Public Library 4 (left); *Aramco World Magazine* 13; Department of the Army 16; George R. Collins 18

Chapter 2
From the Collections of Henry Ford Museum and Greenfield Village 21, 23, 25 (bottom); American Automobile Manufacturers Association 24; Library of Congress 25 (top), 26 (bottom), 30

207 (inset); YAD Vashem Photoarchives—
Courtesy of U.S. Holocaust Memorial Museum
214; Dwight D. Eisenhower Library 215 (both),
216 (bottom); Unusual Films—courtesy of
Tim Keesee 216 (top); Harry S. Truman Library
222 (bottom); MacArthur Memorial, Norfolk,
Virginia 223, 224 (top); U.S. Energy Department and Resources Administration 225; NYS
Department of Economic Development 226

Chapter 11
George R. Collins 227, 234 (both); Tonto National
Monument 230; Corel Corporation 235 (top);
National Park Service, photo by Richard Frear
235 (bottom), photo by Cecil W. Houghton
237 (bottom); Robert S. Brantley and Jan
White Brantley 236 (top; copyright 1992);
Unusual Films 236 (bottom), 241 (right), 242,
245, 249, 252 (courtesy of Joan Mulfinger),
253 (bottom right), 254 (bottom right), 256;
Virginia State Travel Service 237 (top);
George R. Collins 237 (middle); Stephen Chris-
topher 238 (top); Ewing Galloway, Inc. 238
(bottom); Conservation and Renewable Energy
Inquiry and Referral Service 240; Tim Davis
241 (left); U.S. Marine Band 246; B.W. Carper
248 (both); Burton Pretty on Top 251 (both);
Basketball Hall of Fame 253 (top, bottom left)

Chapter 12
Young America's Foundation 257; Florida State
Archives 259 (top), 268 (top); Library of Congress 259 (bottom), 260 (top), 262 (bottom);
NASA 260 (middle); National Archives 262
(top, middle), 267 (both), 268 (bottom), 269
(right) 271 (bottom), 279 (left); John F. Kennedy
Library 264, 266 (bottom); Unusual Films 265
(all), 283; UPI/Corbis-Bettmann 266 (top), 271
(top), 274 (top); NASA 269 (left-both) 270
(both), 278 (right); Gerald R. Ford Library 272
(both); United Nations/Photo by J. K. Isaac
273; Jimmy Carter Library National Archives
274 (bottom), 275 (both), 276 (both); The
White House, photo by David Johnson 277,
photo by Michael Evans 278 (bottom), 279
(right), 282; Ted Rich 278 (top); George Bush
Presidential Materials Project 281 (top); German Information Center 281 (bottom); U.S.
Marine Corps 284

Resource Treasury
National Park Service, photograph by Richard
Frear 285, 324 (bottom inset), photograph by
Fred Bell 331 (right); Rise Studio, Rapid City,
South Dakota 324 (top, bottom); Manda Cooper
325 (both), 331 (left); Library of Congress 326
(top); Unusual Films 326 (bottom), 327 (both);
Dwight D. Eisenhower Library 328 (top); Na-
tional Archives 328 (bottom); David Valdez,
The White House 329 (left); George R. Collins
329 (top right), 330 (top); Defense Audiovisual
Agency 329 (bottom right); Architect of the
Capitol 330 (bottom); National Gallery of Art
331 (Lincoln portrait)